"*From one musician to another, the most comprehensive "how to" for wedding musicians. Anne Roos is witty and real. A must have for success in this business.*"

—Deborah Magone, blues and rock guitarist

"*Don't think for a second that performing at weddings means you are doomed to play the 'Hokey Pokey' for eternity. As Anne Roos points out so well, providing the music for matrimony can be lucrative and creatively rewarding. Using her years of experience, she spells it all out for you: how to promote yourself, book the gigs, make clients happy, and get paid. This book is a gem for any musician wanting to carve a profitable niche playing weddings.*"

—Bob Baker, author of *Guerrilla Music Marketing Handbook*

"*Musicians are wonderful artists, but they need to think about 'marketing' too. Anne Roos' logical guide can help musicians package their product and launch their services into the $160 Billion wedding industry. Her book is easy to read and a solid resource.*"

—David M. Wood, M.B.A. Harvard, President, Association of Bridal Consultants

"*If you're a musician who's been working in the wedding market for years, this book will open your eyes to dozens of ideas on how to grow your business. If you're new to the industry, read this book from cover to cover before you book one more gig. It will put you miles ahead of your competitors and open the door to revenue-generating ideas you never knew existed.*"

—Joan Stewart, The Publicity Hound

"*As I learn to play the harp, I am intrigued to realize I can make money doing this! Anne's book truly has it all: from learning to understand the bride and her special day, to selecting just the right music, to helpful lists that will insure I am prepared for anything that comes my way!*"

— Marie Bledsoe, harp student

The Musician's Guide to Brides

How to Make Money Playing Weddings

by Anne Roos

Illustrated by Jerry DeCrotie

Hal Leonard Books
An Imprint of Hal Leonard Corporation
New York

Published in 2008 by Hal Leonard Books
An imprint of Hal Leonard Corporation
19 West 21st Street, New York, NY 10010

Book and cover design: Stephen Ramirez

Editor: Sandy Lawson

Produced in Association with Mike Lawson, Lawson Music Media, Inc.

Library of Congress Cataloging-in-Publication Data is available upon request.

ISBN: 978-1-4234-3874-8

Printed in the USA

www.halleonard.com

To my meditation teacher, Swami Chidvilasananda,
who taught me to listen from within when I perform

Dedication

There are a number of individuals whose input was invaluable during the writing of this book. I'd like to thank:

- Marina Ledin, Victor Ledin, Wanda Perschnick, Fred Smith, and my husband, John, for their thoughtful feedback.

- Roxane R. Fritz, attorney specializing in entertainment law in the state of California, for clarifying legal information and her Creating a Band Name addition to the text.
  and
- Steve Tetrault of GigSalad.com for his contribution to the Appendix.

I'd also like to thank the many wedding professionals throughout the US and Canada who participated in interviews and answered questions about wedding musicians.

A very special thanks to those who were particularly articulate with their responses. These professionals are quoted throughout this text:

Joanne Barnes, Agent and Manager, Arts Management Services, LLC
Reverend David Beronio, Lake Tahoe Wedding Ministries
Karen Brown, Master Bridal Consultant, Karen For Your Memories
David Bugli, Musician in Greenridge Music and Millennium Bugs
Bill Burns, DJ, Music Magic
Natalie Cox, Harpist, Classical to Go
Seán Cummings, 8th Generation Professional Bagpiper
Destiny, Sound Sculptress, Harpist from the Hood
Tobey Dodge, Wedding Planner, The Wedding Connection by Tobey Dodge
Norma Morse Edelman, Wedding Coordinator, Wedding Casa
Gwyneth Evans, Concert and Celtic Harpist
Rabbi Jonathan Freirich, Stateline, Nevada
Buzz and Sue Gallardo, Wedding Fair Producers, Business Network Expositions
Timothy Goldsmith, Musician, Red Davidson Trio
Kerry Ann Hawk, Wedding Coordinator, Blue Sky Event & Travel Management
Jeffrey Leep, Entertainment Agent and Musician, Leep Entertainment
Reverend Janice Midkiff, Ceremony of Love
Ed Miller, Officiant
Gerard J. Monaghan, Co-Founder and Former President of the Association of
    Bridal Consultants

Pastor Rob Orr, A Beautiful Lake Tahoe Wedding

Jean Picard, Master Bridal Consultant and California State Coordinator for the
    Association of Bridal Consultants

Derek Tarpey, Lake DJ

Kathy Vaughan, Wedding Coordinator, A Beautiful Memory

Stephen Vardy, Sound Engineer for Harpist Alison Vardy

Van Vinikow, The Supreme Being of The String Beings String Quartet/Trio

Lora Ward, Wedding Coordinator, A Day to Remember

And thanks to the Association of Bridal Consultants for their suggestions and resources.

Contents

Contents

Preface

More than twenty years ago, people approached me with comments like, "Wow, you're playing the harp! Could you play "Greensleeves" at my cousin's wedding?" I was shocked and embarrassed, thinking, "Hey, I'm just a student!" Up to that point, I was taking lessons for my own enjoyment, as a way to unwind after a day of stressful work. I hadn't considered playing for pay, but since brides started inquiring about my wedding fees, I figured I was missing out on a great opportunity. So, with little concrete help and advice, I guessed at a fee to charge and nervously took my first job. I did okay, but I would have felt more comfortable performing at the ceremony and working with my client, had I received more coaching and advice.

The advice I needed was not just concerning what music to play and when to play it. I needed to know what the bride expected of me and how to communicate smoothly with her. I discovered that once I had an easy working relationship with brides, the wedding jobs just came to me, and my calendar magically filled up. I now make my living playing at weddings.

This user-friendly, step-by-step handbook will help you get started if you are new to performing at weddings—including how to set your fees, how to create a contract, how to sell your services, what to wear, and more. And if you already have a few wedding gigs under your belt, then you'll pick up on some new ideas within these pages. This book is laid out as a manual, allowing you to jump to chapters that cover your particular interest.

My own experience performing at weddings is diverse, but by no means complete. Therefore, I have interviewed event coordinators, booking agents, celebrants, and ceremony and reception site managers for their insight. They described what makes for a great musician and added their pet peeves. I also polled professional wedding musicians for hints about what works for them and what doesn't. All of the wedding pros that I interviewed have at least ten years of experience under their belts. You'll read their suggestions, success stories, and those unbelievable horror stories we'd all like to avoid.

I've also added useful suggestions for building your wedding music repertoire. If you need more complete wedding music books and wedding music suggestions, you'll find extra resources listed in the back of this book.

The kind of information included within these pages tends to change over time. I welcome all feedback and any suggestions for material to be covered in my future editions. Please contact me with your kind thoughts.

Wishing you the best in your wedding music career!

Anne Roos
anne@celticharpmusic.com

Thank you for coming to our performance today!
*Oh, uh...**and** Tom and Kim's Wedding Reception.*

CHAPTER 1

A Primer for Performing at Weddings

"Music and love are inseparable. Certain music tugs on the heartstrings, makes us remember a loving moment, brings to mind a gentle time or a pretty face . . . It creates an atmosphere for intimacy and connection."
—Mickey Hart, Drummer for the Grateful Dead

THE RIGHT MINDSET— THE BRIDE IS THE STAR, NOT YOU

Performing at weddings is much more than simply playing well. It's more then creating a lovely atmosphere for tying the knot, and it's more than supplying the right party music to get people up and dancing at a reception. Unlike other gigs where you can play any tune you wish within a certain style, this is the bride's big day and she is in charge. She gets to select the special music that will make her day magical. This requires clear communication between the bride and her musicians.

This might sound easy at first. So, you just explain to the bride what selections you can perform, she chooses, and then you show up at the wedding and play. Just like any other gig, right? Not so fast . . .

The bride is unlikely to have hosted or coordinated other big events in the past and therefore will be inexperienced in event planning. Because of this fact, she may have very different expectations of what you can and cannot play, where you can set up, how to pay you, and so on.

The wedding itself, and the planning of it, can be an emotional rollercoaster for a bride. Often she'll hold a picture in her mind of her perfect wedding, and she'll do anything for her wedding day to match her fantasy. She'll enter into wedding planning with these expectations, while she is wrestling with the expectations of her fiancé, her parents, and her future in-laws. Sometimes a bride will crack under this pressure, rendering her nervous, indecisive, or overly concerned with non-essential details. (For instance, I remember a bride who needed to know the temperature of the fruit punch to be served at her reception . . .we'll get into unreasonable demands and how to handle them in a later chapter.)

Relax! It's rare that a "bridezilla"* will hire you. The vast majority of weddings are trouble-free, happy events, complete with a gracious bride. Who would want to play at these gigs if all brides were impossible to work with?

Accept the very real stress a bride may be under and hold her hand through this process. Educate her about what you need from her, from music selections to the kind of performance area that you require. Don't assume she is experienced with party planning. It's also good to do this even with a bride who will be having a smaller wedding, eloping, and getting married for a second time, or simply renewing her vows. This bride may be more flexible and relaxed, but she still needs to have the same level of communication with you as a nervous and excited bride with big wedding plans.

Wedding musicians are an important member of a team of wedding vendors* consisting of the celebrant**, the event coordinator, the banquet manager, the photographer, the videographer, and any number of other service providers. We all work together to make the bride's day memorable. Wedding musicians are part of the bride's "supporting cast". We are not interested in upstaging or stealing the spotlight from her. She is the star on her wedding day.

*A "bridezilla" is a bride who is so wound up about her wedding that she becomes difficult, obnoxious, and in some cases, hostile. Etymology: 1995; blend of "bride" and "Godzilla"

* A "wedding vendor" is a wedding professional who provides a service or product to brides. This term is frequently used in wedding-related businesses, and in this text, I will also substitute this term with "wedding professional", as the context fits.

**A "celebrant" is the minister, justice of the peace, priest, rabbi, etc., who officiates at a religious or civil ceremony, especially a wedding. This term is often incorrectly interchanged with the term "officiant". An "officiant" refers to priests or ministers who perform religious ceremonies, and since weddings can be non-denominational, without any religious references, I prefer to use the term "celebrant".

It can be a relief to know that all eyes are on the bride, particularly for musicians with a bit of performance anxiety. Typically, you'll be supplying background music to an audience who will be perfectly happy if you are not a virtuoso, as long as you play smoothly.

Here's another great fact about playing at weddings: You don't need to be famous in any way to make an income from these gigs. You don't have to have a huge fan base, release recordings, tour the country, perform in concert venues, or publish original music to be a successful wedding musician.

If you are just starting out and have yet to perform for an audience, you'll need to get out there and play before taking on wedding jobs. Become accustomed to playing in front of an audience, even a slightly inattentive one. Play in a coffee shop or some other non-threatening venue and air out your present repertoire. Gradually get into playing at weddings using the suggestions within these pages. Then perform at weddings on weekends while keeping your regular day job—this is how I got started.

My first experience with inattentive audiences was at the Southern California Renaissance Faire in Agoura as a pass-the-hat performer some 25 years ago. I relaxed to the fact that most people were paying more attention to their friend's period costumes than to whether I'd miss a note while playing "Greensleeves". So, with new confidence, I began playing at weddings.

If you've been performing for a while, wedding gigs will be a great way to supplement your music income when you aren't touring or recording. At this point in my career, I make my living performing at weddings, and that income helps to support my recording activities. You'll already know some of the basics in this book, and I'll be presenting suggestions to make performing at weddings a better experience for you. Plus, you'll be reading suggestions from other wedding professionals—a few secrets of the trade that might strike you as eye-opening.

Enjoy performing, have patience and understanding with the bride and her loved ones, and the money will follow. A bride who is happy with you and your services will shout your name from the rooftops. She'll tell her friends and relatives, and she'll blog it all over the Internet (a number of bride chat rooms exist online).

WHAT IT TAKES TO PLAY AT WEDDINGS—YOUR PERSONALITY AND SKILL SET

Below are ten general abilities and attitudes that will help you to be a successful wedding musician. Master these, and you'll start receiving a steady flow of referrals, inquiries, and bookings:

1. **Be content with taking directions from the bride and those she appoints to oversee her wedding, no matter how strange you think her expectations of you may be.** Follow instructions with a kind smile and a nod, without being argumentative. Aim to please.

2. **Educate the bride about the services you have to offer.** Keep the lines of communication open so that there is absolutely no doubt in the bride's mind that she can count on you.

3. **Politely stand your own ground when necessary**. Be firm regarding such issues as requesting pay, seeing that you are provided with your performance requirements, and squelching impossible demands (for example, refusing ridiculous requests, such as Chuck Berry's "My Ding-A-Ling", from inebriated wedding guests. Yes, this is a true example of a request I received—and the gentleman wanted to hear this tune on a harp, no less!).

4. **Possess a willingness to offer helpful suggestions about how to select wedding or reception music, without actually making up the bride's mind for her.** In other words, even if you disagree with the bride's musical taste, or you don't like playing the songs she has chosen, let her know why. If she insists, play what she wants to hear anyway. Understand that she is creating her own personal memories with the music she chooses.

5. **Accept the fact that you will be performing background music while people are talking and mingling.** You are not a "diva"—You don't have to be the center of attention.

6. **Perform smoothly and with confidence.** Understand that if you display a lack of confidence, the bride and the other wedding professionals on your team will have a lack of confidence in you, too.

7. **Look good. No, look GREAT!** Smile. Look like you are having fun when you play. Take good care of yourself and the clothes that you wear. Take good care of your equipment, too.

"The most important gift you can give a bride is your own self-confidence. Placing yourself in her shoes, it's not hard to understand how a musician who is confident and reassuring can be an oasis in a desert of worries."—Timothy Goldsmith, Red Davidson Trio

You are much more than a musician, for any bride can substitute a live musician, quartet, or band with a handful of CDs or an iPod with stereo speakers. You are an entertainer. Everyone forms first impressions by how you look, before you ever play your first note.

8. **Realize that you can learn from bridezilla stories, those horrible nightmares about crazy brides that you, other musicians, and wedding vendors experience from time to time.** Turn lemons into lemonade—Ask yourself, "How can I avoid that particular situation?" This kind of contemplation helps to set parameters for what you are and are not willing to do at future wedding gigs.

"People with positive expectations generally enjoy positive results. So by all means, think big, dream big, fully expect to succeed."—Bob Baker, "Artist Empowerment Radio" podcast

9. **Know that a positive attitude makes you a magnet for enjoyable, high-paying wedding gigs.** You'll be viewed as a calm professional. Brides will appreciate that your feathers don't get ruffled too easily. Better yet, other wedding vendors will see that you can handle situations that come up at a wedding with ease, and they will want to work with you again. They'll refer you over and over.

10. **Love what you do and success will come.** Show your love of what you do with gratitude. Thank the bride, your clients, other wedding vendors, and everyone who crosses your path.

DO WHAT YOU DO BEST—CREATE A REPERTOIRE

Do what you do best, and you'll love what you do. The music you play that resonates within you carries your own fingerprints. Even if other musicians can play the same songs as you do, what you bring to these songs is uniquely your own.

To land lucrative wedding gigs, you need to find your niche among the competition. This is known as "positioning" in marketing lingo. It means researching what makes you different from the rest of the musicians and capitalizing on these differences. Compiling your wedding repertoire is the first step to making you stand out.

"You are more attractive when you break bread with a competitor. . . . The goal [is] transforming this competitor into a collaborator"—Stacey Hall & Jan Brogniez of Perfect Consulting Unlimited, experiential consulting and training company, from their book, "Attracting Perfect Customers"

How do you find out what your competition plays? There is no better time than now to enlist some allies. Make friends with other successful musicians in your geographical area and hear them perform. Get together and jam. Check out their websites. If some musicians give you the cold shoulder when you approach them in friendship, they may be viewing you as a threat, and that's their problem. Your competition can be your friends, and I'll come back to this fact again and again in this book.

Seek advice and direction from someone you trust and respect—find a mentor. Pretty soon, the line between giving you this advice and doing you a favor totally disappears.

Mark H. McCormack explains in his book, "What They Don't Teach You at Harvard Business School" the value of having a mentor:

"Both mentors and confidants can lead to very effective business relationships . . .Pretty soon, the line between giving you this advice and doing you a favor totally disappears. Making a confidant . . .means sharing your personal feelings from time to time, passing on information that doesn't affect you but may be helpful to him, or encouraging him to confide in you."

You'll receive a variety of very useful information from mentors. The mentors I've had throughout the years have ranged from fellow harpists who have given me repertoire advice, to wedding coordinators who have instructed me on some etiquette dos and don'ts, to a booking agent who has helped me hone in on what clients look for on web sites, to a wedding minister who has given me sound investment advice. And it becomes a two-way street—they ask me for information and suggestions for their own situations.

Being friends with your competition can be of mutual benefit. You might trade some valuable sheet music for gigs. Who knows? In the future, you might even team up and play some gigs with a musician who may be your "competition" right now. When they are already booked for a wedding gig, they may tell the bride to phone you. And in time, that rock guitarist across town may become a booking agent in ten years and be in the position to send you on some very lucrative gigs. Or maybe he'll become a music supervisor for an independent film company and give you a call to license some of your music. You simply cannot afford to waste your energy trying to find ways to bring your competition down. Keep competition on a friendly level.

Right now, in terms of repertoire, you can find out from your new musician friends what songs the local brides are requesting. Choices will vary according to whether the bride is getting married in a house of worship or in a more casual setting. Requested repertoire will also vary between each house of worship. You may also find that the area where you live has local wedding favorites (for instance, if you live in Honolulu, you'll need to know "The Hawaiian Wedding Song").

"Skaters know that it's never in their best interest to look at the competition, because there is nothing you can do to change how well or badly someone else skates. You can win only on your own performance."—Linda Kaplan Thaler and Robin Koval, from the advertising firm of the Kaplan Thaler Group, quoted from their book, "The Power of Nice"

Once you have an idea of what your competition plays, you can fine tune and build your own repertoire. You should be capable of playing at least two hours worth of music without repeating anything. Three hours is even better. Be prepared to perform your entire repertoire cleanly, but you don't have to be a technical wizard.

You can sight read or play from memory. It doesn't matter. Wedding guests are not going to care if you have a music stand in front of you. What does matter is that you "position" yourself differently than other musicians in your area. For example, if you are in a string quartet and your competition plays only Classical music, you won't want to specialize in just Classical music. You'll want to add some music that your competition doesn't play, like pop standards such as Andrew Lloyd Webber show tunes, for instance.

"There is no "standard" repertoire. It is a function of the bride's personality."—Reverend David Beronio

Variety is the key here; it will get you hired for more jobs. Why do you think so many wedding music performance jobs go to DJs? They can play virtually anything the bride requests. Stretch your chops—learn holiday, ethnic, Classical, and modern popular music. Learn to use fake books* to accommodate your clients' requests. Brides love to hear music they already know. They want to hear their favorites on their wedding day.

Focus on the type of music that you play solidly, while simultaneously offering a large variety of titles. Your competition may be your friends, but to make a profit as a wedding musician means that brides single you out among other entertainment options.

Get acquainted with how your music will fit into the flow of weddings. Here are the typical wedding activities, listed in the order that they usually occur at a wedding:

The Wedding Ceremony

Most brides will select traditional Classical pieces, like the *Bridal March* from "Lohengrin" by Richard Wagner (aka "Here Comes the Bride") and Johann Pachelbel's *Canon in D*. However, also be prepared with additional non-traditional music that can be offered to a bride who wants a more unique sound for her wedding.

---

*A "fake book" is a book of music that is usually used as a framework for improvisation. A fake book is filled with "lead sheets", which only contain the melody line, corresponding chords for each measure, and lyrics.

1. **Pre-Ceremony or Prelude Music**—This soft background music is played while guests are being seated, or sometimes, it is played during a pre-ceremony cocktail hour. This music establishes the atmosphere and mood that the bride wants to create for her wedding. A bride may simply select a category or type of music that she wants (for instance, Classical music), or she may wish to select a particular tune to be performed.

For smaller groups of invited guests, fifteen minutes of pre-ceremony music will suffice. However, when the guest list swells above fifty people, it is more fitting to play for at least a half hour before the ceremony begins. It is my experience that I can play, on the average, about six tunes in fifteen minutes and about a dozen tunes in thirty minutes. Of course, this is an average, when I consider that most tunes that I play run anywhere from two to five minutes in length. If you are a member of a string quartet, you may only be able to get through a couple of pieces if you are playing entire movements.

2. **Optional—Music for the Seating of Mothers and Grandparents**—Once all the wedding guests are seated, there may be a formal seating of mothers, grandparents, and any other people important to the bride and groom before the ceremony gets underway. One selection is played for their seating, and it is usually a tune that is easy to walk to and may be a favorite of those who are being seated.

3. **Optional—Music for Lighting of the Unity Candles**—When the bride elects to have a unity candle in her wedding service, the mother of the bride and the mother of the groom walk up the aisle and light the two tapers on either side of the unlit unity candle. The lighting of these tapers symbolizes the two families. One selection is played for this element, and it is usually a tune that is of easy walking tempo. It may be a favorite of one of the mothers or it could be a church hymn.

Note: Sometimes the mothers do not light the side tapers before the ceremony begins—The bride and groom light the tapers during the ceremony and then proceed to light the unity candle together.

4. **Processional Music**—Typically, processional music begins with the appearance of the celebrant and the groom. Sometimes, the groom is joined by the groomsmen at the altar, and the bridesmaids walk up the aisle unaccompanied. Or, the groomsmen may walk arm-in-arm with the bridesmaids.

The processional may also include flower girls, ring bearers, and even pets (I've seen flower dogs and ring bearer dogs, and once, someone walked up with the bride's pet cockatoo).

Traditionally, the processional selection is a majestic piece that is easy for walking. For non-traditional weddings or smaller numbers of attendants, this selection does not need have a majestic sound, but it should still retain a steady andante tempo. This piece ends when the entire wedding party reaches the altar. Just one tune is needed for the entire processional, from the time that the celebrant appears to the time that the bride is ready to make her entrance.

5. Music for the Bride's Entrance to the Processional— Traditionally, the bride enters to fanfare music that announces her arrival (most often, "Here Comes the Bride"). Again, other music may be chosen to suit the bride's taste, as long as it sounds good played at an easy walking pace. This piece ends when the bride reaches the altar. The bride sometimes elects to enter to the same piece of music as her maid or matron of honor, if there are no other members of the bridal party. **Note:** This is the most important tune of the entire wedding ceremony—just ask any married woman what music they remember from their wedding day, and they will all recall the tune they heard as they walked down the aisle.

Important Note: You or someone in your ensemble must be able to play all the processional music with peripheral vision. In other words, you must be able to keep one eye on your music and instrument and another eye on where the bridesmaids and bride are in the room. Otherwise, you run the risk of playing your music for the bridesmaids too long, well after the bride has entered the room, or you are still playing for the bride after her father has given her away and the celebrant is ready to start the ceremony. A pet peeve of many celebrants is that the musicians are still playing at processional volume after the bride has arrived at the altar. Practice your processional music in such a way that you can look away from your sheet music and wind it down at any point in the piece. If you are in an ensemble, rehearse so that one musician has the job of watching the processional and giving everyone the cue to end the tune.

You might find it easier to rely on your memory instead of your peripheral vision. It will be easier to see where people are in the processional if you don't have to stare at your sheet music. If you plan to put aside your music stand, memorize "*The Bridal Chorus*" (also known as "Here Comes the Bride") by Richard Wagner. However, not every bride will want to enter to this march. In fact, the Jewish religion frowns upon using it because the composer was ardently anti-Semitic. Therefore, memorize other popular tunes for the processional, such as *"Canon in D"* by Johann Pachelbel. I've included some great choices for processional music in Appendix A.

6. **Optional—Ceremony Music**—During the ceremony itself, the bride may select special pieces to be performed behind specific wedding traditions, for instance, during:

- the lighting of the unity candle (Catholic)
- candle ceremony (non-denominational, but often still called a unity candle)
- communion (Catholic)
- a scriptural or poetry reading
- the pouring of sand ceremony
- the presentation of roses to the parents
- exchanges of garlands (Hindu, Hawaiian, Eastern Orthodox), crowns (Eastern Orthodox), gold coins (Spanish or Latino), kola nuts (Nigerian), and roses (any faith)
- tea ceremony (China) or sake ceremony (Japan)
- circling the table (Eastern Orthodox)
- bride circling the groom (Jewish)
- handfasting (African, Celtic, Egypt)
- lazo (Latino-a rope or rosary is wound around the shoulders)
- the seven steps (Hindu)
- the honey ceremony
- crossing sticks, sweeping and jumping the broom (African-American)

and a multitude of other ethnic and religious traditions, or new traditions invented by the bride and groom.

The key is to be prepared to perform behind any ceremony tradition, or even to perform between ceremony traditions, during a meditation (this is one of the few moments at the wedding when you will have a captive audience, with everyone attentive to your entire performance).

Some couples request music to be performed lightly as background music behind the entire wedding ceremony or during the exchange of vows. Only one tune should be selected for background music, and you can play it several times through as theme and variations. This selection will usually have a special meaning to the bride and groom, or it will be a religious selection appropriate for the ceremony they have chosen.

If several tunes are played as background wedding ceremony music, there is a danger that attention will be diverted away from the words of the ceremony. (The last thing that I want to hear from anyone was that the music was, "Too much" during the ceremony). You should be able to "noodle" off of any one song selected during the ceremony. It's easy to noodle—just improvise a melody using the same chords in the chord chart. If you are new to this kind of improvisation, use a tape recorder as a practice aid. Play the chords into the recorder, and then play the recording back and fool around with a melody line.

You'll only need to practice noodling at a slow rhythm, or even rubato or without rhythm, because this kind of noodling is done during the ceremony. You may need to noodle because the lighting of the unity candle might take longer than expected—the flame went out or the wicks are not lighting. Or sometimes, a priest or rabbi will motion to you to play something during a ceremony, even when the bride did not inform you that ceremony music was needed.

On rare occasion, you may need to noodle when the bride or her attendants are taking so long to get to the altar that you have played through the entire processional selection and it would sound strange to play it over again. An example of a song that you won't want to play a second time through would be Schubert's "Ave Maria"—this song sounds odd when truncated and should be played all the way through.

7. **Recessional Music**—This is just one selection, a triumphant, almost fast-faced piece played as soon as the newlyweds walk back up the aisle as husband and wife, followed by their wedding party (parents, grandparents, bridesmaids, groomsmen, ring bearers, flower girls, and generally, anyone wearing a boutonniere, corsage, or carrying a bouquet). By the time the seated guests begin to exit the wedding area, the recessional tune may be followed by other selections of the bride's choosing.

A Note About Tempo: You'll notice that I mention the pace of music quite a bit. People subconsciously match their gait to the music that they are hearing, at least for the bride's entrance and the processional. On occasion, I have sped up the tempo of a processional tune when the attendants were taking baby steps and walking unnaturally slow. This tact may help them to move along. During the ceremony, any music that is too loud or bouncy will detract from the ceremony, and you will lose points from the celebrant if they have to raise their voice over your music. The recessional selection can be played as fast as you like because the wedding party will not be matching their gait to your music—they are ready to go off and party. Pacing and dynamics are important to keep in mind as you create your repertoire, because some tunes don't sound quite right when slowed down.

8. **Post-Ceremony Music (Also Known as "Interlude Music") or Cocktail Hour Music**—At this point, the guests are filing out of the wedding area, and the bride and groom may be greeting everyone in a receiving line. Guests are served cocktails and hors d'oeuvres while formal photos are being taken of the newlyweds and the wedding party. This is usually a transitional period, just before the reception kicks off. Appropriate music is mellow and mildly rhythmic tunes that are suitable for mingling. As with pre-ceremony music, the bride may give you a type of music to play or she may supply you with a list of her favorites.

The Wedding Reception

Cocktail and dinner music can be of a soft variety, but if the bride wants Classical music, select more up-tempo melodies than were played during the ceremony. Dance music should include music that every generation can accept. The goal is to bring people together, especially on the dance floor.

The order of wedding reception activities may vary, depending upon the geographical region of the wedding, the ethnicity of the bride and groom, their religious backgrounds, and the logistics of dinner set-up at the reception venue. The bride and groom may take a spin around the floor when they enter the reception and there can be dance music played between courses. Or, the toast may be given as soon as the bride and groom enter, and there is no dancing until after dinner is served.

Regardless of the order, if you'll be playing at wedding receptions, prepare your repertoire to cover the following activities:

1. **Entrance of the Bride and Groom**—With a large number of guests, an emcee (also known as a master of ceremonies) should take over to keep the flow of the reception and make general announcements. One of the musicians, usually the bandleader or head of the ensemble, informs the guests that the bride and groom are about to enter the room. Usually, the attendants will

enter first, and they may enter to their own musical selection. Then they are followed by the wedding couple's grand entrance. A selection can accompany this entrance, often some great fanfare piece. For smaller numbers of guest in attendance, or less formal weddings, no announcement is needed, and a particular selection for the couple's entrance is optional.

2. **Family Traditions Within the Reception**—Sometimes, the candle ceremony is reserved as a family tradition and included as part of the reception activities instead of during the wedding ceremony, especially if the ceremony takes place outdoors and it is impractical to have a unity candle outside in windy conditions. No music is played during the toast and prayers for the couple and before the meal.

3. **Music for Dining**—If you or one of your band members is making announcements, and there is a buffet service, you may want to call people up by table after checking in with the wedding coordinator or banquet captain. Begin with the bride and groom and their wedding party. The banquet staff and guests will appreciate having an orderly dinner service, without long lines winding around the reception room.

Continuous music is played during the meal, without interruption, for at least an hour's time (or longer, depending upon the number of guests to be served, the number of courses, and whether it is a sit-down or buffet service). The music should be easy to talk above and not the kind of music that urges the guests to get up and dance (at least, not yet). Again, it is my experience that I can play about a dozen tunes in thirty minutes, so this gives you some idea of how much music you need to have at the ready to perform for receptions.

4. **Bride and Groom's First Dance**—The bride and groom may have their first dance just after they make their entrance to the reception or they may opt to have their first dance after dinner has been served. This decision could have a lot to do with logistics, since buffet tables may be located on or near the dance floor and would need to be cleared before dancing can begin. Also, the wedding party may be hungry after the ceremony and would prefer to eat before dancing. Regardless of the reason, the bride and groom's first dance signals the call to dance for the rest of the guests. This song is the most important of all the reception songs; the wedding couple will remember their first dance song for years after their wedding day.

Another important note: A member of the band usually announces the dances and even gives dance instructions if the dance is of an ethnic nature (line dances, the Hebrew hora, etc.).

5. **Family Dances**—After the bride and groom take their spin around the dance floor, next comes the father-daughter dance, followed by the dance for the groom and his mother. Other combinations may follow, including the parents of the couple, the siblings dancing with each other, and so on. Then, the rest of the guests are invited by the emcee to join the family on the dance floor. There are variants to which of these dances may occur, and in what order, depending upon whether all the immediate family is present at the reception, and depending upon whether the couple wants to include stepparents.

6. **The Cutting of the Cake**—This tradition usually occurs near the end of the wedding reception, but depending upon the couple's ethnicity or what is commonly done in their geographical locale, these traditions may occur earlier in the reception. In fact, I have seen the cake cut at the beginning of the wedding reception, when the photographer was not hired to stay through the reception and wanted to get some cake-cutting shots before their time was up. Also, when the reception consists only of cake and champagne and not a full meal service, the cake cutting activity will occur right after the toast and there may be no dancing at all. Regardless of when the cake cutting happens, the bride may select special songs to be played just before or during these traditions. I tend to shy away from playing during the actual cake cutting, because the guests love to hear anything the bride and groom exclaim as they feed each other cake and champagne.

7. **The Throwing of the Bouquet and the Garter Toss**—These traditions may also occur towards the end of the wedding reception, or they may occur as a break during the dancing. Like the cutting of the cake, the bride may choose particular songs leading up to or during these traditions. Most often, a drum roll works well for the wind up and toss of these items. Again, it's the emcee's job to get all the unmarried women on their feet to catch the bouquet, and all the single men to catch the garter.

8. **The Last Dance**—This signals the end of the reception and the end of the wedding celebration. It's a special request from the

bride and groom, and everyone is invited by the emcee to join the newlyweds on the dance floor.

Keep all of these wedding elements in mind as you create your repertoire. If you are familiar with certain religious or ethnic songs and melodies, incorporate them into your master song list, too. The more variety you can offer the bride, the bigger the possibility she will hire you.

You'll need to create an inventory of appropriate wedding songs that you already have under your belt, as well as a list of songs you'll want to learn. Below is a brainstorming activity to help you determine your repertoire. As you go through this exercise, refer to Appendix A for some specific wedding music suggestions. Also check out the **Suggested Reading and Other Resources** at the end of this book, too.

Brainstorming Activity for Creating and Updating Your Repertoire:

Step 1: Take out a few pieces of paper, and some colored pencils, too. On one page scribble down the kinds of music that you play right now, making a list of your present repertoire. Be as detailed as possible. Don't stop to analyze whether your music is appropriate for weddings. Just write down the titles of every tune you know how to play comfortably, music that you know you can perform in front of an audience without stumbling or breaking into a cold sweat.

"The wise musicians are those who play what they can master"—Duke Ellington, American bandleader and influential figure in jazz and swing

If you play different genres of music, say you can play jazz guitar and know some bluegrass tunes, use the different colored pencils to differentiate between the types of music that you play. Maybe use one color for up-tempo tunes and another for slow ballads. You can also separate the types of music you play by ethnicity or whether they are secular (religious) or non-secular. Take time to go through your sheet music books and include everything in your list. Take as long as you like to complete this page.

Step 2: Review this list and place things in an order that makes sense to you, an order that you could perhaps share with a potential client, a bride. Place all the pre-ceremony music together, the reception music together, the possible bridal entrance tunes together, and so on. You'll want to be prepared to offer the bride several choices for each wedding activity. Remember: Not every bride wants to enter to "Here Comes the Bride". Use the **Wedding Music Inventory Worksheet** to sort out when certain tunes may be most appropriate to play.

Avoid filling in the worksheet with titles that you feel are inappropriate for weddings. Also, don't include tunes that you absolutely hate playing. You'll get a lot more enjoyment out of wedding gigs when you play music that you like.

For example, although I play "Danny Boy" at many concert and pub gigs, I don't care to play it at weddings because it reminds people of funerals and wakes. So, I'll play this song at a wedding if my client insists, but I'd rather not.

Step 3: Start on a new page. Make a wish list of all the kinds of music you'd like to learn to play. Write down specific titles. These may include tunes you are still working on, tunes that you're not ready to perform in front of an audience quite yet. This list will help you to determine if you should continue working on these tunes or abandon them for other music that will give you a better chance of landing you wedding gigs.

When you're done with this list, compare it with first list of songs you know. Do the songs you want to learn fit in with the types of songs you already know? Will they flow together nicely? Are these tunes appropriate for weddings? For instance, if you play for receptions, are they danceable? Put these tunes in order, with your first choices at the top of the page.

If you are in a band or ensemble, do this entire brainstorming exercise with your band members. They may have tunes in their personal repertoires that could be worth adding to your group's song list. This exercise will also help to confirm that all the members of your group have the same goals. If they aren't interested in performing at weddings and receptions, then the truth will certainly come out through this brainstorming activity. The key to this exercise is to make sure that each member of your group is on the same collective track. Musicians who share the same goals tend to get along well together and have longevity as a group.

If you're thinking about forming a band or ensemble with other musicians, sit down with them and do this exercise. You'll know what to practice together and will have a game plan for building a repertoire and a practice schedule. If you are forming a band and are searching for a good name for your group, refer to the **Creating a Band Name** supplement provided at the end of this chapter for some helpful pointers.

You are now going into business, so it's time to make it official. File for a business license once you have a band name, an ensemble name, or even if you are a solo act and using your own given name. Savvy brides may want to research to see how legitimate you are and may check to see if you are licensed.

Brides love menus of information. When they ask you, "What do you play?" you'll now be prepared to share your repertoire list with them.

DON'T LEAVE HOME WITHOUT IT—NECESSARY EQUIPMENT

While you are beefing up your repertoire, you can also be acquiring the equipment you'll need as a wedding performer. Good equipment takes a monetary expenditure, and budgeting for this expenditure is important. Only purchase equipment you need right now, at this very moment. If you are presently playing as a soloist on acoustic guitar in a wedding chapel that holds twenty-five people, you don't need to purchase a P.A. (however, you could continue to shop for one and keep it on a wish list).

"Don't be cheap—Study and then invest in great equipment for the long haul"—Destiny, Harpist from the Hood

It never ceases to amaze me that talented musicians will spend thousands of dollars on excellent instruments, only to show up to gigs with cheap equipment: amps that buzz and hum, toppling wire music stands, and clothespins to hold their sheet music to their wire stands. This makes them look and sound mediocre at best, for all the money that they spent on their instruments.

Equipment purchasing advise: Save your money. Buy the best to sound your best and look your best. Don't buy any equipment you don't need right now.

Amplification—The next biggest investment besides your instrument. I think Stephen Vardy, sound engineer for harpist Alison Vardy, sums things up best here:

"I find most people go through an acquisition path with sound gear. They all seem to need to start cheap and nasty . . . Then they start acquiring more gear patchwork as their wallet starts to loosen. Eventually they understand good sound and tire of the fiddly patch-work . . . It is a very inefficient and costly process of learning, but people eventually equate quality sound with monetary expenditure and good design."

"It will never matter how well you play—If the sound system is distorting you, you'll sound dreadful."—Derek Tarpey, Lake DJ

What a complete waste of money, buying cheap equipment just to make do. You are better off renting a good system until you can afford to buy one yourself. You only sound as good as your sound equipment sounds. Your sound system needs to make your instrument sound better than it would when it's played acoustically, not worse.

Ask yourself if you really need a sound system. If you don't play to sizeable groups or if someone else in your band or ensemble supplies all the cords and amps, why spend the money? Wait until the need arises and then go shopping. **Here are some steps to take when you are ready to buy a sound system:**

1. Determine if you need a battery-operated amplifier, a tube amp, a P.A., or some other sound equipment for your own particular instrument and for the wedding locations where you will need it.

2. Visit large, full-service music stores. Take your instrument with you. Ask the salesperson to plug your instrument into various systems and play from the full range of notes that your instrument can handle. Play them loudly and softly. Listen to which system sounds the best to you.

3. Do some online research at the equipment manufacturer's web site, too. You'll find out the weight of the system you have in mind, the electronic specs, and the ease of use. Get even more information by emailing directly from their website or calling their toll-free number. Google the sound equipment that you are researching to find out which web sites may be selling it. Finally, you'll want to visit sites like amazon.com, musicians-friend.com, and zzounds.com, because these retail sites post customer reviews that can help you make up your mind.

4. When you think you have found the amp you like the best, calculate the cost of all the peripheral equipment needed: equalizers, cords, microphones, pick-ups, pre-amps, direct boxes, monitors, computerized accompaniment, and more. Look at the cost of the entire system before you commit. You'll end up spending hundreds or thousands of dollars on quality sound equipment, so seriously contemplate whether the system you have your eye on is going to serve you well for years to come.

5. Finally, when you are ready to buy, don't just settle on the price listed on the manufacturer's website. Don't purchase it from the first catalog you receive in the mail, either. Do an Internet search for the pieces of equipment that you want. Then compare the prices you find on the net with the prices in your catalogs. Finally, find out if your local music store will slash the price even lower (sometimes you'll get a big discount if you are

interested in buying the last system on the showroom floor or a display model). Visit stores that may be going out of business and liquidating merchandise.

6. If you're thinking about buying used equipment, make sure the equipment is in good condition before purchasing, and haggle with the seller for a lower price.

Purchase the very best sound system that money can buy right from the start. Even if you are not able to land a great discount, you'll save money in the long run, since you won't be buying one piece of junk after another. And you'll sound great.

Always have a spare: I learned this valuable equipment rule the hard way, only very recently. . . .

I've always known from the start to carry extra strings for my harp, extra tuning wrenches, extra cords, and extra batteries. However, I discovered that it is imperative to take two of EVERY item that I cannot do without (oh, except for my instrument, since I play a harp . . .But if I played another instrument, say a flute, I'd bring other flutes and recorders as back-ups).

I was performing at an outdoor wedding where the wind was howling. My little battery-operated amp can usually plow through windy conditions, but on this particular day, I couldn't get any sound out of it at all. I tried all the inputs on the amp. It was charged up, so it had power. I checked to see if my equalizer was working, and everything else seemed in order. So, I played the loudest I could possibly play. It was no good. The guests, the wedding party, everyone could barely hear my instrument. I assumed my amp died.

After the ceremony, the minister told me that the mother of the bride said to him, "I can't hear the harp. Can you hear it?" The minister covered for me and told her, "I heard it just fine", but he didn't hear it at all. I was very thankful for what he said, but I was also very embarrassed.

I had extra cords with me, but I didn't think to use them, because I thought my amp was failing. My friend Bill Burns, the DJ at this wedding, helped me determine that the problem was with a faulty cord, and we substituted another cord I had on hand. Voila! I had sound!

Bill explained to me, "You need to have two of everything with you at every gig. You even need to bring a second back-up amp. You can't rely on others to save your rear end when equipment fails. And it will fail."

The moral of the story is to bring that back-up amp and anything else you simply cannot do without at a wedding gig. Pretend you are loading up Noah's Ark when you pack up your car.

With all this being said, here are essential items that you'll need:

1. **Your instrument, of course.** You should have a protective, waterproof case for it, either a soft gig bag or a hard shell case. Pack with your instrument all of the items that you directly use with your instrument (a full set of strings, drum sticks, bows, rosin, etc.).

2. **Your favorite seat to sit upon.** Your comfort is tantamount to having a good time performing. Bring your favorite portable chair, bench, or stool. If you don't, your client is apt to offer you something that will be uncomfortable. A client once offered me a chaise lounge chair to sit upon while performing. Can you imagine playing harp while sitting on one of those things? I couldn't either, and thankfully, I brought my own folding chair instead.

3. **Strong, waterproof bags for your sheet music.** In case you need to scribble a line or two of music at a gig, also keep some blank manuscript paper, a pencil, and an eraser handy at a gig. Post-it sticky notes are good, too, because you may need to write some last-minute cues on your sheet music. My favorite sheet music gig bags are Tuxedo Bags, made by Humes & Berg. These cordura bags are indestructible, and they'll fit tons of sheet music. (Humes & Berg also makes a wide selection of cordura soft cases for instruments.)

"Band leaders should always have at least one extra music stand in their trunk!"—Van Vinikow, The "Supreme Being" of "The String Beings" string quartet/trio

4. **A music stand.** Invest in a solid metal music stand, and save the cheap wire stand as a spare. A solid stand is less likely to fall over in the wind or when someone backs up into it, and if you play a cello, double bass, or harp, you'll avoid scratches on your instrument. You'll also be able to place large books or heavy binders on a solid stand without their falling off. Manhasset has a solid, fold up stand called the Voyager. It's more money than a wire stand, but it's worth the added investment.

5. **A soft case for your music stand.** It's a nuisance when a wire stand suddenly opens up while carrying it, and it is pretty painful to drop a Manhasset stand on tender feet. These are reasons enough to have a soft carrying case for your music stand.

6. **A tough waterproof bag on wheels.** Place all your small peripheral items in this bag. What works best for me is a 20" rolling carry-on flight bag that I purchased from a factory outlet store. Purchase it in person, not online, so that you can see the capacity, the design of the interior, the number and size of pockets, and the quality of the bag. Don't purchase a bag that will fall apart in a few months. It needs to be rugged.

Fill this bag with:

a) **An electronic tuner and an optional alligator clip cord or another cord to connect it to your instrument pick-up.** It is easier to tune in noisy environments if you can plug your tuner directly into your instrument pick-up.

b) **Extra batteries for your electronic tuner.**

c) **A fix-it kit for your instrument: wrenches, pliers, wire cutters, you name it.** I place all this stuff in a Dobbs kit (a men's travel toiletry kit) so that I can easily find it inside the rolling gig bag.

d) **Gaffer's tape and masking tape.** Don't bring duct tape, because it will leave a sticky mess wherever you use it. Gaffer's tape looks just like duct tape and is just as strong, but it can be easily removed without gummy residue. I have used gaffer's tape for anything from sticking a loose pickup back inside my harp, to taping down cords on the floor to avoid accidents, to fixing the hem on a gown. It's truly indispensable. Masking tape is also very useful to have handy, just in case you need to write on it. I also use masking tape to cover unused input or output holes on my amp when I'm performing outside (it keeps bugs and sand from ending up inside my amp).

e) **Sheet music clips to hold down your music in breezy conditions or to keep your music books open.** Don't use clothespins; they look too tacky for a well-paid musician to use at weddings. You can purchase see through clips at standard music stores or any number of online retailers.

f) **A doorstop.** Keep doors open while you are loading and unloading musical equipment.

g) Instrument polishes and polish cloths. You'll be amazed to see the gunk that can get on an instrument, especially when performing outside.

h) Personal emergency items. In the summer, I take mosquito repellent lotion with me, along with antihistamine, since I am allergic to mosquito bites. I also bring along sun block. In the winter, I take hand warmers with me, the ones that can be purchased in camping stores. I place them in my pockets so that when I have some downtime at a wedding, I can keep my hands warm. Aspirin and Band-Aids are year-round emergency items for me, along with a nail file, Kleenex, and cough drops. I usually keep them in my purse or car, but they can also be contained in the rolling gig bag. You might have others items necessary for your own personal comfort that you'll want to drop into your bag, too.

i) Extra business cards and brochures. You may wish to keep business cards in your wallet or purse, but it's good to know that you have more in your rolling gig bag if you run out.

If you are using amplification, also store the following items inside the rolling gig bag:

j) Lots and lots of extra batteries for all of your electronic devices.

k) Power AC adapters to recharge your electronic devices. If you are using a battery-operated amplifier, these adapters will save you if your batteries run low.

l) Warranties and instruction booklets for your tuner and amplification devices. When your equipment malfunctions, you'll be able to trouble-shoot on the spot.

m) A wide assortment of cords. Over the years, I have collected cords that I don't presently use with my equipment. I still carry them with me to all my gigs. Why? I can plug into house sound or into onsite P.A. systems that will enable my harp to be heard well in that particular location. Some of these spare cords will just do the trick, fitting right into a sound system built for the wedding or reception site.

n) Velcro straps for tying up your cords neatly.

o) **Equalizers, direct boxes, and special effects pedals.** These items can easily fit into a rolling bag.

p) **Microphones, transducers, pick-ups, etc.** If one of these is already installed in your instrument, bring an extra one, in case it fails (remember Noah's Ark . . .)

Things you can keep in the trunk of your car, your vehicle's glove compartment, or your garage, until you know you'll need them:

1. **Instrument stands.** If you can place a guitar stand or a fold-up stand for an electronic keyboard into the rolling gig bag, by all means do so. If not, find another bag for this item and take it with you on a wedding gig where you'll be changing instruments or when you're taking breaks.

2. **A music stand light.** Even in the daylight, you could end up playing in a dark corner of a reception hall. Sometimes, brides want to be married in the evening by candlelight, and you'll have quite a challenge if you're unprepared. You can start with one of those little battery-operated book lights and place it inside the rolling gig bag. I've graduated on to a larger light, made by the ConcertLight company, which will illuminate my entire music stand. It comes in it's own waterproof carrying bag.

3. **A long, bright orange, wind up extension cord.** Get an extension cord that is at least 150 feet in length. If you do need electricity, you'll be able to use it even if you are far from the nearest outlet. Since it's a hideous bright orange color, there is less of a chance that an accident-prone guest will trip over it and sue you. If you can fit this item into the rolling gig bag, then it will be one less item to carry.

4. **Amps, monitors, speaker poles, speakers, and all your big sound stuff.** If any of this equipment does not come in a waterproof gig bag, keep clean, extra large garbage bags in your car. In case it rains, cover these expensive electronics with the plastic garbage bags as you transport them to and from your vehicle.

5. **A weather tarp.** Keep this item in your car at all times. You'll find that you can use it as a carpet underfoot in case you have to perform on wet, muddy grass or dirt. The tarp is also useful

"Always come with extra extension cords, just in case someone has used the outlet you planned to use and you have to draw power from a longer distance than you had planned."—Tobey Dodge, wedding planner, The Wedding Connection by Tobey Dodge

for covering up your equipment while it's in your car. The blue side up will hold heat in for the contents underneath; the silver side up will reflect the sun off your instrument and equipment on hot days.

6. **Carpet samples.** Go to a local carpet store and ask for remnants, samples of carpets they are discontinuing that are about the size of doormats. Select some neutral colors and then place them under any and all of your equipment. They'll keep your instrument and music stand from sliding across a hardwood floor, and they'll keep them clean when you are playing on dirty surfaces. You can also place them strategically over power cords to prevent guests from tripping. Carpet samples look a lot nicer than a weather tarp. Reserve the weather tarp for when you need to play on truly wet or muddy ground.

7. **A 3' × 5' sheet of plywood (or maybe a couple of sheets of plywood, if you are in an ensemble).** Use the plywood for deep sand, the kind you'll find at the beach. It will give you a level performing surface and prevent you, your chair, your music stand, and perhaps even your instrument from sinking into the sand at a crazy, unnatural angle. Make sure the plywood is thick enough to support you and your equipment (at least ½ inch). A long, thick plywood board can also double as a ramp for rolling extra-heavy equipment out of your vehicle.

8. **A fold up cart to transport your equipment.** Wedding DJs use these all the time. Why shouldn't musicians? In fact, save your back and place as many items on wheels as possible, unless you have Sherpas working for you.

9. **A portable beach or café umbrella.** If you play an acoustic instrument and are asked to perform where there is no shade, having your own portable umbrella will save your instrument and save your gig. The umbrella that I use is inserted into a hollow plastic base that I fill up with water. It is very lightweight. If you find yourself performing at a lot of outdoor weddings, shop for a portable umbrella in garden shops and stores that carry seasonal summer merchandise.

10. **A space heater.** Think I'm kidding? Nope. If I know I'm going to be performing for hours in a cold room on a winter day, and an electrical outlet is available, I'll bring my space heater with me. I've found it of greatest use inside damp wineries. If this

doesn't keep you warm, do what harpist Alison Vardy, does: bring a hot pad with a high, medium, and low setting to sit upon!

And finally, here are a few items that defy categorization:

The one most hygienically important equipment item: hand sanitizer. Your clients and their guests may sneeze and cough into their hands and then turn to you and shake your hand in appreciation of your wonderful musical abilities. They will also shake hands with you when they have just finished eating barbeque chicken wings and fried egg rolls. Yuck. You simply cannot avoid shaking hands with them as a universal gesture of greeting and thanks.

A wedding minister I know swears by the effectiveness of hand sanitizer, because he is shaking hands all day. He convinced me that it should be part of my equipment list. And I found another use for it—I discovered that it's also great for a quick clean up before performing, when no running water is available or the bathrooms are a long hike from the wedding site.

Whether you get the liquid kind that comes in a tiny plastic bottle or the little individually-wrapped towelettes, bring hand sanitizer with you everywhere. Keep plenty in your small rolling gig bag, your purse, a jacket pocket, and the glove compartment of your car.

The one most indispensable equipment item: a cell phone. If I'm driving in circles, trying to find the wedding location, I make a call. If I show up onsite and the wedding coordinator is nowhere to be seen, I give her a call. My cell phone also displays the time, so if I forget my watch, I have another means of checking the time (but I turn off the ring function at the wedding).

Many years ago, I showed up for a church wedding and no one was there when I arrived, except the photographer. There were no wedding flowers or decorations, and there was no sign that a wedding was about to take place. We couldn't figure out what was going on. Where was everyone? The bride, all her guests, and the minister suddenly burst upon the scene ten minutes before the ceremony was scheduled to begin. They scurried around the church, placing flowers at the altar and bows on the ends of the pews. A couple of men rolled down a white runner, and up walked the bride. I was astonished, and so was the photographer. We were concerned that we arrived at the wrong church, and the bride somehow forgot to tell us about a last-minute change of wedding location. If we had cell phones back then, we would have been able to check on the bride's whereabouts and verified that we were indeed at the correct wedding location.

As obvious as it may seem to bring a cell phone with you, I hope it is just as obvious that it should remain turned off for the duration of the wedding. As soon as you arrive at the wedding, shut it off. Do not turn it on again until after you have left the wedding site, unless you take a break and leave the room to make a call. All phone calls you make at a wedding should be out of earshot of the wedding guests and staff. I know several wedding pros who intentionally leave their cell phones in their cars; they can retrieve them if they need to, and they never have to worry about their cell phones ringing during the exchange of vows.

Now it's your turn to make a quick assessment of your equipment. Fill out the **Equipment Inventory Worksheet and Checklist** at the end of this chapter. List ALL of your items. Include extra equipment, keeping in mind to always have a spare. Use this list as a checklist for loading your car for a wedding gig.

The last page of this inventory is your wish list for the equipment you'd like to purchase. Keep this list at your desk, taking notes about competitive costs of different brands and where different items are available for purchase.

Here's one more piece of equipment to include: A small duffle bag, small rolling carry-on bag, and/or garment bag for your change of clothes. To keep your formal clothes neat, you won't want to be setting up and breaking down your musical equipment in them. You'll want to use this bag to store a change of shoes, deodorant, a lint brush, a make-up bag and jewelry for women, and a necktie for men.

This leads to another important investment in your wedding equipment. . . . Your attire.

ALL DRESSED UP WITH SOMEWHERE TO GO

Scientifically, our sense of hearing is considered secondary to our sense of sight. First impressions are made by what we look like, not by how well we play. If you look like dynamite, neatly dressed and groomed, then even if you are having an off day and not performing at your best, your audience will give you a second chance. The converse is also true—If you look like you just rolled out of bed, have a five-o'clock shadow or hastily applied your make-up, and your clothes are ill-fitting or display stains from last week's gigs, then you

"My most essential wedding music equipment includes a reliable car, a cell phone, and a computer."—Seán Cummings, 8th generation professional bagpiper

"No musician should ever wear anything that would draw negative attention or comments."—Karen Brown, Master Bridal Consultant, Karen For Your Memories

can play every note perfectly, and your audience may not think you are all that great.

This discussion goes beyond personal hygiene. Take your wardrobe into consideration. Dress conservatively. Even if everyone, including the bride, is wearing blue jeans, this doesn't mean that you should, too. You won't see the banquet staff or the minister dressed in blue jeans. They don't dress like the guests. Why should you? Dressing like a professional means you'll be paid like a professional.

The rule of wedding attire is: You can never be overdressed only underdressed. When in doubt, always dress more formally.

Known as "concert dress" on the orchestra scene, black and white are the standard colors for musicians to wear at a wedding ceremony. Picture how a pianist in a four-diamond restaurant would be dressed. Picture what chamber orchestra members wear on stage. Then you'll have the right idea.

The standard uniform for male ceremony musicians is a black suit with a necktie. Eventually, you may wish to invest in a tux as you perform at more weddings.

The safest wedding ceremony attire for women is a black dress. Purchase one calf-length black dress (or a black skirt and blouse) for less formal weddings, when the bride informs you that the bridesmaids will be wearing tea length dresses. Reserve a full-length black dress or gown for the more formal weddings, when the wedding party is wearing floor-length dresses.

Even in the summer, a sleeveless black dress looks elegant (and use a wrap if you are playing in a house of worship). You'll never have to worry about clashing with the bride's chosen colors. Dress it up with simple jewelry like pearls or rhinestones. A pretty hat is also a great addition, especially to shield your eyes from the sun if you are performing outdoors.

Invest in ethnic or period costumes for theme weddings. A Scottish piper is expected to wear a kilt, of course. If it is a luau wedding, or country-style denim and diamonds wedding, or some other kind of theme wedding, then wear theme clothes. If you want to match the bride's colors, it's perfectly acceptable. Men can choose the same color tie or cummerbund, and ladies can wear a dress or gown, that matches the bridesmaids' colors. However, you'll still get more mileage out of the dark suit and black dress.

"As a bandleader, I always bring extra bowties. We all make human mistakes, and it's easy to forget these kinds of things."—Jeff Leep, Entertainment Agent/Musician, Leep Entertainment

If you are in an ensemble or band, your outfits should match each other in color or style. It's entirely appropriate for mariachi band members to wear traditional clothing instead of tuxes. Even if you are in a punk band, your group should dress like a cohesive unit (yes, punk bands play at wedding receptions, too). The bandleader can dress themselves apart from the rest of the group, with a little flash of color on their necktie or shirt to indicate to guests that they are the one in charge of the group.

Only wear your performing wardrobe for performing. Try not to wear your good clothes for loading and unloading musical equipment at a wedding gig. Change into your performance clothes after you set up. At the very least, if there is nowhere to change, wear comfy shoes to haul your equipment, and save your nice, scuff-free shoes for performing. I don't wear my gown and three-inch heels when I'm carrying my amp or when I'm driving to the gig.

By the way, acquiring the appropriate wardrobe for wedding gigs should not break your wallet. I purchase all my performance dresses and gowns at consignment stores. Gorgeous prom dresses and bridesmaid dresses can be found at unheard-of prices, and they were probably worn only once. I've also found matching costume jewelry at consignment stores. What I don't find there, I can usually find at end-of-wedding-season sales at bridal boutiques.

Men can also locate inexpensive suits at consignment stores, but since you may be wearing the same suit over and over again, I'd suggest purchasing one or two new suits that you'll just reserve for wedding performances. If you are ready to invest in a tux, check with local tux rental shops to see if they have any styles that are being discontinued and are on sale. However, be careful about buying a heavily used tux. You might get a great discount, but will it last without the pants splitting?

Women—Heed this warning: Never, ever wear white to a wedding. Remember, the bride is the star, not you. Only the bride wears white, and you must never detract attention away from her on her wedding day.

I once played at a wedding where the bride loved white so much that she instructed all her bridesmaids to wear white, too. Imagine my confusion trying to figure out who the bride was at this wedding! This bride also wanted me to wear white, but I quietly declined and wore the standard black.

"I do not allow sunglasses. Period. Only for jazzers or rare eye diseases"—Van Vinikow, The "Supreme Being" of "The String Beings" string quartet/trio

Men and women: Avoid wearing sunglasses, especially during the ceremony. Photos are taken non-stop, video cameras are rolling, and people want to see your eyes. When performing outside, insist on being in the shade—It's better for your eyes and you won't need sunglasses. Besides, it's also better for your instrument.

Wedding Music Inventory Worksheet

Instructions: Fill in the music you already know how to play within the appropriate spaces on this worksheet. If you have a lot of titles to list, continue on a blank page.

The Wedding Ceremony:

1. Pre-Ceremony or Prelude Music

2. Optional—Music for the Seating of Mothers and Grandparents

3. Optional—Music for Lighting of the Unity Candles

4. Processional Music

5. Music for the Bride's Entrance to the Processional

6. Optional—Ceremony Music. For each tune you list, name the tradition where the tune would be used (for instance, "Simple Gifts" for the candle lighting ceremony)

7. Recessional Music

8. Post-Ceremony Music (Also Known as "Interlude Music") or Cocktail Hour Music

The Wedding Reception:

1. Entrance of the Bride and Groom

2. Family Traditions Within the Reception

3. Music for Dining

4. Bride's and Groom's First Dance

5. Family Dances

6. Other Dance Selections

7. The Cutting of the Cake

8. The Throwing of the Bouquet and the Garter Toss

9. The Last Dance

Creating a Band Name

By Roxane R. Fritz, Attorney at Law

Choosing a name for your group is something that should be done very carefully. It will likely be something that you will use for years to come. If you're planning on playing for weddings, you want to make sure there isn't a negative connotation to your name. Few brides want to tell people that they have "The Pirates of Death" or "Satan's Love Child" playing at their wedding. Having a pleasant sounding name will help your image right off the top.

The most important thing you'll want to do is to make sure the name you choose is not already taken. A band name cannot be protected by copyright, but it can be trademarked. This can be done on a State level or nation-wide through the federal government. There is also something called a "common law" trademark, which you get simply by using a name for a period of time.

While you probably won't be worried about trademarking your name until you have been around for a while, you do want to make sure that you won't get a letter to "cease and desist" from using your name from a lawyer or another business. There are several ways to check on the name you want to use. The first is to do a simple "Google" search on-line. If there is someone else in the entertainment business using the name you chose, go back to the drawing board and start over. Also, check to see if the domain name is available for your name. If there is someone in another unrelated business using the name, for example, a carpet company, you are probably alright. You can do a search of the name you want to use to see if it is federally trademarked at www.uspto.gov.

Changing the spelling of a name already in use will not help. For example, you can't use the name "The Beetles" just because it is spelled differently. If your name "sounds" too close to another name so that the names can be confused, you could be in violation of a trademark.

The best thing to do is find a name where you can get the web domain name as .com which will be the easiest way for people to find you and help you build your business.

Once you decide on a name, you should file a fictitious business statement in the city or county where you live. This is a requirement to do business in most areas, and will also help protect your name in that area.

Equipment Inventory Worksheet and Checklist

"If you have to ask for any piece of equipment or furniture, you are not sufficiently well-prepared."—Stephen Vardy, Sound Engineer

Fill in the spaces with all the equipment you own that you'll want to bring to your wedding gigs.

The obvious equipment:

❏ Your instrument (s): List instruments below

_____   _____
_____   _____
_____   _____

❏ Your instrument case and items to pack into your instrument case:

_____
_____
_____

❏ Things to sit upon:

Chairs—How Many: ____,   Benches—How Many: ____,   Stools—How Many:___

❏ Sheet music bags and items to pack in sheet music bags

How Many Sheet Music Bags: ___

What to pack:

_____
_____
_____
_____
_____
_____
_____
_____
_____

❏ Music stand and music stand carrying case—How many music stands: ___

Rolling gig bag and items to pack into rolling gig bag:

❏ Electronic tuner(s)

❏ Clips or cords to use with tuner(s)

❏ Batteries for tuner(s). Types of batteries needed: _____

❑ Instrument fix-it items:

_____

_____

_____

❑ Sticky stuff: ❑ Gaffer's tape, ❑ Velcro tape, ❑ Masking Tape, Other tape:_____

❑ Sheet music clips

❑ A doorstop

❑ Instrument polish and polish cloth

❑ Warm weather personal emergency items:

_____

_____

❑ Cold weather personal emergency items:

_____

_____

❑ Extra PR: Business Cards, Brochures, and Other PR items: _____

Items needed for amplification to include in the rolling gig bag:

❑ Power AC adapters for electronic devices: _____

❑ Warranties and instruction booklets for tuner, amps, and all devices:

_____

_____

❑ Cords: How many and what kind:

_____

_____

❑ Velcro straps. How many: _____

❑ Equalizers, direct boxes, and special effect pedals. What kind and how many:

_____   _____

_____   _____

_____   _____

_____   _____

_____   _____

❑ Microphone inventory:

_____
_____
_____
_____

Stuff to be left in the trunk of the car, your vehicle's glove compartment, or in your garage until needed:

❑ Instruments stand(s): How many and for which instruments:

_____   _____
_____   _____
_____   _____

❑ Music stand light(s)—How many and are they battery-operated or need electricity?

_____

❑ A long, bright orange, wind up extension chord

❑ Inventory of amps, P.A., monitors, speaker poles, speakers, and all other big sound stuff:

_____
_____
_____
_____
_____
_____
_____

❑ A weather tarp

❑ Carpet samples

❑ Plywood Sheet(s)

❑ A fold up cart to transport equipment

❑ A portable beach umbrella

❑ A space heater.

Other important items:

❑ Hand sanitizer. Where will you store this item? : _____

❑ A cell phone

Your Wish List for New Equipment

What do you NEED to purchase?

❑ _____

Brand or Manufacturer and Model:

_____

Specs for Equipment (Electronic Specs, Weight, Ease of Use, Etc.)

_____

_____

_____

Peripheral items needed with this product:

_____

_____

Where can it be purchased?

Retail Stores and Prices Quoted:

_____

_____

_____

Catalog Sources and Prices Quoted:

_____

_____

_____

Online Sources and Prices Quoted:

_____

_____

_____

Online Customer Ratings for Product:

_____

_____

_____

Photocopy this page for each piece of equipment you have in mind, staple these pages and keep them at your desk as you do your research.

Yes Dear, that is my price. I am an accomplished and experienced organist with great references. Of course; If it's too much, you could always look in the "Clearance Section".

CHAPTER 2

The Bottom Line: Setting Your Fees

"Price is what you pay. Value is what you get."
—Warren Buffett

ALL KINDS OF FEES FOR ALL KINDS OF SITUATIONS

Putting real thought into your pricing structure, from the outset, will cause you to be confident about what you charge. Then brides will perceive your prices as reasonable and you will get booked. The bride must believe that she is getting something of value for her money.

You won't find any solid numbers in this section, just some guidelines about how to arrive at those figures yourself.

Setting fees is such a soft science. You'll want to keep these variables in mind as you design a fee schedule:

1. **To the bride, what you charge is what you are worth.**
   Charge enough money and the bride will think you are worth hiring. Undercut other musicians in your area and your abilities will be perceived as substandard. If you appear to be hungry for work, brides will get a whiff of this and try to bargain down your prices. If you want to keep on friendly terms with fellow wedding musicians, your fees should be in line with what they charge.

To find out what other musicians in your area charge, contact wedding coordinators and booking agents. Finding these people is easy: do a search on a local Internet wedding directory or do it the old fashioned way, with the Yellow Pages. When I was first starting out, I made friends with colleagues who, to this very day, continue to open up to me about what my competition is doing. Best of all, they refer my services all the time.

Once you have determined the range of fees that are charged in your region, set your fees at the lower end of this range if you are new to performing at weddings.

If you are an experienced musician with years of performances under your belt, you can charge rates at the upper end of this range. Brides will be thrilled to pay for your experience. They plan to only get married once and they expect everything to go perfectly. Brides will pay a premium for your abilities and professionalism.

Be careful not go overboard by setting your prices well above your competition. If you indeed have the credentials, the bride will think you are a fantastic performer. She may also assume that performing at weddings is beneath you. I know of a very accomplished instrumental duo that purposely priced themselves well above everyone else because they just didn't want to play at weddings anymore. They charged a premium to do something they didn't want to do. They now are involved in other musical endeavors.

2. **You can charge more than most other musicians in your area if your performance is truly unique.** If another musical style, instrumentation, or band with your abilities cannot be found within several hundred miles of your home, then you can also charge more than most other musicians in your area. This is the basic law of supply and demand—If there is a demand for what you can do and there is no supply of musicians who can do it, you have a monopoly. For instance, if there is a sizeable Greek population in your area, and you are a member of the only Greek dance band for miles and miles around, then charge what the market will bear.

3. **What the market will bear depends upon the size of the local population as well as the socio-economic status of the residents.** Even if you are a member of the only Greek dance band for miles, if you live in a low-income, sparsely populated rural town, be reasonable. Brides need to be able to afford hiring your band. Conversely, if affluent residents live in your

city, you can charge more and will still get booked. The cost of living, the effects of inflation or depression, and the general economic outlook are all geographical factors to take into account when creating a pricing menu.

If you live in a resort community: Wedding destination areas attract brides of various economic backgrounds. If you reside or plan to perform at resort areas, the socio-economic level cannot determine your fees. Brides travel from all over the world to get married where I reside, here at Lake Tahoe, and I have no idea what their financial status is when they book my services.

A Caution: Some wedding musicians charge according to the wedding venue, because they think if a bride can afford to get married at a private, exclusive golf club, she has a larger budget than a bride who gets married on a public beach. This philosophy is flawed, though, because the bride may have used up her budget to get married at the golf club and has little or no budget for music, whereas the bride who is getting married on the beach may have plenty left over to spend on live music.

4. **Price to make ends meet for you.** If you aren't charging enough to make it worth your while, what's the point? You're not in this for free. Weddings are not pay for play, play for tips, or a way to practice, air out your repertoire, and learn to play in front of people. Weddings can be a viable source of income. Your equipment costs money, your music education cost money, and your car and the gas it takes to get to your gig costs money. If you use a roadie, a sound tech, or other personnel, pass their costs along to the client, too. Additionally, your time is of value. What is it all worth to you?

5. **Quote fees according to the amount of hassle involved.** As a harpist, it is a lot more bother for me to get to a wedding, set up, tune up, and perform, than say, a pianist, for instance. Therefore, my fees are comparable to those of other local harpists and understandably above those of local pianists, who just walk in with their sheet music, sit down at the piano, and are ready to play.

If loading zones are nonexistent, you've got to trudge up three flights of stairs to the performance area, or if the staff at the particular wedding venue is impossible to work with, then you have reason to raise your fees for weddings at those particular venues. For whatever reason, if it's a lot more trouble to perform at certain wedding sites, then charge more to perform there. If you really hate the location then don't take the job. Otherwise, you'll dread playing there and it will show in your performance and your dealings with the bride.

Here at Lake Tahoe, a local ski resort hosts summer weddings at their private restaurant on a mountaintop. Access is via tram, then via bus over a road riddled with potholes. Not only is it exhausting to transport my harp and equipment up there, it takes me a full hour just to get to the wedding site, and another full hour to get back down to the parking lot afterwards. I still perform at this ski resort, because the wedding coordinator and staff are so pleasant and go out of their way to help. So, I tack on an additional fee to pay for the extra time and work it takes to perform up there. And brides pay it.

Some experienced wedding musicians will charge extra money to a bride if they think she has the marks of turning into a bridezilla. Certainly this falls into this category of pricing according to the hassle factor, but it's hard to tell if a bride will sprout horns and a tail at an initial meeting, when you are explaining your fees. In the extreme case when a bride is behaving irrationally at the outset, do you really want to perform for her at all?

6. **Bundle free services within your fee schedule.** We all like to get a little extra freebie when making a large purchase, and brides are no exception. Items you can include in your quotes may include free consultation, free amplification, free mileage (within a certain radius of your home), free wedding calendars, free mp3 downloads of your audition material, and so on.

No one wants to be "nickeled and dimed"—You'll scare away brides by itemizing every single cost. Roll all the costs into your packages, so you aren't quoting a bunch of fees for your performance. Just think of how the cable companies are making money—They bundle TV, Internet, and phone costs together, throw in some perceived freebies like extra channels and discounted long distance rates, and the consumers think they're getting a good deal.

7. **Package and price your services to sell.** Design three basic performance packages. Why three? See below:

The Highest Cost Package—This contains your most performance time available for a wedding and all extra services you're willing to provide. Because it's your premium package, you'll want to price it as such.

The Lowest Cost Package—this enables brides who have very small weddings or very small budgets to afford your services. This package is your minimum—your minimum of how much time you will perform and the minimum of what the bride can afford to pay you. This package is the answer to the bride's question of, "What is your minimum?"

When customers are provided with three choices, they become more meaningful in their decision-making and are more likely to avoid the lowest-priced option"—Doug Hall, CEO of the Eureka! Ranch think tank

The Best Value Package—This package is in the middle of your price range. When a cost-conscious bride finds out that there isn't that much included in your lowest cost package, she'll be willing to pay a little more to receive more value.

In Chapter 9, I'll offer some pointers about selling these packages to brides, but for now, let's just stick to developing your price list.

8. **Discount wisely.** Discounts are viable when they are offered to wedding coordinators and booking agents. They are booking your services on the bride's behalf instead of the bride contracting with you directly.

I regularly offer a small discount to wedding coordinators and booking agents for two reasons. First of all, they continue to recommend my services to brides, instead of recommending my competition. This results in dependable repeat business. Secondly, the discount makes sense because they are doing all the sales work for me, selling my services to brides. They are convincing the bride to hire me. My phone regularly rings with the coordinator or booking agent saying, "I have a wedding job for you. Are you available?"

Otherwise, when it comes to performing at weddings, no discounts. Period. In her book "Price Yourself Right: A Guide to Charging What You're Worth", direct marketing copywriter Jane Francis explains why you should avoid discounting:

"In a nutshell, discounting starts price wars. What do you do if your competitors discount their prices? The clients start focusing on the prices that are being charged, not the perceived value."

Here are some caveats about discounting:

a) **Discounting may be a symptom of a lack of confidence on your part.** Have confidence in your abilities, and your clients and potential clients will have confidence in you.

b) **If you do provide a discount, have a solid reason for doing so.** For me, I can concretely explain why I offer small discounts to wedding coordinators and booking agents. I also have a discount policy when I am exhibiting at bridal fairs—If a bride books my services, signs my performance agreement, and gives me a deposit right there at the fair, I'll give her a small discount. It is a sales enticement that works. A small discount gets the bride to decide to book me that day, instead of waffling for weeks about her decision.

c) **Stick to the fee schedule.** Make your fee schedule your "business policy". When a bride asks if I have a special discount because she is booking far in advance, I respond that it is not my policy to offer a discount for that reason. It sounds official and final, and the bride doesn't argue.

d) **Don't discount to friends and relatives.** In my experience, this becomes a messy practice, because they figure they can pay you whenever (or never). If your friend is a new acquaintance, charge your normal fees. Have her sign a contract just like any other client. She'll understand that performing is a source of income for you and will pay you accordingly. If it's a close friend or a dear relative who wants you to play for her wedding, just give your performance to her as a wedding gift. She will be overjoyed, and you won't have to go shopping for items on her gift registry. When you give your performance as a gift, you can behave like a guest, mingling, eating, and dancing with everyone else.

e) **Capitalize on your uniqueness instead of your pricing.** The more you look the same and sound the same as your competitors, the more likely brides will start focusing on pricing instead of what you have to offer. Then, you'll feel like you are being forced to offer a discount.

Your instrumentation, your repertoire, and your attire are only part of what makes you unique. Your creative fee schedule can also make you stand out among the crowd. Here are the types of fees you'll want to consider:

1. **Performance fees.** Create three packages and determine what you would like to offer within those packages. Even give these packages special names. Be creative, because brides will associate your packages with you and not your competition.

Will you have separate fees for certain types of wedding ceremonies? For example, will you have one package for couples that are having a full Catholic Wedding Mass vs. a simple church wedding?

Will you charge per hour or per job? What will be your performance time minimum? If you charge per hour, will you be willing to charge for partial hours, say 2½ hours? If you charge hourly, will you charge more the first hour and then a flat fee for each following hour?

Will you charge different rates for receptions vs. ceremonies? Will you devise packages for reception performances as well, or will they simply be on an hourly basis?

What will you bundle into your packages to entice the bride? Free consultation, free mileage within a certain radius, free amplification, free set-up time are some examples.

2. **Overtime rate.** Will playing beyond the scheduled time be charged hourly or with a flat rate?

3. **Rehearsal fees.** Will you charge to attend the wedding rehearsal? Will you turn down wedding rehearsals? Please don't say, "I don't charge for rehearsals". Trust me, you'll live to regret it, as every bride will expect you to set up and play for her giddy wedding party the day before the wedding. Your time is worth money.

If the bride wants you to perform with or accompany her friend or relative, or with someone else you don't know, will you do it? How much would you charge for rehearsing with these musicians? Will you add an extra charge to your performance fee as well?

Will you charge a flat rate for rehearsals (say, $50) or an hourly fee (say $50 per hour)?

4. **Fee to perform new songs.** Will you add an extra fee if the bride wants you to play music that is not part of your repertoire? Or will you turn down a client who gives you a shopping list of requests that you don't currently play?

5. **Cartage fee.** Will you charge an extra fee if you have to haul your equipment to more than one location? For example, if you are hired to play at a wedding ceremony in a church and play at the reception at a restaurant, will you charge extra to pack up at the church and set up at the restaurant?

6. **Mileage/travel fee.** Will you charge for mileage from the moment you back your car out of the driveway, or will you waive your mileage fee within a certain radius from your home? How much per mile will you charge? I base my mileage on the current allowable IRS deduction rate. Will you also charge an hourly fee for drive time?

7. **Set-up fee.** Will you charge extra if you need to arrive far earlier than is necessary? If you are in a band, when will it become necessary to charge a set-up fee, beyond what you include in your performance packages?

8. **Extras.** Will you charge for amplification? When will it be necessary to charge for amplification? Will you charge for special attire if you have a wardrobe of theme costumes for the wedding? Will you charge for stage platforms or other items that could be provided by the client and would cost you extra to rent?

9. **Hassle fees.** What will you charge if you have to perform at certain venues that are difficult to access, have no loading zones, etc.? What charges will you need to pass along to the client for performing at certain venues (parking fees, toll bridge fees, etc.)?

10. **"Roadie"** * **and sound tech costs.** What will you be paying your assistants? You will need to pass this fee along to your clients, including it as part of your performance packages.

I am leaving the most important fees for last . . .

THE MOST IMPORTANT POLICIES TO CONSIDER— COLLECTING A DEPOSIT AND YOUR CANCELLATION POLICY

These policies are an integral part of your fee structure. A bride determines the fairness of your business practice by the rules you set for collecting the deposit and handling cancellations. If she believes your policies are unreasonable, then she will think twice about hiring you.

Without a deposit and a cancellation policy in place, you make it very easy for your clients to think nothing of canceling your services

---

*A "roadie" is a person who is employed by bands, ensembles and musicians to load, unload, set up equipment, and run errands. Etymology: A person who travels on the road with musicians.

at the last minute. You'll receive nothing for the time and effort you put into working with the bride, not to mention the fact that you might have turned down other work for this same date.

Require a deposit to book a wedding job. The deposit is the client's statement of intent to hire me to perform, beyond a signature on the contract. The deposit also implies that the client indeed has the funds available to pay for my services. If a deposit check bounces or if it is late, this is an indication to me of how I'll need to proceed to collect the balance due (In Chapter 11, I'll discuss ways of ensuring that you will be paid . . .)

What amount will you require as a deposit? Will you require a client to give you a percent of the total amount due (for instance 50%), or will you request a flat rate as a deposit regardless of the total amount owed (for instance $100)?

When will the balance of the payment be due? Will you require the entire total before the event date (say two weeks before) or will you collect the balance due on the event date? Other vendors who are supplying products expect the total amount to be paid in full prior to the wedding date. For example, the baker needs to purchase ingredients and do most of their work prior to the wedding date. As musicians, we are offering a service, and it may be difficult justifying to a bride why we need to be paid in full before her big day.

You may be able to justify payment in full before the wedding date if you are a big name in your community and are in high demand. In other words, you regularly turn down gigs due to a calendar full of bookings. If you employ a crew of roadies, sound techs, and lighting techs for your wedding performances and need to guarantee payment to them in advance, then this is another viable reason to demand full payment up front.

In my poll of experienced wedding musicians, about half of them insisted on prepayment prior to the wedding date, and the other half received their balance due on the big day. It is clearly up to you what boundaries to set regarding prepayment in full.

The only situation when it is unreasonable to require a deposit is when a couple is hiring you to play within a few short days, or even hours, of their wedding. Sometimes, I'll get a phone call from a panicky bride who suddenly realized that she forgot about booking music for her wedding. Or maybe she had another entertainer booked (usually a friend or relative), and they cannot make it to the wedding or don't want to perform. Other times, there is no panic involved—It's simply an elopement, and the couple decides to hire musicians at the last minute.

For whatever reason, if there is only enough time to run performance agreements back and forth via fax machine, I am willing to be paid in full on the wedding date. But my caveat is that I must receive this payment *prior* to unloading my car and setting up, and this provision is in writing, as part of the faxed contract.

The cancellation policy—Having a cancellation policy in place is your safety net in case the wedding is called off or your performance services are no longer needed.

At this point, I highly recommend that you consult with an attorney or legal professional to cover all the bases of what can happen in terms of cancellation. If there is any dispute over who is owed money, how much money is owed, and when it is owed, you'll want to settle this outside of court.

Here are some questions to ponder: What will the client owe you if they cancel three months before the performance date? Or one month? Or two weeks? Or on the morning of the wedding? Obviously, it will be easier to rebook the date with a lot of advance notice of cancellation.

How must your client notify you of cancellation for it to be valid? Is a phone call sufficient, or will you require a statement in writing (via email, snail mail, or fax)? What if the client claims they called and left a message and you never got it? For this reason, getting it in writing is always your best bet.

Will you refund the deposit in the event of a genuine emergency, or will your deposit be nonrefundable under any set of circumstances? How will you define what an emergency is?

What will you do for the client if you are the one who has to cancel the date? Will you refund their deposit? Will you help them find a suitable replacement musician or band? Will you pay them a penalty if you have to cancel and you are unable to find a suitable substitute musician?

WHAT WILL BE THE METHOD OF PAYMENT FOR ALL YOUR FEES?

The last portion of your fee schedule includes how you will accept payment. Will you accept payment by check, cashier's check, money order, or will you accept cash only? If you are set up to receive credit card payments, will you take a payment by credit card? Maybe you'll decide to accept payment by one means for the deposit, say by check, and then accept cash only for the balance due on the wedding day.

If you wish, you can accept payments by credit card. It is an easy means to collect money, and brides are fairly used to making deposits for hotel rooms and other amenities by credit card. If you go this route, some musicians have reported satisfaction with using PayPal.com, where a detailed invoice can be sent to a client via email. You don't need to have a website to use PayPal. Simply enter the amount into an online virtual terminal, and the money automatically goes into your bank account.

Personally, I am reluctant to use PayPal, because of all the phishing* surrounding this company. In fact, I am not an advocate of accepting credit card payments for performances. If a dispute arises and a bride wants her money back, my concern is that credit card companies will side with the cardholder—They want to keep the cardholder's business. I do, however, accept credit card payments for the sale of my CDs, a small price to pay if someone were to ask for a refund.

How do I know this? When I purchased a computer from a mail order company many years ago and the computer would not boot up, I tried to get a refund from the mail order company. They refused to refund my money because they said I waited beyond their return period. So, I went to my credit card company. They got on the phone with the computer company, and they told them to refund my money. After some haggling, the charge was reversed on my credit card. My credit card company has always stood by me. (By the way, this is why you should pay for all expensive musical equipment by credit card— it is easy for the merchant to reverse the charges on your card if you want to return it, and there is a paper record of the transaction).

* "Phishing" is the act of luring unsuspecting Internet users to a fake web site in order to steal passwords, financial or personal information, or introduce a virus attack. This is done by sending an authentic-looking email, with the real organization's logo, that directs recipients to this fake website by claiming that they will lose their account privileges if they do not do so. Etymology: 1996, as in "fishing" for a user.

I've given you a lot of food for thought in this chapter. Do your research. Discover what your competition is doing, what they are charging, and what kinds of payment and cancellation policies they ascribe to.

If you are a member of a musician's union (here in the U.S., The American Federation of Musicians), they may dictate the minimums you should be charging. You'll need to check with them before you make your pricing policies public.

In the end, after you have taken all of these points into careful consideration, trust your gut feelings. Set fees you can be comfortable charging. If a bride asks you, "How much do you charge?" and you stutter to get the answer out of your mouth, you have to go back to the drawing board and rethink your rates.

A concert harpist I know moved from Houston to Sacramento. In Houston, she played for a very affluent crowd. When she moved, she discovered Sacramento brides were unwilling to pay the fees she charged in Houston. This harpist could not bring herself to lower her rates, so she prefers to live with the fact that she doesn't get to play as often as she likes.

The bottom line is to be comfortable with the fees you are quoting.

Set up? Oh, we'd like you right out at the end of the diving board...
*you don't have a **problem** with that, **do you?***

CHAPTER 3

Writing a Performance Agreement—Essential Items to Include and Non-Essential Items You May Want to Add

"Boldly guarantee that you will deliver what you promise."
—Doug Hall, CEO of the Eureka! Ranch corporate think tank

Stories abound about the musicians who have been "stiffed*" and are henceforth, sour about performing at gigs. Dig a little deeper into these stories, and you'll often discover that the disgruntled musician never bothered to put anything in writing.

The contract is a written promise. For you, the performer, it is a written promise that your needs will be met at the wedding or reception and you will be paid. For your client, it is a written promise that you will provide the performance that they expect. It is the only way for both of you to be certain that you are covering all the needs that each of you have.

Note that I am using the term "client" here, because this is the person who you will work for, your "boss". He, or more commonly for a wedding it will be a "she", is the person who signs the contract. More often than not, your client will be the bride, but it could be her mother, her future mother-in-law, a friend or relative of the bride, a booking agent, or a wedding coordinator. The contract you devise

*A musician who is "stiffed" is one who has not been paid money due for a performance.

should be universal—something that can be used with any and all wedding clients.

If you want legal protection, you need a written contract. I have known several musicians who perform at weddings as a hobby and refuse to put anything in writing. They didn't want to report anything to the IRS for taxes, and they insisted on being paid in cash and avoiding a paper trail. Wouldn't it be better to insure payment for a job by using a contract? What recourse does a musician have if the client tries to weasel out of paying by claiming at the event, "Ooops, I forgot my checkbook"? Or what recourse does a cellist have if a child pushes their instrument over while they're on a bathroom break? Or what if the client instructs the harpist to set up on a diving board platform when they arrive at the wedding site? I'm not making up these situations—They have all happened to my musician friends or me.

You get the picture. You need to put each job in writing in the form of a written agreement. However, I am not an attorney nor in any way a legal authority, and nothing in this book should be construed as giving legal advice. What follows in this chapter are ideas and suggestions. Decide if they are pertinent to the contract for you or for your ensemble or band. Then, make up your own contract using the **Contract Worksheet** at the end of this chapter.

Next, after you have reviewed the worksheet, make an appointment to see a contract attorney or entertainment law attorney. Most lawyers charge by the hour. You'll save a lot of money by creating your own contract first and then taking it to the lawyer to let them poke holes in it (instead of having your attorney make one up for you from scratch). My attorney instructs me to email or fax documents to her. She'll look them over, "redline"* them, and send them back. I make final corrections and then send them to the printer for hard copies (you can keep them on your computer, but in the event of a computer crash, hard copies and back up CDs are essential).

Keep your clients in mind as you devise a performance agreement template. Address their concerns as well as your own. You may wish to start with a simple contract form and as time goes on, add new terms

---

*To "redline": In MS Word and other word processing programs, there is a feature where you can have changes to a document noted with an underline or a strike through, usually initially in red. The term "redlining" means to show proposed changes to a document, which can then be accepted to change the document.

to your contract when you discover you need them. In this way, your contract will eventually evolve into an indispensable business tool that you'll feel very comfortable using. Even if you feel ill at ease with your contract now, begin to use it with all your clients. Have faith that it will protect your interests. As long as your contract includes items that are important to your clients as well as to you, your clients will feel a sense of protection, too.

If you belong to the Musician's Union (The American Federation of Musicians), you may be required to use their contract form. You can still add extra terms that are important to you and your clients. Check with your union to see if you need use their contract just for union jobs or for all jobs.

Many musicians rely on electronic contracts, which can be emailed. To get an actual signature, you'll have to print it out at some point. Also, if you meet with a potential client in person, you'll need to have hard copies. Make sure your contract looks good in print, as well as on your computer, and number the pages.

When a client books you, you'll need to print three copies of the contract if you intend to send the contact by postal mail. Sign all three copies, sending two to the client and saving one for your own records. Instruct your client to sign both copies, mailing one back to you and saving one for her own records.

Have your contracts printed with your own letterhead information from your stationary at the top. Make sure to include your phone number, fax number, email address, and website address. This way, they'll know how to reach you when quickly glancing at the agreement. If you don't have any letterhead, using a self-inking address stamp will do fine, and write in any extra contact information not included on your address stamp.

It's a good idea to use a stable mailing address where people can always find you. I also suggest listing a post office box and a cell phone number if you happen to move a lot or are on the road playing other gigs when you aren't performing at weddings. Another argument for having a separate phone number and P.O. box for your business is that they provide security and privacy, particularly for women.

Here's an explanation of items to include in your contract. Use the **Contract Worksheet** at the end of this chapter in tandem with the following items.

ESSENTIAL CLIENT AND EVENT INFORMATION FOR YOUR CONTRACT

The client's name, and the time, date, and location of the wedding performance are the most critical information to collect.

1. **Client's name and contact information.** Know how to reach your client, the person who is signing the contract, under any circumstance. Include spaces for their mailing address, email address, and their day, evening, cell phone, and fax numbers.

2. **The names of the bride and groom.** Even if neither the bride nor the groom is your client, it's good to know their names so that you can congratulate them at the end of the wedding gig.

3. **The contact information for the bride and groom.** As I mentioned, the bride and groom may not be your clients, but your client (the wedding coordinator or booking agent) may instruct you to contact the bride and groom directly for music selections.

4. **Date and day of the week for the wedding.**

5. **Type of event.** Are you being hired to perform for a wedding ceremony, a Catholic Wedding Mass, a cocktail reception, a full wedding reception, or even for the rehearsal dinner? Specify this on the contract.

6. **The location of the wedding ceremony and/or reception.** Include enough space for two locations, just in case you are hired to perform for both the ceremony and reception, and they are in two different locations. If the ceremony and reception are at two different locations, you might want to have your client give you an estimated distance in mileage and time so you can calculate any additional costs and plan accordingly.

7. **Is the client to provide you with a map and directions to the location(s)?**

8. **Event day phone numbers.** These are emergency numbers to have on hand in case you can't find the wedding location, are running late, or need to find out if there is a change of venue due to bad weather. Leave enough space to write at least two phone numbers: the phone number at the location, the bride's or groom's cell phone number, the mother of the bride's cell

phone number, the wedding coordinator's number, or even the minister's number.

9. **Name of your on-site contact.** This person can tell you where to set up when you arrive and may also be the one who hands you your payment (!)

10. **Your arrival time.** Brides like to know when you will arrive. Your on-site contact will be expecting you. Schedule enough time to set up, before you need to start playing. (As a soloist, I need at least a half hour to set up, but if there are loading zone issues, stairs, or if I have to set up elaborate sound equipment, I allow at least an hour.) If you are performing for a wedding ceremony, arriving early is professional. If you are performing for a wedding reception, you may need to arrive even earlier to set up before guests are seated for the ceremony, if the ceremony and reception take place at the same site. Even if the ceremony takes place outdoors and the reception is indoors, reception musicians absolutely cannot run sound checks once prelude music begins for the ceremony, so being very early is essential.

11. **Your performance schedule.** These are the times you will begin and end your performance. If you'll be playing for the reception and will playing sets, you'll want to add the length of your set as well as the length of the breaks to your contract.

12. **Ceremony time.** If you are a ceremony musician, this is an important piece of information. If the ceremony starts more than ten minutes late, and wedding activities have been scheduled too closely together, you may run into overtime.

13. **Number of guests.** You'll be able to get a sense of which price package to quote when you know this number—the more guests, the longer they take to get seated and exit the ceremony area, and the longer they take to eat at the reception.

14. **Required amplification.** Often, the number of guests will also help you decide whether you'll need to amplify or not. Of course, this question is best answered by knowing the acoustics of the wedding venue and the loudness of the instruments. As a rule of thumb, amplification becomes a necessity for me, a Celtic harpist, when there are 50 or more people at an event. Of course, if your band includes electric guitars, amplification is a necessity. If you find that you don't need amplification for

a gig, or the venue will allow you to plug into "house sound", you won't have to haul a lot of extra equipment.

If amplification is required, and your equipment needs electricity to run, make sure the proper outlets are available. Include a space on your contract for the approximate distance between the performance area and the outlets. This way, you will know beforehand what kinds of cords and how many extension cords to bring.

15. **The due date for the client or bride to supply music selections to you.** If you include on your contract a deadline for the absolute last date that you can receive selection requests, the client or bride will be more inclined to remember your needs. Receiving the selections well ahead of the wedding date allows for practice and makes me feel confident when I'm performing.

16. **Special Instructions.** Leave several blank lines for additional instructions. This can include all kinds of statements like: "Client requests to meet with the Artist two weeks before the wedding date. She will phone Artist to make appointment"; "Artist is invited to dine at reception. A vegetarian plate will be provided", or even; "Bride does not want "Stairway to Heaven" played, even if her brother requests it".

"Don't expect to be fed for a one hour gig. My deal is three or more hours, they must feed the animals. I say that the meal has to be CONSISTENT with the guests' meals, otherwise, they might give you a tuna sandwich when the guests are eating sushi."—Van Vinikow, The "Supreme Being" of "The String Beings" string quartet/trio

ESSENTIAL FEE INFORMATION FOR YOUR CONTRACT

Let's move on to the fees you need to include on your contract. Refer to a full discussion of how to set your fees in the last chapter.

Itemize your fees, leaving blanks to fill in if a fee pertains to a certain wedding gig. Don't print your fees on your contract, because if you change your rates, you'll avoid having to reprint your contract.

1. **The wedding package that you are quoting to your client.** Remember those performance packages you designed in the last chapter? Leave room on the contract to describe the package that your client has chosen, and a space for you to include the price of that package.

2. **Overtime rate.** Write this charge on the contract, even though you aren't applying it until the need arises. Your clients should have in writing, ahead of time, what they will be charged if they need you to play longer.

3. **Rehearsal fees.** Also include the day of the week, date, and time that the rehearsal begins.

4. **Cartage fee.**

5. **Mileage fee/travel fee.**

6. **Set-up fee.**

7. **Additional or miscellaneous fees.** Include a space to add other fees that don't fall into the above categories, such as additional amplification or renting a P.A., or simply parking and valet charges.

8. **Any other terms.** Leave a big blank space to include information such as discounts to wedding chapels and explanations of barter trades.

9. **The total amount due.**

10. **The amount of the deposit due and the date when you must receive the deposit.**

11. **Accounting for payments received and payments due.** Leave enough space to record the amount of the deposit received, the check number and the date it was received. Also leave space to record the balance due and the check number when you receive payment.

12. **Instructions for how a check should be written to you.** Does the client write your name, your band's name, or your business name when paying you by check?

13. **Instructions about when the balance of the payment is due to you.**

14. **The type of payment you'll accept.** If you elect to take credit card deposits or payments, include enough room on your contract to write the pertinent data that you'll need to process the payment (everything from the card number and expiration date to the billing address).

15. **If the contract is not signed and returned with the required deposit by a certain date, you have the right to cancel and book elsewhere.** Include room to write this date on the contract. Thus, if you don't receive the signed contract and deposit within a reasonable amount of time, the client understands that you will not hold the date for them.

16. **Will you charge interest if the balance isn't paid on time, and if so, how much interest?** It is difficult to collect interest on a late balance, but including this item in your contract simply helps to insure that you will be paid on time.

17. **Instructions to sign.** Quoting from my own contract as an example, "By signing this agreement, Client indicates that this entire agreement, including the additional terms to this agreement on the back of this page, have been read and understood." More about the additional terms in the next section . . .

18. **Directions for where the client sends their deposit and the original copy of the contract, signed by the client.**

19. **Date and place where the contract is signed.** The date is important for your own records, and the place becomes important if there is any legal action. Court appearances may be held in the jurisdiction where the contract is signed.

20. **Your signature and date, and your client's signature and date.** It is helpful to the client if you place a big "X" next to where they need to sign. You can also purchase little removable stick-on arrows that say "Sign Here", to point to where the client needs to sign.

ADDITIONAL TERMS FOR YOUR CONTRACT

Stuff happens, and you need a game plan when it does. This is the information in the fine print, your rules and regulations about performing for this client. I don't suggest that you print it off in a tiny, barely-legible font. Instead, have it all printed on the reverse side of your contract, avoiding a second page for the contract. It's entirely okay to use a second page if you wish, though.

You'll want your clients to know what you expect from them, what you'll do if your needs are not met, and what you'll do if the wedding is cancelled, or if you have to cancel your services. Here are some clauses that are essential to include:

1. **Specific performance area and/or equipment that the client needs to provide for you.** How much space do you need? Must that space be level and dry? Do you need an accessible loading zone and how close must it be to the performance area? Do you need electrical outlets, and if so, what is the maximum

allowable distance from the performance area to the outlet? Are there any other performance area particulars that the client needs to address?

2. **Any stipulations about performing away from heating and air-conditioning ducts or needing shade from direct sunlight or shelter from adverse weather.** This clause educates your clients that your instruments and equipment are sensitive. You can further explain that instruments will go out of tune in the wrong environment, and electrical equipment, such as amps, cannot withstand rain.

3. **Failure to furnish suitable performance conditions shall be considered a breach of contract on the part of the client, and the client will be responsible for 100% of the contract amount.** This is what happens if your client cannot find anywhere else for you to perform, other than that swimming pool diving board platform I mentioned earlier.

4. **Failure of the client to provide music selections within a certain time limit before the wedding.** This clause is important, because the client should know what happens if they neglect to give you their music requests. In my contract, I indicate that if I am not advised of what to play at least five business days prior to the performance, I reserve the right to perform whatever selections I think are appropriate (usually, any music I have memorized, so that I don't have to bring a music stand and sheet music to the gig).

5. **Client assumes the risk of cancellation if you are unable to perform because of weather conditions and no acceptable alternative has been made. In this event, the client will be responsible for 100% of the contract amount.** If you are hired to play outdoors and it pours rain, and if the client can't or won't provide you with a better performance area, then the client still owes you for the performance.

6. **You reserve the right of final decision with respect of content, theme, arrangements, style, and equipment used for the performance. In other words, the client accepts the general nature and scope of your repertoire as satisfactory.** This clause prevents a client from weaseling out of paying your balance due because they didn't care for your rendition of "Unchained Melody".

7. **You will only accept music instructions from the client or another person appointed by the client.** This clause will save you time and time again, because even if it is clear that the bride is your client and she will make all the music decisions, her mother, the groom, and other friends and family members may contact you to give you their requests. With this item on your contract, there will be no confusion about which person has final say over the content in your music list for the gig.

8. **You'll take regular breaks at each hour of play.** Also mention the maximum length of your breaks in the contract.

9. **Your cancellation policy in the event of death, illness, or genuine emergency on the part of either you or your client.** Events that would be covered by this clause include road closures due to law enforcement or fire protection agencies, and blizzard conditions or avalanche control (I live in snow country). If I can't get to a wedding because of an act of Mother Nature, I simply refund the entire amount. If the bride and groom need to call things off for reasons that are beyond their control, such as the groom being called off to war or a bride hospitalized with chicken pox, I will also refund their money. I think it's good Karma to return money when the bride and groom fully intended to have me perform, but fate wouldn't let it happen.

10. **Your cancellation policy in the event of a non-emergency.** This clause covers cancellation because the bride and groom called off the wedding. You turned down a lot of other work to play at their wedding. You should be retaining something, perhaps the entire deposit, in the event you can't recover any other wedding gigs for that given date and time. You don't have to refund the full amount if you manage to book another client that same date; it is all up to you and what you state in the contract.

11. **Your policy in the event that you have to cancel a job.** Many weddings are booked months in advance. Sometimes, your personal calendar may change and wreak havoc on your booking calendar.

For instance, what if your wonderful husband buys two non-refundable plane tickets to Hawaii as a surprise without checking with you or your performance calendar? Will you find a substitute musician for the bride whose wedding is in the way of your vacation?

Will you return her deposit? Or will you perform the job anyway, wishing all the while you could run off to Hawaii without paying damages to the bride? (Okay, I admit that it's improbable that you'd still do the job.)

This is an important clause to include because if you do have to cancel and don't have this clause, you'll leave yourself open to being sued for all kinds of damages by disgruntled clients. It doesn't mean that the bride will win her lawsuit against you, but your goal in constructing a contract is to avoid seeing the inside of any courtroom.

12. **Your policy if you suffer any injuries on the job or damage to your equipment by the client or the client's guests.** Carrying property insurance is necessary in case anything happens to your equipment, such as dropping your instrument out of your car. But what do you do when it's the client's fault when a 4-year-old guest runs into your string quartet during cocktail hour, knocking music stands over and scratching precious instruments. It's not just children, either. At one cocktail reception where I performed, the entire room broke into a friendly food fight, tossing hard dinner rolls across the room at each other like softballs. I quickly moved out of harm's way, hastily carrying my harp into another room.

Do you think the client should pay for damages? By including this clause, your client will be much more respectful of your instruments and equipment, and they will be mindful of out-of-control guests.

By the way, if you don't have property insurance yet, you can contact your home or rental property insurance company and include a rider for your equipment. It may be less money, however, to shop for group property insurance available through several musician organizations, such as the American String Teacher's Association, the National Recording Academy, or the American Federation of Musicians.

13. **Any changes to the performance date, time and location should be made in writing.** As this is the information that is material to your contract, make it legal. Even if you are informed of changes by phone, you can still confirm everything in writing by sending a follow-up letter detailing the date of the phone call and the items in the contract to be updated. You can start the letter with: "This letter refers to our telephone conversation of November 1, 2007" . . .And end it

with something like this: "In the event your understanding differs, please contact me in writing". This assures that you've created a paper trail of any changes.

14. **If both you and the client mutually decide to cancel your services for the wedding, are there any damages to be paid to either party?** This clause is useful when you and the client decide that things aren't working between the two of you. Not everyone's personalities are a perfect fit.

15. **In the event of any lawsuit, the prevailing party will receive all costs of the suit, including the attorney's fees.** This clause, and any other legal types of sentences that your attorney deems important, should be added at the end of your list of additional terms. There may be more terms that are particular to your city, state, or country of residence that are essential to include in your contract. For instance, if you often perform in counties other than where you live, you might also want to put a clause in the agreement that in the event of litigation, the lawsuit must be brought in the county where you reside.

NOT-SO-ESSENTIAL TERMS TO INCLUDE IN YOUR CONTRACT

Here are some items that I have added to my contract over the years. For me, they are essential, but for you, they may not apply:

1. **An Invoice Number.** I include a place at the upper right hand corner of my contracts to add an invoice number. Originally, I added this feature because large corporations, such as Hyatt Hotels, would hire me to perform for weddings and like to run the invoice through their accounts payable departments. If I didn't include an invoice number, my paperwork would get lost in the shuffle and my payment would be delayed. Now, I include an invoice number on all my contracts, because it means that the contract is not just an agreement of services to be rendered, it is a bill to the client.

2. **The Time by Which You Must Leave.** Particularly when you are performing for receptions, it may be important to know what time you have to pack up and leave. Some reception facilities will book their banquet rooms for more than one wedding in a day, and they have strict rules that everyone must vacate by a certain time so that they can clean up.

3. **Requested Performance Attire.** If you have some clothing choices or costume choices to offer the bride, include a space to write this down on the contract. Over the years, I have collected Renaissance fair costumes, Dickens fair costumes, 1920s period flapper dresses for the local Gatsby festival, and an assortment of other fanciful clothes. I've also picked up some great gowns at my favorite consignment store. So, if a bride has a particular theme for her wedding or reception, or she is into a certain color scheme, I can make her happy by visually fitting into her wedding. Asking about attire also gives me a sense of how formal the wedding will be.

4. **The Name of the Celebrant.** If you are a ceremony musician, this information can be very helpful. If you know the individual who is performing the ceremony, you will know what your cues will be for playing selections during the ceremony, for instance, behind the lighting of the unity candle. If you don't personally know the celebrant, having their name will enable you to address them properly when discussing your cues.

5. **Particular Music Selections.** I like to write music requests directly onto the contract. Even if those selections are preliminary, when the client reviews their contract closer to the wedding date, they will know exactly what was discussed at the time of booking. If the client doesn't have any specific music requests when they booked the wedding, they will see big, empty blanks on the contract to indicate that they need to provide me with this information.

If you are a reception musician or a member of a reception band, it may be difficult to find space to include the client's music requests on the contract. So, you may wish to use an entirely separate form for the reception music list.

6. **If you are in an ensemble, you may want to stipulate whether a client can add additional pieces to your group.** For instance, if you are in a jazz trio, with piano, bass, and drums, and the client wants you to add a sax player to the group, will you do so? How much will you charge for each additional musician? Provide a space to write any instructions about extra instrumentation and the fee for adding each extra piece.

7. **Instructions about gratuities.** There seems to be no set rule for proper amount of tip for musicians. Sometimes, clients will ask me about this, and I usually respond that they can tip

according to how happy they are with my performance. Next to the "Total Amount" on my contract, the words, "Total does not include gratuity", so that my clients understand that a tip is welcomed. You could print, "We suggest an optimal 10% gratuity to the band leader at the end of the reception," but not all wedding resources are in agreement as to the amount of gratuity wedding musicians should receive. Why limit the amount of gratuity you could receive by stating it on the contract?

And Some Not-So-Essential Additional Terms for Your Contract. . . .

> **1. Terms regarding taking requests.** If you do take requests at a reception, you may want to establish some rules like, "Requests will only be entertained by the client, unless the client instructs Artist to take requests from all attendees."

I will take requests that are not in my repertoire, but they must be submitted at least 90 days prior to the performance so I have plenty of time to write an arrangement of my liking. Also, I must be provided with piano/vocal/guitar sheet music along with a CD or mp3 of the song to be played. Brides want their request to sound close to the rendition they are used to hearing. I do not guarantee that I will be able to perform the special request, because the song may not translate well to the harp, even after I have taken time to write an arrangement for it. And, I state that I may charge an additional fee if the bride wants me to perform a number of songs outside of my repertoire.

What rules do you want to set if you are willing to take requests? If you won't take requests outside of your established repertoire, then you may not need to bring up the subject of taking requests in your contract at all.

> **2. Rules about performing with vocalists or instrumentalists who are not in your ensemble.** As a soloist, I will perform with others (such as the best man, who plays the trumpet, or the niece who sings in her church), but I have a set of rules for doing this, too.

It usually becomes evident during a rehearsal if the bride's friend is comfortable with being accompanied by a harp. Some can't follow a beat, hold a pitch, or read music at all, and that just doesn't work for me. And then other times, the bride's friend determines at the end of the rehearsal that he'd rather sing a Capella, or without instrumental accompaniment. I stipulate that a rehearsal must take place at least twenty-four hours prior to the wedding performance, and I have an hourly charge for rehearsal time. It's difficult to get a rehearsal accomplished on the wedding day, because the bride's friend may be part of the wedding party and involved with the bride and her relatives. I always reserve the right to refuse to perform with the bride's friend. I state it in my contract that the client cannot cancel the contract because I won't perform with the bride's friend.

Once, a bride wanted me to accompany her best friend, a "professional singer". I set up a rehearsal appointment, and that morning, the bride's friend phoned to tell me she was running late. She could barely speak. She had laryngitis and still wanted to run a rehearsal! I told her that the rehearsal was out, firstly, because she shouldn't be singing in that condition, and secondly, because I didn't want to catch anything from her. She still insisted on coming over. She came over, banged on my front door for fifteen minutes, and then finally left. I phoned the bride, told her what happened, and she said that it was fine for me to play the song as a solo. The bride's girlfriend still had laryngitis at the wedding, so I wouldn't have accompanied her, anyway. This whole episode made me think, "What if the bride insisted that I accompany her girlfriend? What if the bride would try to cancel my services or refuse to pay me because I didn't agree to perform with her friend?"

Because of these sticky situations, I know of a number of wedding musicians who will not perform with any of the bride's friends at all. Period. And they put this condition into their contracts. But it isn't absolutely necessary to do so, because your contract is between you and the client and no other performers.

By the way, if I am performing with another professional musician whom I know, then I simply waive (or excuse) any rehearsal fees. It's a pretty sure thing that the wedding performance will go smoothly with another pro that I know, and any rehearsal is usually a pleasure.

These are my rules, but what will yours be? For instance, if you are the leader of an established string quartet, and you won't accompany someone else or won't perform with substitute musicians, state this caveat in your contract. Or conversely, as a bandleader, you will allow guests to sing karaoke with the band, consider this fact too, and your rules governing your decision.

3. **Rules about sharing your equipment with others.** Many, many times I am asked whether I have a wireless microphone for the celebrant and whether they can be hooked up to my sound system. For me, the answer is no, but for other

musicians, they are willing to provide this service free or at an extra charge.

I am also asked to provide additional mics for people I am accompanying. In this case, I have one extra mic, because if I am playing a duet with someone, I want both of us to sound good (or else it makes me look bad).

What equipment, if any, will you provide to others? If you don't even own amplification equipment, and you perform as an acoustic soloist for small gatherings, of course you don't need any rules about sharing equipment that you don't have.

4. **Make it clear that you are not a licensed booking agent.** I don't run contracts for other performers, even if I know they are solid and dependable. I don't represent anyone else. I only include others in my contract if I'll be performing with them, because in this case, the client is hiring me within an ensemble, not as a soloist.

A bride may not understand the fact that I cannot book a reception band for her when she has booked me as her wedding musician. This is why I include this statement in my contract, but it certainly isn't necessary.

5. **An empty "For Office Use Only" box.** I use this empty box on the back of my contracts to record dates of when I've had phone discussions with my clients. This can be very useful, for instance, to note when the client has supplied me with a final music list. If I somehow misplace this list, I'll know my client has completed it and I've simply misfiled it. Also, if you have not been paid a balance due at the end of a performance, then writing down the dates of phone discussions can help you to determine when you've waited long enough and might want to take legal action. You might think of other uses for this empty box—giving yourself a little extra room for notes is always a good idea.

A contract should be a "living" document, one that can grow and change as you learn from different situations that come up. After something unexpected comes up at a wedding, review your contract and ask yourself, "What could I have put in this contract that might have helped avoid this situation?" Don't be afraid to address difficult issues in your contract.

Personalize your contract. Fill out the **Contract Worksheet**. Again, once you have a mock-up of your performance agreement in hand, I urge you to visit a local contract or entertainment law attorney. If you have a carefully planned contract, you'll be protected and will avoid many of the horror stories you may have heard from other musicians.

INSTRUCTIONS FOR THE CONTRACT WORKSHEET

You'll notice that the worksheet is a template. The essential material to include in your contract is printed in black, and the non-essential is in gray. Use extra pages for additional terms that you'd like to add.

You'll also notice that the contract is actually called a "Performance Agreement". This is the term to use with your client. Why? You'll find out in Chapter 9 (The Nitty Gritty—Selling Your Services to the Bride).

If you are wondering how to enforce all the rules you have now established in your contract, including the bride's payment schedule, you'll find that information in Chapter 11 (Bride Relations—Avoiding Problems)

Performance Agreement

Invoice #: _____

```
Your letterhead, including all your contact info, goes here, for example:

                        JANE MUSICIAN
                   Name of Jane's Ensemble or Band
                        P.O. Box 5900
                        Allegro, CA 99999
                      Phone: (555) 555-1212
                       Fax: (555) 555-3414
                    Email: info@JaneMusician.com
                       www.JaneMusician.com
```

Client Information:

Name & Address _____ Fax # _____
_____ Day Phone _____
_____ Eve Phone _____
_____ Cell Phone _____
_____ E-mail Address _____
Fiancé's Name or Wedding Couple's Names: _____
Their Contact Information: _____

Event Information:

Type of Event: _____ Date: _____ Day: _____
Name of Celebrant(s): _____
Location(s): _____ Event-Day Phone #1 _____
_____ Event-Day Phone #2 _____
_____ On-Site Contact: _____
Arrival Time _____ Performance Schedule _____
Ceremony Start Time: _____
Reception: Length of Sets: _____ Length of Breaks: _____
Musician must leave by: _____

Client to supply map or directions to location? _____ Yes _____No
Number of Guests: _____
Amplification Required? _____Yes _____ No,
Amplification to be Provided by Client? _____Yes _____No
House Sound Available? _____Yes _____No
Distance Between Outlets & Performance Area: _____
Other Sound Specifications: _____
Artist's Wedding Attire: _____

Music Selections for the Ceremony:

Pre-Ceremony or Prelude: _____

_____

Seating of Mothers & Grandparents: _____

Processional Music: _____ Bride's Entrance: _____

Music During Ceremony: _____

Recessional: _____

Post-Ceremony Music: _____

_____

_____

Music Selections for the Reception:

Cocktail Hour Music: _____

_____

_____

_____

Entrance of Bride and Groom: _____

Music for Dining: _____

_____

_____

Bride and Groom's First Dance: _____

Family Dances: _____

_____

_____

_____

Cutting the Cake: _____

Throwing The Bouquet: _____ Garter Toss: _____

Other Dance Selections: _____

_____

_____

_____

_____

The Last Dance: _____

_____**will supply music selections to Artist no later than** _____

Special Instructions: _____

_____

_____

_____

_____

Fees:

<u>Description</u>	<u>Fee</u>

Name and describe your highest cost package here, detailing all the services it includes: _____

_____

_____ $_____

Name and describe your best-value, middle of the price range package here, detailing all the services it includes: _____

_____

_____ $_____

Name and describe your lowest cost package, detailing all the services it includes: _____

_____

_____ $_____

Name and describe any special reception package here: _____

_____

_____ $_____

Hourly Rate beyond packages described above: $ _____ Per Hour $ _____
Overtime Rate: $ _____ Per Hour $ _____
Rehearsal Fee: $ _____ Per Hour $ _____
     Rehearsal Day: _____ Date: _____ Time it Begins: _____
Cartage Fee (transport for performance at more than one location) $ _____
Travel/Mileage Fee: $ _____
Set-Up Fee: $ _____
Fee for Extra Musicians: _____

_____

_____ $_____
Additional Fee: _____ $ _____
Other Terms: _____

_____

_____ $_____

TOTAL $ _____
Total Does Not Include Gratuity

All Checks are to be made payable to _____

__% DEPOSIT IS REQUIRED WITH SIGNED AGREEMENT, OR $ _____

Deposit Received: $ _____   Check # _____   Date Received: _____
Balance Due: $ _____   Check # _____

Credit Card Number: _____ Expiration Date: _____
Name On Credit Card: _____
Billing Address: _____
_____
Amount Charged for Deposit: $_____ Date Charged: _____
Authorization Code: _____
Amount Charged for Balance Due or For Total Amount: $ _____ Date Charged: _____
Authorization Code: _____

Instructions to Sign:

When Balance is Due to Artist: _____
Late payment of balance will accrue an interest of _____ % per month.

By signing below, client indicates that this entire agreement, including the Additional Terms to This Agreement, have been read and are understood and agreed upon.

This agreement is entered on _____ **at** _____

X _____/_____   _____/_____
      Client Signature   **Date**   **Artist Signature**   **Date**

Additional Terms to This Agreement

1. Requirements of your performance area and any equipment that the Client needs to provide to you: _____
_____
_____
_____
_____

2. Stipulations about suitable temperature environment: _____
_____
_____
_____
_____

3. Client is responsible for 100% of the contract amount if you aren't provided with suitable performance area/conditions. Your wording: _____
_____
_____
_____
_____

4. What happens if the Client does not provide music selections by the indicated due date? : _____
_____
_____

5. Terms regarding taking requests: _____
_____
_____
_____

6. Rules about performing with vocalists or instrumentalists who are not part of your ensemble: _____
_____
_____
_____

7. Rules about sharing your equipment with others: _____
_____
_____
_____

8. Making it clear that you are not a licensed booking agent: _____
_____
_____

9. Client assumes risk of cancellation if you are unable to perform because of weather conditions and no acceptable alternative has been made. In this event, the Client will be responsible for 100% of the contract amount. Your wording: _____
_____
_____
_____

10. You reserve the right of final decision with respect of content, theme, arrangements, style, and equipment used for the performance. In other words, the Client accepts the general nature and scope of the Artist's repertoire as satisfactory. Your wording: _____
_____
_____
_____

11. Artist will only accept music instructions from the Client or another person appointed by the Client. Your wording: _____
_____

12. You'll take regular breaks. How often will you take breaks and for how long will you be on break? : _____
_____

13. Your cancellation policy in the event of death, illness, or genuine emergency, on either the part of you or your Client: _____

_____

_____

14. Your cancellation policy in the event that the Client cancels for reason of non-emergency: _____

_____

_____

_____

15. Your policy in the event that you have to cancel a job: _____

_____

_____

_____

16. Your policy in the event that you suffer any injuries on the job or damage to your equipment by the client or the client's guests: _____

_____

_____

_____

17. Any changes to the performance date, time and location should be made in writing. Your wording: _____

_____

18. If both you and the Client mutually decide to cancel your services for the wedding, are there any damages to be paid to either party? _____

_____

_____

_____

19. In the event of a lawsuit, the prevailing party will receive all costs of the suit, including the attorney's fees. Your wording: _____

_____

_____

_____

20. Any other additional terms you would like to add to this agreement:

_____

_____

_____

_____

_____

_____

_____

_____

_____
_____
_____
_____
_____

17. Additional terms that your legal representative suggests you add to your contract:

_____
_____
_____
_____
_____
_____
_____
_____
_____
_____
_____
_____

"For Office Use Only" Box

**Fill out this form completely,
then submit it to a local contract or entertainment law attorney
for review and final draft.**

*My card? Certainly! While we're at it...
here's a few copies of my flier **and** a promotional T-Shirt!*

CHAPTER 4

Get The Word Out: Creating Promotional Materials

"Life isn't about finding yourself. Life is about creating yourself."
—George Bernard Shaw, playwright

WHO ARE YOU?—DETERMINE YOUR OWN IDENTITY TO SEPARATE YOU FROM YOUR COMPETITION

Unless your potential clients have had the good fortune to see you perform, they are at a loss to know anything about you at all. This is where promotional materials come in. They create an image of you and your music to new clients. If you are just starting out, great promotional materials will help you build your reputation. If you have a solid reputation to begin with, great promotional materials will help spread the word far and wide. Promotional materials are the net you use to catch new clients.

Here's an example of how promotional materials work. Think about how perfumes and colognes are sold. An image or story is shown in commercials of the kind of man a woman can attract by wearing a certain scent, be he a knight in shining armor or a hairy-chested hunk. Or perhaps the perfume story is a dream sequence of what a woman can accomplish by wearing a certain cologne. Or sometimes the dream sequence makes no sense unless its symbolism is interpreted in Freudian terms. In any case, you cannot smell the scent through your television set. The idea is to get you, the consumer, hooked on the identity the perfume company has created so that you will run to the store and buy it by the gallon for yourself, your girl-friend, or your wife. If the perfume company's ad has succeeded, the actual scent can even be secondary to the image that has been created in your mind.

How does this relate to your promotional materials? The key is: Design your promotional materials to create an identity for you and your music. Just by reading your business card or brochure, or receiving a letter on your stationery, you can sway prospective clients to decide, subconsciously, that *you* are the musician or band to hire. Business cards, brochures, and stationery are much more than pieces of paper with a name, address, and phone number on them—they are your paper ambassadors.

Creating your promotional materials is part of the bigger creative plan of marketing. Advertising, selling your services, and relating to your clients also fall under this umbrella of marketing. Right now, we'll zero in on creating your unique promotional package.

The first step in this process of creating your own distinctive marketing materials is to review how you are positioned against your competition. (Remember, we discussed "positioning" back in Chapter 1, in respect to building your repertoire).

"Effective Marketing is about touching people. It's about creating awareness and clearly communicating who you are and what you do, It's about starting and maintaining relationships . . ."—Bob Baker, Artist Empowerment Radio Podcast

Here are some questions to answer to help you to hone in on your unique identity:

1. What makes you different from all of your competition?

_____
_____
_____
_____
_____

2. List all the obvious benefits that your clients are looking for when they hire you. Be sure that some of what you have to offer to your clients is unique, and perhaps even difficult for your competition to duplicate. (For example—"Only bagpiper in the tri-state area", "Dance instructions provided", "Dresses in authentic period costumes", etc.)

_____

_____

_____

_____

_____

_____

_____

3. Focus on just one of the benefits that you listed above, the benefit that stands out, the one that sets you apart from your competition. Redefine your benefit to attract more clients. For example, instead of saying that you play jazz dance music for receptions, you can say that you play "Cool Jazz for Swinging Receptions". Try to keep this statement at ten words or less.

_____

_____

"By focusing your marketing on doing one thing great, you increase your odds of long-term success by 60 percent."—Doug Hall, author of "Jump Start Your Marketing Brain"

You have now arrived at the one difference that will be meaningful to brides, your target clients. This is your business identity, the vein that should run through all the marketing you do, and therefore, the essence of what to include in your promotional materials.

Before you start creating your own materials, start a collection of your competition's business cards, brochures, and fliers. You may be able to find these materials at the local Chamber of Commerce, bridal boutiques, and other places that display promotional materials from wedding vendors. Also, collect samples of any materials that you intrinsically like to get a sense of the typestyles, papers, and graphics that you may want to use.

Building your identity in the marketplace and collecting samples of your competition's materials are the necessary steps to take before investing time and money on your own promotional pieces.

You'll notice that many of the pieces you have collected will have logos or some kind of uniform look about them. You don't necessarily have to go all out and spend money to have a logo created by a graphic designer. Use a particular illustration or clip art that is in public domain, a graphic symbol, or a particular typestyle will visually represent your music and your service to your clients. They will lend a uniform image to all your printed materials, as well. Every printed item will tie in nicely, making your presentation look professional.

A collection of promotional materials is commonly known as a "press kit" or a "promo package". Typically, you will not be sharing wedding-related promotional literature with the press, so I'll stick with the term "promo package". The package will be of most use to wedding coordinators, banquet managers, and booking agents who will want to have your information on file to share with prospective clients. You probably won't end up sending your entire promo package to brides or clients—They may only need your business cards and brochures.

The contents of wedding promo packages differ according to who is going to receive them. The one thing common among all promo packages is that they answer the questions, "Who is this performer?", "What do they play?", and "Why should I hire them?"

The following items are musts in your arsenal of promotional materials . . .

THE "OOOO!" REACTION—WHAT PEOPLE SHOULD SAY WHEN THEY SEE YOUR BUSINESS CARD

Very early on in my career, I experimented with different business cards, trying to find a card that would stand out, a card that would not get thrown away after I handed it to someone. I didn't have a lot of money to spend on cards, but I wanted something that had a classy look and feel, because to me, harp music is classy. I found a wonderful deep burgundy paper that looked almost like velvet. I printed my information with silver ink on that card, and when I passed it out, people exclaimed in glee, "Ooooo!" I knew I was on to something. They were intrigued about my music and asked me questions about my music, fees, and availability, all because of the look and feel of that little card.

In truth, you'll want to hear that reaction from all the materials in your promo package. Get this response from your business card, and then design the look and feel of all your other materials around it.

Here are just a few guidelines to having them printed:

1. **Stick with the standard business card size (2" × 3½").** It should fit into a wallet easily. Avoid having your business cards printed on paper, or other materials, that are too thick.

2. **Include your name, area code and phone number, email address and website address.** Optional additions to your card may be your cell number, fax number, and mailing address. If

you are in a band or ensemble, print the name of the group and the contact name or leader of the group, if it isn't you.

I only include one phone number on my business cards: my toll-free 800 number. And I do not include my mailing address. Why? Because I want my potential clients to fall in love with the idea of hiring me, before they find out that they may need to pay an extra fee for me to travel to their wedding. They don't need to know where I am located when they receive my business card.

Don't forget to include the identity statement and any artwork that also appears on your stationery. Running out of room on your card for all the necessary information? You can also use the back of your card. However, I caution against doing this, only because sometimes people will want to write down notes about you on the back of your business card, and they find that blank space useful.

If you want to include a lot of information on your business cards, consider printing "tent cards". These cards fold in half to be the same size as standard business cards. You can print all kinds of extra information inside of the fold. Tent cards can also stand up on tables, which may come in handy for table display in a bridal boutique or at a bridal fair.

3. **Be creative with special colors of ink, card stock, and typestyle to match the identity you want to convey.** For example, if you specialize in early music, your cardstock could look like parchment paper and you could choose a gothic typestyle. Just be sure you choose a font style and size that is easy to read!

Business cards do not have to be an expensive investment. In fact, if you are just starting out and have few funds for printing promo materials, you can get by with just your business cards and some matching stationery. If you have a laser printer, you can print business cards from your computer. A number of word processing programs come with business card templates, and the card stock can be purchased at an office supply store. If you go this do-it-yourself route, make sure your cards and stationary look as good as if they were designed and printed by a professional print shop. If not, your business cards will send an underlying message to potential clients that you are "cheap", implying that you are not a professional class act.

If you decide to shop at a discount office supply store, they usually offer business card and letterhead printing services, but their selection of inks, typestyles, and papers may be limited. I have found some very unique online catalogues that sell beautiful matching business cards, stationery, and envelopes. Do a Google search on the terms "business cards" and "stationery", and you'll find a number of ready-made designs to have imprinted with your information.

The letterhead you choose should be created around your business card design. Again, think in terms of sending a uniform message to your client about who you are.

Be generous when passing out your cards. Business cards, when properly designed to cause the "Ooooo!" response, are your strongest promotional commodity.

"The idea is not to save money on design, but to get it right the first time and have it feel like your other marketing."—Jay Conrad Levinson, author of "Guerrilla Marketing Weapons"

EVEN MORE INFORMATION FOR YOUR CLIENTS— BROCHURES AND BIOS

Brochures do a lot more than business cards. They convey information to brides who want to learn about you. A good brochure will sell a bride on the benefits of hiring you to perform. It must be persuasive, giving a bride many reasons for booking you for her wedding instead of continuing to shop around. Brochures are also image-builders. The style and colors of your brochure should match those of your business cards. Again, aim for that "Oooo!" response.

"A brochure can also build image and establish credibility. Anybody can have business cards printed for $10 and claim to be a company. But a sales brochure establishes immediate credibility and says to your prospects, "This is a real business, not a fly-by-night organization.""—Robert W. Bly, author of "The Perfect Sales Piece"

A brochure is not a flier. A flier does not have the same look and feel as a brochure. Certainly, fliers can be very informational and very inexpensive to design and reproduce, but they look a lot cheaper, too. "Cheap" is not the image you want to convey to potential wedding clients.

To produce a polished-looking brochure, I highly recommend hiring a professional graphic designer. Even if you have the software templates to produce brochures yourself, experienced graphic designers have the background to know artistic placement rules. A graphic designer can make the brochure match the look of your business cards and stationery. At your request, they can also shop around at different printers for the most competitive printing rates.

Your brochure can have no folds, one fold, or several folds, depending on how much you have to say. It is important that your brochures fit into a standard display rack (3½" × 8"). This way, you can display them at your neighborhood Chamber of Commerce and any other locations that allow you to display brochures (I have mine on display at bridal boutiques, tux shops, and even at my local gym).

Your brochure could have a backside that is blank so that it can be addressed and stamped and mailed as is. In other words, it is a "self-mailer". Or, if you intend to print information on all sides of your brochure, be sure it can fit into your standard number 10 business letterhead envelopes.

What should you say in your brochure? Think about how your music can fill your clients' needs. The more information your clients have, the more comfortable they will feel about hiring you. Use the third-person voice, as if you had someone else write all about you, or as if the information in your brochure originally appeared in a slick bridal magazine.

Include the following information in your brochure:

"Your headline dictates your positioning in the mind of your prospect—and attracts prospect attention or apathy. It is the most important thing you say to a prospect."—Jay Conrad Levinson, author of "Guerrilla Marketing Excellence"

1. **A headline.** You want this statement to catch the reader's attention and cause the reader to want to learn more about your services. You may want to use your identity statement as a headline.

Try your hand at writing some headlines here:

_____

_____

_____

_____

_____

_____

2. **Your contact information: your name or your band's name, area code with phone number, email address, and website address.** Your address may be included or not, depending on how you intend to distribute your brochures. If the brochure will be a self-mailer, just print your return address on the blank side of the brochure, and there will be no need to print it elsewhere. Include this information on the front of your brochure, and even on several other panels of your brochure, for good measure.

3. **Copyright notice.** Put a © with your name and the year on the brochure, usually on the back of the brochure or in some inconspicuous place. This is giving copyright notice and will help to insure that your competitors do not swipe the printed information and artwork in your brochure.

4. **The benefits of hiring you to perform.** Review your competitions' brochures to decide what to include. Not all of the benefits you list have to be uniquely your own. For instance, your competition may list that they provide amplification free of charge. It may be prudent for you to do the same, just so that your clients know you also have a sound system available. However, also add the unique benefits to hiring you. Your clients will believe they are getting more value for their money.

Some of the benefits to list could include: the style of music you play, some of the tunes you play, your particular attire, and free services that you include, such as free consultation, free amplification, free demo CDs, and so on. Make a list now, as a way of brainstorming:

_____
_____
_____
_____
_____
_____
_____
_____
_____
_____
_____
_____
_____
_____
_____
_____
_____

5. **Testimonials.** These are positive quotes from key people. If you are just starting out, you can use verbal quotes from friends, mentors, and your music instructor. If you have been performing a while, use quotes from the thank-you notes you received from past wedding clients. You can also include brief excerpts of quotes from reviews of your public stage performances and your CDs, but remember your target client, the bride. It will be most important to her that other wedding clients of yours have something positive to say about you. Be honest in all the quotes you provide and respect your client's intelligence. People can see through boastfulness. If they think you are making stuff up and are full of boloney, will they hire you?

If the testimonial appeared in a newspaper, magazine, or some other public source, include the name of the periodical, the particular issue and date of issue, and the author. You can even include online reviews of your music, too. If you are lifting quotes from thank-you notes, include the names of the people who wrote the note to you and their city and state of residence. Respect your past clients' privacy—do not print their addresses. Go a step further to honor their privacy and print the first initial and last name of each past client who wrote you a thank-you note. If printing their full names, please get their permission to do so, first.

List some testimonials that you've gathered here:

_____

_____

_____

_____

_____

_____

_____

_____

_____

_____

_____

_____

_____

6. Educate your potential clients. What can you tell your future clients about your instrument and the kind of music that is your specialty? Do a little research and include a short paragraph. And if you have been performing for a while, offer brides suggestions about how to select their music, how to hire musicians, or any other kinds of free advice. Give them a little free information, just for picking up your brochure and showing an interest in you. Offering advice establishes you as an authority in your field.

You could quote other sources, such as bridal magazines, but it is better to write something original. In other words, avoid listing Modern Bride's most recent suggestions to the bride about, "How to Select Your Ceremony Music". You want to be deemed the authority, not someone else.

Write down some ideas for educating your wedding clients here:

_____

_____

_____

_____

_____

_____

_____

_____

_____

_____

_____

_____

_____

_____

_____

_____

6. Your experience. This is also known as your bio, and this deserves an entirely new section . . .

YOUR BIO—TELLING YOUR STORY

The word "bio" is obviously short for the word "biography". I like the short, abbreviated term better, because this is exactly what a bio in a brochure should be—short and to the point. Tell a story and make it interesting. Be very conversational, writing it as if a friend of yours is telling a bride all about you. Avoid slang. In a brochure, you only have a few paragraphs, so mention only the information that you believe will impress the bride. Your bio is the final clincher to impel her to pick up the phone and call you.

"You are most attractive when you establish your expertise."—Stacey Hall and Jan Brogniez, authors of "Attracting Perfect Customers: The Power of Strategic Synchronicity."

Mention your personal achievements in these brief paragraphs. Describe what made you fall in love with playing music for weddings, how you got started, and where or how you received your music education. Let your bio read like a short magazine column about you, and even include a quote from yourself. For example: "Anne says, "I look forward to performing at ceremonies, because each is so sweet in their own way.""

Just a few paragraphs about your wonderful experiences that led up to your performing for weddings is all that is needed for your brochure. Give it a try on the following page:

First paragraph:

_____

_____

_____

_____

_____

_____

_____

Second paragraph:

_____

_____

_____

_____

_____

_____

_____

_____

Third paragraph:

_____

_____

_____

_____

_____

_____

_____

Need another sheet of paper or more lines? Then your bio is probably too long for your brochure.

You could write a longer version of this bio, but it won't fit into your brochure. Instead, post it on your website or print a paper copy on your letterhead stationery for those booking agents who want more complete information about you. This extended version still needs to read like an interesting story, like a full-length article in a bridal magazine, but don't let your bio be longer than two pages. This longer version of your bio is the one that is included in most press kits; so keep it on file in case you need to supply it to a bridal magazine or for a wedding insert in a newspaper.

JUST THE RIGHT SHOT—THE USE OF PHOTOS

The photos that you print on your brochures or business cards, or that you post on your website and save for press releases and paid advertisement, must all accomplish one thing: they visually must tell who you are. This snapshot of you needs to fit into the bride's imaginary picture of her perfect wedding day. How can you visually make yourself fit into her picture?

Here are some general thoughts about photos:

1. **A professional photo makes you look professional.** Shop for a photographer who has produced the "look" that you want. View their portfolio. A good photographer will be able to get the photo to reveal something about the subject's personality.

Get the most out of your money by having shots taken that could be used for your wedding promo package as an 8" × 10" glossy, inside your brochure, on your business card, on your website, and for any print advertisements. Your goal at the end of a photo session is to receive at least one multi-purpose photo. Let your photographer do all the touch-ups, colorization, sepia, and further magic. Then, ask your photographer to provide you with a digital copy that is the correct file size to be posted on your website and sent via email to advertisers, booking agents, and others. Also have larger files of the photo delivered to you via CD or DVD. These photos can be printed.

I am not an expert with the exact pixels to request, how to use software programs like PhotoShop, and other technical photography information. I leave these things up to my professional photographer, who can help to supply exactly what is needed for my website or for printed materials. If you are a do-it-yourselfer, I caution against allowing your photos to look amateurish in exchange for a few dollars saved.

To save money, if you have already gotten your feet wet performing at weddings, you may want to select one of the professional wedding photographers you know. Simply as a professional courtesy, they may discount their rates for you. In addition, they know that if they do a great job for you, they can depend upon your referrals for future wedding work.

2. **Include your instruments in all your photos.** The kinds of band shots you see on MySpace.com do not cut it here, where the band members are standing around, looking cool, without an instrument in sight. A bride wants to see exactly what you'll

look like when you perform for her, which means she also needs to see what your instrument looks like. If you are in a band, your wedding PR photo should show everyone holding his or her instruments. It could be a still shot or an action shot, with everyone playing. It doesn't matter as long as your instruments and your faces can be seen plainly.

3. **Dress like you would dress when you are performing at a wedding.** Look the part. A bride wants to see how you will show up at her wedding. Will you show up in a tux and cleanly shaven, or will you be wearing the trendiest shirt, unbuttoned to your waist, with your hair gelled so it sticks straight up? Which picture fits the bride's fantasy the best?

People of all ages are invited to weddings, and you need to dress to the most conservative faction. Show your face in all shots: no sunglasses or hats to hide your eyes. No visible tattoos, rings through your nose, etc, either. They won't sit right with grandpa, and he may be the one who is paying for the wedding and making the final decision of whether to hire you.

4. **Recruit the services of a make-up artist, if needed.** Women should wear heavier make-up for photo sessions. With digital photography, you can see exactly what the camera sees right after the picture is snapped. You'll have instant feedback about how your make-up looks. But when the photographer is snapping away, there won't be any time to review your make-up in each shot.

If you are uncomfortable or unfamiliar with applying your own make-up for your photo sessions, consider hiring a make-up artist. Ask your photographer for a few recommendations, and then shop for the one with the best price. Make sure the make-up artist doesn't just apply make-up before the shoot, but remains in the photographer's studio throughout the shoot to touch you up as needed.

Gentlemen, you may not think these words of advice apply to you, but you are wrong. The last thing you want in a photo is a shiny forehead. A good make-up artist will simply powder your face and remove any glaring imperfections that the camera sees.

Professional photography software, like PhotoShop, can get rid of some imperfections, but it takes a very experienced photographer to know how to use it correctly. It's better peace-of-mind to know that you have gone into the photo session with the best look possible, rather than relying on the photographer to fix your face after the shoot.

5. **Your band or ensemble must look like a cohesive group.** This goes further than making sure everyone is dressed like they are in the same band. Facial expressions should be the same, too, with no one member looking off in a different direction wearing a scowl when everyone else is looking into the camera with a pleasant smile.

6. **Update your photos anytime your appearance changes.** These changes include changes of personnel in your band or ensemble, significant weight changes, dramatically different hair styles or colors, wearing contact lenses instead of glasses, and so on.

7. **Show that you love what you do.** Your wedding PR photo is not one of those photos that are taken of models in high-fashion magazines, where they look posed with serious looks on their faces. Look like you love playing for weddings!

AUDIO AND VIDEO DEMOS—DO THEM RIGHT OR DON'T DO THEM AT ALL

When a potential client is intrigued by the services you have to offer for their wedding (perhaps because of your wonderful business cards and brochures), the very question they are likely to ask is, "Do you have a demo?" No discerning bride is going to hire you without hearing what you sound like, unless your services are being booked through a wedding coordinator or booking agent whom she trusts.

Investing in the production of a good demo will cement your reputation. Some of my brides have told me they love my demo so much that they listen to it over and over again on their computers at work or in their CD player in their cars! They play it for all their friends and relatives. And my demo is only fourteen minutes long. A good demo not only gets me hired for weddings, it also creates referral business and fans. When I released my first CD, past brides were among my first customers.

"Sending a poor demo is worse than sending none."—Patricia Shih, author of "Gigging: A Practical Guide for Musicians"

Clients will be playing your demo and comparing it to demos from other wedding and reception musicians, before they make a decision. If the recording quality or your playing doesn't measure up to that of your competition, then of course, you won't get the job. But much worse, this recording is out there for all to hear. It can bust your reputation. For this reason, if you are thinking about creating an audio demo, do it right or don't do it all. Wait until you are a polished performer before recording. And if possible, squirrel away some money to invest in a high quality production.

If you are new to performing, relax. You can still get away with a simple audio demo recorded in a quiet living room, but you need to disclose this fact to your potential clients when you hand them your demo CD. If warned about the recording quality, they will instead zero in on listening to your performance on the CD. So, play cleanly, smoothly, and flawlessly, and a homemade CD will pass as a suitable demo of your abilities.

Recorded demos are still referred to as "demo tapes" and "video demos", even though cassette tapes and videos are becoming obsolete at the time of this writing. The media of choice is now CDs and DVDs. In certain settings, however, there are uses for looped videotapes that play continuously, over and over. These can be played in a small monitor at bridal fairs or in hotel banquet offices. The sound can be muted until a bride is interested in listening along with the visual presentation.

As a wedding or reception musician, there are ways around using audio or video demos, particularly if you are a soloist or perform in a small ensemble. Brides need to have an opportunity to audition you, so create that opportunity for them. If they live in your area or will be traveling to your area, you can set up a private appointment to meet with them in person, at your home. Before you meet with a bride, ask her to select some tunes from your repertoire list, so that you will have a chance to practice them before you meet with her. When you meet, play through her requests and then, go into your sales pitch (which will be covered later, in Chapter 9). If you bowl the bride over with your performance, she will probably book you right then and there.

One caution: A bride may get so carried away with your lovely presentation that she'll want to stay and hear more music. She isn't paying you for a private concert; so only reserve an hour for your meeting. If she wants to hear more, explain that you were only prepared to play the tunes that she had pre-selected. Or just tell her you have another appointment.

You can arrange for a live audition over the phone, too. This works best for soloists. Make a phone appointment with the bride, instruct her to select some music from your repertoire, and ask her to call you at the determined time. Do just as you would in a live audition, except you can wear your jammies in a phone audition.

Set up your phone so that the bride will be able to hear you clearly, either by using a cordless phone placed on a table next to your music stand, or by using a speakerphone. Don't use a cell phone, if you can help it, because a poor connection will make you sound less than desirable.

With the advent of computers that come with built-in cameras, it is possible to run a live demo as a videoconference. I caution against this, only because the camera may not offer a true, clear image. Depending upon the computer connection, the bride may end up viewing an audition that stutters and is a blur. As this technology is perfected, video conferencing may eventually become yet another way to supply an audition for a bride.

If you are ready to invest in a quality audio demo for your promo package, keep in mind that this demo is for landing a wedding gig. Come at this from the bride's prospective. She wants to hear what you will sound like at her wedding.

Here are suggestions for creating an audio demo specifically tailored to your wedding clients:

1. **Hold your listener's attention.** Keep the demo short—less than fifteen minutes is best. This translates to three or four complete songs. Or, you could display your diversity by having a number of 30-second samples of tunes, fading out at the end of each sample.

2. **Familiar music is what brides will want to hear.** Play the music that is most requested by your brides on your demo. For ceremony musicians, brides are most interested in hearing what you can play for their entrance, be it "Here Comes the Bride", "Canon in D", or the current modern popular music favorite.

3. **Include pieces you would normally perform, so that a bride will get a true sampling of what you would play for her wedding.** Your demo isn't the place to challenge yourself to play the most difficult songs in your repertoire. You are creating a demo of what you already play, not a CD to be released on the market sometime in the future. Keep it simple.

4. **Your recording should sound as close as possible to what you sound like when you play live.** Therefore, avoid sweetening your recording with special effects like over-dubbing or reverb, which wouldn't be included in your live performance.

5. **Record a voice greeting at the beginning of your demo.** It can be generic, for any bride, telling her a bit about yourself and how to contact you for booking information. I also suggest ending the demo with your contact information, too. If you have editing software on your computer and are burning your own discs, you may even be able to record a personal message to the bride, before sending off the demo CD.

6. **Start with your best song.** People with short attention spans will always listen to this song first, then make a decision whether to listen to the rest of the demo in it's entirety, skip through all the songs for a quick sampling, or take it out of the CD player and trash it.

7. **Versatile performers should record different demos for different clients.** If you play several genres or styles of music, or if you play different selections for ceremonies vs. receptions, record several niche demos instead of trying to cram everything you can do into a fifteen-minute CD. For example, if you are a soloist and are also a member of a reception band, make one demo for prospective clients interested in hiring you as a soloist and another highlighting your band.

8. **Look for a recording engineer who has experience recording the instrument you play, recording your band's instrumentation, and recording your genre of music.** Request recorded samples from the engineer, so that you can hear what music sounds like when recorded in their facility. If the engineer lacks experience, they will spend a good portion of your recording session time setting up and adjusting your mics instead of actually recording your tracks. You will be paying for their tinkering around with mics, and you'll be wasting money.

To find good engineers, ask your musician friends which studios and engineers they recommend. Visit with the engineer and take a tour of the studio before you reserve studio time.

If you know someone who has a soundproofed in-home studio, with digital editing equipment and state-of-the-art equipment, their rates are likely to be lower than those of commercial recording studios. Lower cost may also mean lower quality, so listen to their recorded samples before you decide to use their services.

You can choose to have your audio demo available to potential clients as a CD or as a downloadable mp3 sound file. I recommend both.

Some brides do not have access to a computer, unless they are at work, where they cannot do any personal business (or plan for a wedding). A number of wedding coordinators prefer the CD demos, because they simply hand them out to their brides—In this fashion, your CD demo is like an audio business card.

As a downloadable mp3 file that you place on your website, you save money because you don't have to duplicate CDs or mail them to brides. You can make CD demos from your computer mp3 files by burning them onto a disc. This method is fine if you don't get many requests for CD demos, since it can take some time to burn discs en masse. Another concern is that unlike CDs that are commercially reproduced, CDs burned from your computer may not play on all CD players.

Some booking agents, wedding coordinators, and banquet managers at resort hotels may not be satisfied with receiving audio demos from you. They may want to know exactly what you will look like in performance. This is when you'll need to think about having a video demo produced. To have a video filmed, produced, and edited professionally can be a very expensive proposition.

Here is a way to save money: Record the video demo first, and then use its soundtrack for your audio demo.

And here's another way to save money: Extract stills from your video demo to use as promotional photos.

To prepare for creating a wonderful video demo, combine some of the suggestions for taking a good photo with the suggestions for making a good CD. I'll review these points here:

1. **Dress like you would dress when you are performing at a wedding.**

2. **Recruit the services of a make-up artist, if needed.**

3. **Your band or ensemble must look like a cohesive group.**

4. **Show that you love what you do.** Smile until your face feels like it's going to fall off. A good video shows that you enjoy playing at weddings.

5. **Hold your listener's attention.** Keep the demo short—less than fifteen minutes is best. And if the video will only live online, more than three minutes will seem like an eternity. Think of the length of MTV music videos . . .

6. **Familiar music is what brides will want to hear.**

7. **Include pieces you would normally perform, so that a bride will get a true sampling of what you would play for her wedding.**

8. **Your recording should sound as close as possible to what you sound like when you play live.**

9. **Start with your best song first.**

When you are ready to record a video demo, look for an experienced cameraman who can produce a broadcast quality video and has access to digital editing equipment. View a sample of their work. Avoid bouncy, home video recordings filmed with camcorders. YouTube.com-style videos are fine for emerging bar bands, but they don't have the kind of polish needed for a wedding demo. Even when viewed online, the quality of the video and your performance must stand out.

Another money-saving tip: Incorporate video clips of your live performances at weddings into your demo tapes. As long as the film quality is apparent, you can save a bundle in shooting costs. You'll need to get permission from the bride to use the video as a demo. As a gesture of goodwill, you will also need to credit the videographer in the film.

Of course, like all your other promo materials, include your contact information (phone numbers, website, email, etc.) in the video. Slate this information at the beginning and at the end of the video demo. You could even post your contact information in the lower left- or right-hand corners of the screen in the video, as commonly done on MTV videos and during television programs.

Keep this information in mind for producing both audio and video demos:

1. **"Good documentation of pieces and timings . . . is important."**—Bruce Egre, recording engineer for the Ohio Chamber Orchestra. Booking agents are often too busy to listen to unsolicited recordings in poorly labeled packaging. You don't

need to spend a lot of money on jewel cases and j-cards. Just insert your CD or DVD into a paper envelope, made for discs. Include those timings either on the paper sleeve or on the face of the disc itself.

Don't forget to include your contact information—your name, mailing address and phone numbers—on the face of the disc and on the outside envelope for the disc, too. This way, if the disc gets separated from the envelope, the bride will still know how to contact you. This will make it easy for clients to contact you for booking information, and it will make it easy for brides to know where to return the disc.

2. **If your demo includes snippets of copyrighted material, include on the packaging of the disc, "For audition purposes only. Not for broadcast or sale."** You never know if someone will try to sell your demos on ebay! As long as you are not selling your demos to make a profit off the recordings, there is no problem including copyrighted songs and arrangements for clients to audition you.

"If you do build a great experience, customers tell each other about that. Word of mouth is very powerful."—Jeff Bezos, founder and CEO of amazon.com

3. **Don't be stingy with your investments.** Give them away to anyone and everyone who requests them. Your most serious prospects will request your demos and give them the attention they deserve, passing them along to family and friends, landing them in the hands of people you never had the opportunity to contact personally.

PUTTING IT ALL TOGETHER

Use your letterhead stationery to complete the rest of your wedding promo package. Print the following information on your stationery:

1. **Your repertoire list**

2. **Your extended bio.** This is the one that is included in most press kits, so keep it on file for booking agents who want more information about your experience, or in case you need to supply it to a bridal magazine or for a wedding insert in a newspaper.

3. **Testimonials** (if you have so many that you cannot include them in your brochure)

4. **Performance resumé.** Booking agents are used to receiving an 8" × 10" glossy photo with a one-page resumé. For wedding

work, this is rarely requested, given the fact that a short bio and photo(s) are included in your brochures.

5. **A fee schedule.** This is not for the bride's eyes. Only print this information if a booking agent or wedding coordinator requests to receive it. They are in direct contact with the bride, and they need to know what fees to quote on your behalf.

Buy some nice folders with pockets for all your promotional materials. Purchase the kinds of folders that allow you to insert your business card into the folder.

Don't send out your promo packages before speaking to the recipient first, unless you want your packages to end up in a garbage can. Open up the phone book. Search the Internet. Start phoning the kinds of people in your local area who might be able to refer your services as a wedding performer. When you connect with these booking agents, wedding coordinators, and banquet managers, find out specifically what kinds of materials they need. Some may only request your business cards and brochures, while others will want everything and anything that you have to share. Place these items into the folder.

Don't be disappointed if some of the folks you contact are not interested in learning about your services. This is not a reflection on you or your abilities. Some wedding chapels service low-budget brides who cannot afford extra frills like live music, so these chapel owners don't have any use for your information and won't refer you. Some wedding coordinators and banquet facility owners have their own favorite musicians to recommend and are too narrow-minded to add you to their referral lists. And sometimes, you might contact a booking agent who doesn't book entertainment for weddings. I know one agent who prefers to work with corporate clients only, so he turns down inquiries from brides.

When you have made contact with a booking agent, wedding coordinator, or banquet manager who is interested in finding out more about you, write a personal cover letter for the promo package.

Simple rules for cover letters:

1. **Be personal.** Address the letter to the recipient—No "To whom it may concern" or "Dear gentlemen". Spell names correctly. You can type it out on your computer and print it on your stationery, or you can add a personal touch and handwrite it (if you write neatly and legibly).

2. **Always run spell-check before printing the letter.** Spelling and grammar mistakes are inexcusable. I know some booking agents who will throw out a promo package if they can't make sense of the cover letter.

3. **Write the same way you would speak, in a conversational, yet formal tone.** Weddings are formal affairs, and your understanding of this comes across in the tone of your cover letter.

4. **Use no more than three paragraphs to introduce yourself and your promo package.** All the other details about you are included in your brochures, so there is no need to elaborate on your experience in the cover letter.

5. **Finish off the letter with a P.S., a statement that will stand out.** Make a big personal statement by handwriting the P.S.—Thank the recipient for a recent referral, give them your website address if it is not on your stationery, or even request that they contact you when they run low on your brochures or business cards.

At the end of this chapter is a **Sample Cover Letter** to help you get started. If you need more help with writing, track down a copy of "How to Say It" or "A Manual of Style". Keep your favorite grammar and punctuation books handy as desk references when writing any correspondence.

Paperclip your cover letter to the outside of your promo package folder or place it so it is the first thing that your client sees when opening it up.

You can mail the promo package, but it is much better to make an appointment to meet with the recipient in person. When meeting with a new contact face-to-face, you can make an impression that a mailed folder simply cannot. This personal connection will increase the probability that your new contact will mention your name when one of their clients says, "Do you have any musicians you can recommend for my wedding?" Your contact will remember you and the time and effort you took to get to know them.

The added benefit of meeting with people who may refer your services is that you can get a good idea of how they work and how they respond to brides. And if you are meeting with a banquet manager, request a tour of the wedding or reception facility. Take notes at the meeting and on your tour. Check out the lighting, the acoustics, and where the electrical outlets are located. If you discover that there is no loading zone or you will have to climb three flights of stairs to reach the reception hall, you'll know in advance that you may want to charge the bride extra to perform at that facility.

During the personal appointment, ask your new contact about other vendors that they recommend. They may even be kind enough to share their referral list with you. Voila! Now you have even more new connections to make with others who can refer your services—everyone from celebrants to photographers to florists.

Your promo materials will make inroads into networking with other wedding vendors. A professional-looking promo package will conjure up an outstanding first impression on anyone who receives it.

Even if you are only including portions of this package to clients, the fact that your business cards tie in with your letterhead stationery, which tie in with your envelopes, which tie in with your brochures, delivers a powerful subconscious impression. All of your clients, especially brides, will feel comfortable hiring you because they will believe that you know what you are doing. Your promo package will establish this trust at the outset.

Ms. Brandi Jones, Event Coordinator
Happy Cove Resort
P.O. Box 800
Happy Cove, NV 88888

March 18, 2007

Hi Brandi;

    Here are the materials you requested from me today, with the addition of business cards, photo, and current repertoire list. You are welcome to display any or all of these materials. There are sound files on my web site, so I am only including one CD demo tape. You have my permission to duplicate this tape for brides if you wish.

    Here is what is enclosed:

1. Video demonstration tape (approximately twelve minutes in length, DVD format)
2. Audio demonstration tape including a variety of music
3. Fifty (50) brochures that include a biography
4. Business cards with toll-free number
5. Repertoire list (the entire list, which prints out to fourteen pages, is located on my web site at www.celticharpmusic.com)

    Thanks again for displaying my materials. I will phone you in a week to confirm you have received this package.

                  Sincerely,

                  Anne Roos

P.S.—When you start running low on brochures, please give me a call and I will be happy to supply you with more.

And now, for my final number...

CHAPTER 5

The One Item You Should Never Include Anywhere in Print

"Require customers to call you for details. The simple act of making a phone call to you to gain additional information tilts your odds of sales success significantly."—Doug Hall, CEO of the Eureka Ranch! think tank

This information is so very crucial to your ultimate success as a profitable musician that it deserves it's very own chapter!

In order to get brides to take action, to want to book your services, you must give them a reason to phone you, email you, and contact you personally. The way to do this is to purposely leave out a very important piece of information in your marketing materials. And the one piece of information to withhold is: your pricing.

Do not print your rate sheet anywhere—not in your brochures, not on your website, not in any advertisements—not anywhere.

I know that there are some seasoned musicians shaking their heads in disagreement, but please hear me out.

Picture this: A bride has listened to all of your demos on your website, is convinced that you are the one band who can handle playing her first dance at her reception perfectly, and then what does she look for? She searches all over your website for your prices. She ends up phoning you or sending you an email asking, "How much do you cost?" Now you close in on the sale!

Or picture this: A bride just picked up your lovely brochure at her local bridal boutique. She reads it cover-to-cover, shares it with her fiancé who says, yes indeed, that harpist has the experience to play at our little wedding in the park. But, he asks his bride-to-be, "How much does the harpist cost?" She has no idea, so he instructs his little pumpkin to phone the harpist and find out.

No cold calls for you. Brides call you. And when an interested bride phones, you will get all the information you need about her wedding details, explain all the benefits that are included when she hires you, answer all her questions, and only then, reveal your special fee designed just for her needs. She will think, "I get all those wonderful things, my favorite music played on my favorite instruments for just the right amount of time, with free amplification and free mileage and . . . That's all it costs? Wow. I can afford that." And if she can't afford it, then mention your Best Value Package or Your Lowest Cost Package. She may even adjust her overall wedding budget to include you. Hey, she may even adjust the time of her wedding ceremony to suit your schedule—This has happened to me countless times.

Many years ago, I used to sell burglar alarm systems to supplement my income as a musician. The company I worked for would make a bunch of cold calls until they found someone interested in a home demonstration. I'd get a call on my beeper and drive over to that customer's house to make a sales pitch.

The presentation was all about quoting current home burglary statistics and demonstrating how anyone could find a way into any home if they really wanted to. Then, I'd show the customer how my company's system would protect them. It was all about scaring people into buying a home burglar alarm system, and it worked. The price quote was intentionally left until the end of the presentation. By that point, my poor, anxious customers wanted to know how much it would cost to protect their home and valuables, and they were ready to sign up for an immediate installation. These were very expensive systems, costing thousands of dollars. If my customers couldn't afford the total price tag, there was "easy financing" available.

This process worked like a charm, and I made some fine commissions selling home burglar alarm systems, but I couldn't live with myself, scaring people into making a purchase. Gratefully, as a wedding musician, I don't have to use scare tactics to close a sale!

What I learned from that experience is to leave the price quote to the end of the sales presentation. If you mention your prices too soon, your bride will not be hearing about the value of hiring you. Instead, she may be reeling from the price tag.

Here are a few other reasons to leave your rates out of your marketing materials:

1. **Quoting different fees for different customers.** If you are working with booking agents and wedding coordinators, they may either take a commission off of what they pay you, or they expect you to charge a discounted, "wholesale" rate to them. Then they quote your fee to the bride as you would quote it, or jack up the price even higher. Of course, many agents and coordinators make their money this way. (Not all coordinators request a discount from you; instead, some may charge the bride a fee for their time).

If you agree to offer commissions to agents and consultants, you cannot post your regular fees in your brochures and on your website. What if a bride gets a quote for your services from a booking agent, decides to continue shopping, and comes across your brochure or website with your fee schedule posted in plain sight? It will be pretty embarrassing for both you and the agent if you quote something different than they did. And you'll lose referrals from them as a result.

I am aware that there are a number of viable Internet directories for musicians, such as gigmasters.com, that require you to list your fees when you create a profile. These directories ask for a price range, not exact hourly fees. Just quote a very wide range for your fees so that you are covered in case a bride has already received a quote for your services from a booking agent or consultant. This will also cover you when you decide to adjust your rates.

2. **Cost of reprinting.** This is a no-brainer. If you spend money on printing beautiful brochures, and you raise your rates before another printing, what are you going to do? Place an ugly sticker over the fees you quoted? White out the fees on each brochure and write in the new fees? Shred the old brochures, the good money you spent on printing, and have new brochures printed? Avoid reprinting costs by leaving out any time-sensitive information, such as your rate information.

3. **How you are viewed as a professional service provider.** I have never seen an accountant, a lawyer, or even a wedding

consultant print their fees in their brochures or online. They are offering a service, not selling a product at a fixed price. If you were to see a price list printed in the newspaper from an attorney, would you suddenly start viewing him as less than a professional, as someone who is trying to sell his services by price alone and not quality of service?

There is just one instance when you may want to print up your fee schedule, but you won't be distributing it to brides. As mentioned in the last chapter, wedding coordinators and booking agents may insist upon receiving a list of your fees when they request a promo package from you.

For this private rate sheet, use your letterhead stationary and include the following:

1. Print the date at the top of the page.

2. Address the rate sheet directly to the person who is meant to receive it.

3. Explain the discount that you are willing to offer, if any.

4. Detail each price package, listing the benefits included with each package.

5. Offer any other perks to the coordinator or agent at the end of this letter (for instance, a free link on your website).

And most importantly:

6. Place this phrase at the bottom of each page of your rate sheet: **"Please Note: All fees are subject to change without notice. Please phone for a quote."** This phrase will force the coordinators and agents to phone you anyway. So if you have raised your rates, no longer wish to pay commissions, or want to change anything else, the list you gave them is not etched in stone. It's subject to your revisions.

For those of you seasoned musicians who have been posting your prices on your website and still disagree with me, at least add the above disclaimer to the rates that you post. Brides can and will print your online rate sheet. When you update it, brides may insist on paying your old rates because they didn't know you changed them.

Here's one last example of why it is a good idea to keep your prices out of print:

Many years ago, a woman who was writing a book about wedding services here at Lake Tahoe contacted me. She sent a questionnaire to all the wedding vendors in the area, asking everything from how long we were in business, to what our services included, to our rates. Not knowing any better, I gave her my going rate at the time, my minimum. I think she printed it as, "Anne's fees start at $_____." For years after that book was released, I received calls from brides who had bought a copy of that book. The publicity was great, but I was continually disappointing brides by saying, "No, I don't charge that rate anymore. That book is five years old." It was the quickest way to kill a sale.

Much more about selling will be covered in Chapter 9, but in the meantime, you have some early insight into the process of selling and how to get potential clients to phone you.

CHAPTER 6

Beyond Business Cards—Time to Invest in Advertising?

"I figured that if I said it enough, I would convince the world that I really was the greatest."
—Muhammad Ali, Legendary Heavyweight Boxing Champion

You now have your repertoire, your equipment, the proper attire, a performance agreement, and all kinds of promotional materials. But how does anyone actually hear about you? Through publicity and advertising. It doesn't have to cost much money. You can get the word out about your talents as a wedding musician even with a tight budget.

PRESS RELEASES—THEY LEAD TO FREE ADVERTISING!

A press release, or news release, is simply a bit of tantalizing information that you send off to the media. It tells them why they shouldn't pass up the opportunity to mention you in their next newspaper or magazine edition, their next podcast, radio or TV broadcast, or their website e-zine or blog. You write the press release, and you send it. If the recipient likes what you wrote, off it goes into print, broadcast, or over the worldwide web.

Your press releases can round up publicity that money simply cannot buy. Here are six examples of what publicity can do for you:

1. **Publicity brings you wedding business**—It has the power to increase traffic to your website, make your phone ring off the hook, and fill your email inbox with inquiries.

2. **Publicity can get the word out about your musical abilities cheaper than paying for advertisements** (and often, with more media coverage).

3. **Publicity turns you into a wedding music expert.** Brides who read and hear about you will be convinced that you are a professional worth hiring. They will believe that you have a good reputation and shine above your competition.

4. **Publicity gives your clients and your potential clients a chance to know more about you.** It gives them the opportunity to examine you and your talents beyond the carefully crafted information in your brochures.

5. **Publicity for "good works" makes you look good in your immediate community and among your musician peers.** Besides, brides like to hire nice people.

6. **Publicity gives you credentials.** Forever after you appear in a column of "Modern Bride", you can quote the writer directly in all your PR literature. Instant testimonials!

7. **Publicity can bring you fantastic performing opportunities that you would have never received without the media exposure.**

"You are more attractive when you understand that customers are seeking you...They are counting on you to make it easy to find your business in the places they are looking. The question to ask yourself is, 'How can I help them find me faster?'"—Stacey Hall and Jan Brogniez, authors of "Attracting Perfect Customers: The Power of Strategic Synchronicity."

Are you hesitant to get the word out that you are available to play at weddings? If you are new to performing for pay, it's understandable that you may not feel comfortable tooting your own horn. The solution is to think of things in this way: by sending out press releases, you are doing a great service for brides by helping them find you. You are also helping the media reach those brides—You're supplying them with interesting information about you and your music.

When I write a press release, I pretend I am a reporter explaining why the media should take notice of the musician, the subject of my press release. Press releases are written in the third person, which frees me from feeling like I'm bragging about me, me, me.

If you are an established performer, you'll have a bounty of information to share in your press releases, but you must make sure that it is newsworthy and tells a story. If you sound like you are boasting about your accomplishments, your press release will be ignored.

Put yourself in the recipient's place when you write a press release. Think about what he or she wants to print. For example, if you are sending a press release to a wedding magazine about your next performance at the local country club, how can you make it of interest to the editor of this magazine? Mention what you'll do for dining guests: perhaps you will take their requests for current hit love songs, or perhaps you will give them a free private consultation if they plan to get married at the country club. Be helpful to their readers, and you'll increase the chances that your information will be printed.

Of course, you must have something interesting to tell the media. Otherwise, why would they want to pay attention to what you are saying in the first place? Need some ideas? **Here's a laundry list of wedding-related topics for press releases:**

1. **Are you new to the area?** Your press release can announce that you are now available to perform for weddings and receptions.

2. **Do you offer music that is different from anyone else in your area?** Tell the press that their readers can now go out and hear the only Luau band within 50 miles, and tell them that you are available to play for Hawaiian-style receptions.

3. **Any changes or updates in your music personnel or repertoire?** Are you now performing in an ensemble, rather than as a soloist? Or were you with a band and you're now going out on your own? Are you now available to travel to perform? Have you added new music to your repertoire?

4. **Have you just launched a website, a newsletter, or a special blog for brides that includes wedding music information?** Let the media know so that brides will know where to find you.

5. **Have you just released a new CD? Are your songs available for downloading on iTunes? Have you and your music been featured on a podcast?** You may not immediately think that this kind of announcement has any draw for brides, but you'd be surprised. Clients and brides audition you by listening to your recorded music. They don't have to leave home to determine if you have the sound they want. Send a press release

to let the media tell your potential clients how to find your recorded music.

6. **Have you received some offbeat endorsements?** What if the president of Guinness heard your Irish band perform at an event and said, "Brilliant music!" Publicize it, because this kind of testimonial will attract brides and all kinds of clients.

7. **Are you performing at an event where brides can come and see you in action?** Can you supply calendar listings of your upcoming performances to the media? Offer private consultation appointments during your breaks or after the performance for brides who attend.

8. **Will you be exhibiting at an upcoming bridal fair, performing at a bridal boutique open house, or playing for a wedding fashion show?** This kind of direct wedding publicity will put you on the map as a wedding professional.

9. **Are you performing at an event outside of your hometown?** If so, you may be able to get coverage where you do not live because you are a unique act. You may attract brides who are willing to pay for you to travel to their weddings.

10. **Can you offer wedding music information, facts, or statistics in a press release? Can this information tie in with the season or with a topic that is currently in the news?** For instance, if you are appearing at an upcoming January bridal show, you can include in your press release an interesting fact like, "In our region, during the December holiday season, more couples get engaged than at any other time of year. This may be why the yearly bridal show at the local convention center is so popular and so many brides book their services right there." Free, useful, and educational information is a fine way to establish your expertise to the media.

"For my money, I would always rather make a deal with people I like who treat me well."—Donald Trump

There is another class of press release that has the sole purpose of demonstrating to the reader that you are a nice person. I've mentioned above that brides like to hire nice people. In fact, all clients like to hire nice people. A client who thinks you are nice will trust you, your suggestions for their music, and your abilities to deliver exactly what they want for their wedding. The added benefit to being nice is that niceness is infectious, and the bride will be less likely to go bridezilla on you if she genuinely likes you.

Here are some angles to include in press releases to demonstrate to the media that you are just plain nice:

1. **Are you donating your music services to a good cause?** Are you playing piano for the senior center's ballroom dance program once a month? Is your quartet performing during a silent auction benefiting local AIDS research? You are spreading goodwill, and donating your talents to a good cause will get you noticed.

2. **Have you been appointed to a community board or committee? Have you received any awards?** Awards and kudos show that you are well-valued in your community and among your peers.

3. **Do you have some "free advice" to offer to brides?**—Yet another fine way to demonstrate your expertise is to educate. Here are some examples of educating brides in your press releases: You could list the most trendiest first dance tunes this wedding season, you could give advice about how to select a musician, or you could design a wedding timeline for brides to book their entertainment and decide on their wedding music. For more ideas, visit various wedding websites to see what kinds of free information they display for brides. Please remember to mention the source of any quoted information in your press releases.

4. **Are you teaching any classes or seminars?** You will be considered a local music authority by anyone taking your classes and all who read about them. Offer discounts or free first sessions. Special offers may be seen as a gesture of goodwill, a way that you are reaching out to more people interested in learning from you.

This list is just a start. Take one of these ideas and try your hand at writing a press release. There are some basic rules of format to writing press releases, but beyond that, I'm not an authority on the subject. The best authority is Joan Stewart, and she has a free online tutorial called "89 Ways to Write Powerful Press Releases". Sign up for this tutorial at http://www.publicityhound.com/pressreleasetips/art.htm.

Joan's examples and exercises are not specific to wedding musicians, so I've introduced a musician-related **Sample Press Release** at the end of this chapter, along with some information about proper formatting to get you started. This example is something fairly typical—a calendar listing. It won't be immediately evident that the information has anything to do with brides, but do you notice that I mention wedding bookings in the last paragraph?

According to Joan Stewart, here are the six parts of a press release:

1. **Contact Information.** This appears in the upper left hand portion of the press release. Make the website and the email addresses hyperlinks, because more often than not, you will be submitting your press releases via email and posting them on your own website.

2. **The Headline and Sub-Head.** The headline exists to catch the reader's attention, and the sub-head is to entice the reader to continue reading.

3. **The Dateline.** Including the city and state are important pieces of information, especially if you are submitting the press release over the worldwide web.

4. **The Body Copy.** This constitutes the bulk of your press release. One page is all you need for your press release, but if it is a calendar listing, like my **Sample Press Release**, you may end up going onto a second page to display the listing for the calendar. Keeping your press release short is good for another reason: when you paste it into an email, the recipient will not have to do a lot of scrolling to get to the meat of your subject.

Place the most important information at the top of the body copy. You can use "the five w's" (who, what, when, where, and why or how) in the first paragraph, but there is no rule that you have to.

Run spell check several times. Check your grammar, too. Read the press release out loud to check for clarity and avoid redundancy. Misuses of grammar and misspelled words will reflect poorly upon you, and the media may not choose to carry your press release. Even worse, they may be under a deadline and print your press release without making any changes at all, for the entire world to see your grammatical and spelling mistakes.

Avoid slang, jargon, and abbreviations. Your target audience is potential clients, brides, in particular. They come from all walks of life—They may be high school dropouts or may have had post-graduate college schooling. Don't assume your target audience has any prior knowledge of your press release topic. Write in a way that anyone can understand you.

The word "END" appears at the bottom of the body copy, set off with dashes. You can also use the older convention of typing a row of ##### or ***** at the end of your press release, but I prefer the word "END", which makes it obvious to anyone that there are no extra pages to your press release.

> **5. The Call to Action.** This is part of the body copy of every press release. This is where you lead your readers by the hand and tell them exactly what to do. In my **Sample Press Release,** the last paragraph before the information about the calendar listing is the call to action. It is necessary in all of your press releases—Tell the reader that you are available to perform for them and tell them how to book you!

It isn't necessary, but sometimes I like to include a secondary call to action. In my sample, it is listed below the calendar listing. This call to action is written for the editor who is receiving this press release.

> **6. Hyperlinks (or Links).** They are scattered throughout the body copy, and in my **Sample Press Release,** they are underlined. Hyperlinks take the reader to websites where they can receive more in-depth information about topics mentioned in the press release.

Be sure that every link opens to a new window in the browser so that the reader can easily return back to your press release. Before you send off a press release, click on each hyperlink in the body of your press release to make sure that it isn't a dead link. This is a great way to verify that you have spelled out the URL for the link correctly.

Once you have had a little practice writing press releases, you'll want to know where to send and post them:

> **1. Your local newspapers.** They are your best allies, because if you are doing anything locally, they'll want to print it for everyone in town to read. This is especially true in smaller communities.

Brides search within the cities and towns where they plan to get married for all of their services. If you appear in your local paper on a somewhat regular basis, brides getting married in your region are bound to take notice.

> **2. Online wedding sites.** Many of these sites like to print information from wedding professionals as advice to brides.

3. **Craigslist.com.** Since you are generally trying to get your press release distributed to local media to reach local brides, a way to post your press release may be in the classifieds on CraigsList.com. Listings are shown by city and region, so you can target brides who reside in your community.

4. **The "Press Room" section on your website.** Post your press releases, along with hyperlinks to a printable forms of your standard press releases, on your website. When reporters are looking for information about you, they can simply download your latest press release and go from there.

5. **Regional wedding magazines.** They may print your press release information or even call you for an interview. Your press release needs to be very newsworthy and aimed directly at brides to translate into bridal magazine publicity.

6. **Local television and radio producers.** Alert broadcast media of your talents only when you are ready to perform live, on-air. Presenting yourself and your music in front of a live camera takes some preparation, and your reputation is on the line with thousands of viewers and listeners tuned in. This kind of preparation is beyond the scope of this book. To learn more, I'd recommend Richard Laermer's "Full Frontal PR" book for some good pointers for broadcast performances and handling on-air interviews.

Even if the format of your press release is right on, your press release will not get read if you do not observe proper Internet etiquette, or "netiquette". It might not even make it through the recipient's spam filter! So, I've included a **Netiquette for Wedding Musicians** guide in the Appendix at the end of this book. It covers more than just the proper Internet conventions for emailing press releases. I've included ways to avoid offending brides and clients via email.

The Appendix doesn't cover every rudimentary little thing about email, though. I'm assuming that you know how to send and receive emails. If you are new to the world of the Internet, then you may want to buy a good computer how-to book or download some online FAQs (Frequently Asked Questions) about using your particular email program.

This **Netiquette for Wedding Musicians** guide doesn't cover basic non-wedding-business etiquette rules either. If you want to learn more about when it is or is not appropriate to send emails, as well as what to write in general email situations, I suggest taking a look at

Judith Martin's book, "Miss Manners' Basic Training: Communication" or the book "Send" by Will Schwalbe and David Shipley.

The reporter or editor who is on the receiving end of your press release may want to receive it via fax instead of by email. If you are sending it along by fax, always include a cover sheet, even if your recipient says you don't need to. The cover sheet is necessary to make sure your fax gets into the right hands. It also tells how many pages are included in the fax transmission so that the person on the receiving end knows everything came through.

SOME GREAT NOT-SO-FREE ADVERTISING IDEAS

"Advertising is totally unnecessary. Unless you hope to make money." —Jef I. Richards, Professor of Advertising, University of Texas at Austin

You've certainly heard the saying, "It takes money to make money." I think whoever said this was talking about advertising. Of course, this idea can be daunting to anyone on a tight budget. You can stay within your budget and start small, buying a little advertising at a time. Over a period of a few months, if you have bought advertising space wisely, you'll see a profit in the number of bookings you make. It is a fact that advertising is part of being in business and part of making money.

Spending money on advertising works. Look at it like you would look at investing in stocks. But here, you are investing in your own company. In other words, when people buy stocks, they have done a lot of research first. They don't put all their eggs into one basket, purchasing stock in only one company. They spread their money around and create a balanced portfolio. Then, even after the stocks have been purchased, they monitor them for performance. If the stocks don't show any return after a certain period of time, they sell them off. If you go about advertising in this same methodical way—researching the track record of a particular advertising vehicle, spreading around your ad placements in different media, and researching the success of each ad after it has run for a while—you are bound to see a return on your dollar.

Decide which media to concentrate on and then think about designing an ad that is appropriate for that media. **There are certain parameters to consider when determining whether a particular print advertisement placement will successfully sell your services as a wedding musician:**

1. **Who will it reach?** If you primarily perform at wedding ceremonies, would you take out an ad for your services in *Time Magazine*? Of course not. Think about how to reach brides,

specifically. Avoid general advertising vehicles that don't feature wedding sections.

2. **Where will it reach?** Why spend a lot of money advertising your services in national wedding magazines when you're really only performing at weddings in your local area? Confine your advertising dollars to those regions where you want to perform.

3. **How many people will it reach?** Make sure the advertising vehicle is well distributed to brides in your local area. Get statistics on the readership of the newspaper or magazine, and if you are looking into a website, find out the numbers and demographics of their visitors.

4. **How long are readers exposed to your ad?** If your ad will only appear in a local magazine for one month, is it worth the expenditure? Typically, it is best to run an ad in print media for a good six months. Then, determine if the ad has worked for you by the response you have received. You can often qualify for a price break on an ad when you run it over a long period of time.

5. **Are other advertisers happy with the response they've received?** Don't be afraid to contact other people who have been running their ads for a while in the advertising vehicle you are considering. Get in touch with wedding musicians, entertainers, DJs, and anyone offering services to brides that are even remotely similar to what you do. Ask them whether they think the response they have received has been worth the cost of the ad. I have found it refreshing how candid advertisers have been with me when I've contacted them for some feedback on an advertising vehicle.

6. **Is the price of the ad fair, considering the above five points?** Always keep in mind the budget you have set for each particular advertising vehicle. Whatever amount of money that you can allocate may never feel like it's enough, which is even more of a reason to have a grasp of your advertising budget.

Before you pay for any advertisements, here are some thoughts to bear in mind:

1. **Don't fall for the sales pitch.** Sales representatives from different publications will try to get you to buy the biggest, most expensive ad possible. That's their job. Even if you can afford

to buy the largest ad they have available, don't do it. Purchase a modest-sized ad and run it for six months or so instead of emptying your wallet on a large ad that you can only afford to run for a short time. The longer that brides are exposed to your ad, even a small ad, the more response you are likely to receive.

2. **Stay within your budget.** When determining how much you can comfortably spend on advertising, decide how much per month and per year you'll shell out, since website advertising is often based on a one year commitment. Also include in your budget the cost of creating your ads, which leads me to this next caution . . .

3. **Do not let publishers design the artwork for your ad.** To avoid mistakes, supply camera-ready artwork for them. Give this task to the same graphic designer who created your lovely brochures. Be consistent with your theme so that it ties in with your other marketing materials. A good ad arouses curiosity, lures in prospects, and invites them to get in touch with you. Leave the design of your ad to a professional, but do supply them with the text for your ad. I'll get into what to include in the body of your ad shortly.

4. **To save money, "co-op" with other businesses.** Co-op advertising is sharing the space with other advertisers and pooling your money so that the advertisement becomes affordable for everyone. For example, I have shared a one-page ad with a wedding gown shop, along with the photographer, florist, and caterer that they recommend. We all pooled our money together, and a big, one-page magazine ad for all of us became very affordable. If you belong to a local chamber of commerce, you can start there to seek others willing to advertise in the same vehicle that interests you.

Here are some print advertising vehicles worth considering:

1. **The Yellow Pages of your local phone book.** Old-fashioned as it seems in this Internet age, this is one form of advertising you should not pass up. If you do not invest in any other print advertisement, you should invest in this one. The Yellow Pages is the best-distributed print vehicle that you'll find. They aren't just found hanging from metal cords in phone booths (which are becoming obsolete with the high use of cell phones). The Yellow Pages are dropped off at the door of all local residents and businesses for free. They are inside hotel and motel rooms, and most businesses have one stashed somewhere. It reaches many, many people within a specific geographical area, and

it exposes people to your ad for at least a year. (Some Yellow Pages are reprinted more frequently than others, so the length of exposure depends upon region).

The other exposure is that your business name will be listed with your phone company. Therefore, when a bride loses your business card and phones directory assistance for your number, the operator will know who you are.

There are a lot of imitators of your local Yellow Pages. The Yellow Pages that I am recommending is the one that is published by your local phone company, the one delivered to your house twice yearly, or more often. There are other Yellow Pages that are published by companies outside your area that may be soliciting you for advertising within their national Yellow Pages. These are not what I am recommending. Nor am I referring to the Yellow Pages on the Internet. I'll get to a discussion about Internet advertising shortly.

Your local Yellow Pages may have several categories for your listing. Open yours up and see what categories may interest you. Your choices may vary according to where you live. In large cities, there may be a category for "Wedding Musicians", or "Wedding Services". Smaller towns may just consolidate everything having to do with weddings under the umbrella phrase "Weddings". You'll also want to have an additional listing under "Musicians", because brides may think of looking for you there, too. Avoid the "Entertainer" category, since it may include strip-tease acts and other x-rated entertainment.

Be careful with your pennies, though. There is an added cost to every little thing beyond a basic listing. The extra fee for a cross-referenced ad in two or more appropriate categories is worth the money. But if you decide to make your listing in bold, use a larger font for your listing, use a different color of ink, and so on, it adds up. And this is for a text listing; I'm not even talking about the expenditure on a display ad in the yellow pages, which can be staggering. The sales rep will quote you a monthly payment for your ad. Get out your calculator and see what it adds up to for the year. Is it within your budget?

Here is my personal experience with advertising in the Yellow Pages for the past twenty years: I pay a low monthly fee for a simple, one-line listing of my business and my toll-free "800" number. It is only one line of advertising under two sections, "Musicians" and "Wedding Services". That's it. Over years of trying Yellow Page ads of different sizes within the different regions where I've lived, I have come to the conclusion that the extra cost isn't worth it. Very few potential clients phone me because they found me in the Yellow Pages, but it still happens. Why do I list myself there? One of my clients or a potential client who misplaces my number can simply look me up. True, a bride might just Google my name to find my phone number, but not everyone has online access. And the cost is low enough that if just one bride decides to book me after seeing my Yellow Pages listing, the ad has paid for itself.

> **2. Newspapers.** With newspaper advertising, you have some control over how long you want your ad to run. And like the Yellow Pages, you can select a local regional newspaper to reach local brides. Newspapers are also like the Yellow Pages, because you reach a large, general population of readers who are not necessarily brides.

You could advertise in the classified ad section, but here's a better idea…Certain times of the year, your local newspaper may print a wedding services supplement. If you intend to advertise your talents at all in the paper, advertise in this insert. The phone calls you will receive from your ad will be clients interested in your wedding music services—Readers of wedding inserts are either getting married or know someone who is. You'll reach people interested in booking you.

> **3. Magazines.** They are not published as frequently as newspapers, so the exposure your ad gets depends upon whether the reader hangs on to the magazine issue, passes it along to friends, or just throws it away.

I once advertised in a regional magazine that is published twice a year. I bought two years of advertising (for four issues), and a quarter page ad was pricey. It was a gorgeous ad, and people who saw it thought it was wonderful. But over that two-year period, I only received one booking from the exposure. It was a boon for building my reputation, as readers thought I must be very professional, with a pretty ad in a slick magazine. It was great for my ego but not for my pocketbook.

Magazine ads can be one of the most expensive ways to reach people, at least in print. If you choose to experiment with this medium, choose a magazine that has a large readership of brides. Make sure it is readily available on local newsstands and on the Internet. Sometimes, you can get a deal with a magazine where they will list your business information and link to your URL* on their website, all

---

*The "URL" is the Internet address of a particular website. Direct translation of this acronym is Uniform Resource Locator (coined 1990). It identifies a particular file on the Internet, usually consisting of the protocol http:// followed by the domain name.

for the price of an advertisement. The online exposure on a magazine website may expose more brides to your services than the magazine ad itself.

The way to cut the cost of a magazine ad is to co-op with other wedding service providers who are interested in advertising in the same issue.

4. **Radio and Television.** Radio and television advertising is very cost-prohibitive, and commercials only work when they are run frequently when your target audience of brides are listening. Leave this advertising to bridal fair promoters, restaurants, and receptions halls that book weddings.

You can still benefit from the ads that other wedding vendors broadcast. Here's how to do it: Contact any local bridal services that run commercials to make sure they are aware of you. Then when a bride calls them, your services stand a chance of being recommended.

A Few Basics for Writing a Good Ad

It's an art to be able to write an ad that resonates in the bride's consciousness, which makes her feel like she MUST find out more about you and your music. I'm not an advertising executive, so I'll just offer a few points that have worked well for me over the years. If you're stuck, visit your local library or the advertising section of a full-service bookstore for in-depth books on the subject. Or take an extension course to practice the craft of writing advertisements.

1. **What's the purpose of your ad?** Of course, you are introducing yourself to brides. You are also telling them why they should consider hiring you—you are explaining your special benefits to them. This harkens back to your brochure design, but unless you are advertising on the Internet, you will have very limited space to work with. Boil your advertising copy down to exactly what you want to convey. Be brief and avoid hype. Your print ad is not a late-night infomercial.

2. **Write your copy so that a kid can understand it.** If you have any children who are at least ten years old, run your rough draft by them. It's a brilliant way to test your copy. Your ad must make sense to your readers, regardless of their educational level. Besides, if it's too complex, no one will take the time to read it. Make it fun to read and your advertisement will be remembered.

"You can say the right thing about a product and nobody will listen. You've got to say it in a way that people will feel it in their gut. Because if they don't feel it, nothing will happen."—William Bernbach, founder of Doyle Dane Bernbach advertising agency

"We have data that proves that the common phrase "Keep It Simple Stupid" is true!...If you keep the language at 5ᵗʰ grade or less, you have a 70% more effective ability to get the consumer to see your idea."—Dr. Jeffrey Stamp, from the University of North Dakota, as heard on Brain Brew Radio in November 2006, broadcast by Public Radio International.

This method also works for artwork—Jerry DeCrotie, the illustrator for this book, regularly shares his cartoon ideas with his kids. "Sometimes they come up with ideas I haven't even thought about".

3. **Write a headline that stands out.** The headline draws the reader into the body of your ad. Look at the headlines of the existing ads where you'll be advertising. Then, make your ad different so it will stand out. Let your headline introduce the topic of your ad in just a few words. Be sure that the words in the headline are at that 5th grade reading level, too.

4. **Leave room in the ad for a photo.** Even if you are purchasing a small, business card sized ad, include a photo showing you with your instrument. Select a photo that looks great even when reduced down to a very small size. If you are not sure which photo to use, ask your graphic designer to help you select the right one.

5. **Include a "call to action".** Tell the readers how to reach you. List your phone number, email address, and web site.

A final word about print advertising: Be a proof Nazi. When you agree to purchase advertising, find out not only when copy is due, but also when you will receive a proof. Respect the deadline to submit corrections. You may have very little time to proof an ad before it goes into print, so get on it right away. In particular, proof all your copy with a fine-tooth comb, especially your contact information. Once an ad goes into print, it cannot be fixed.

BEYOND THE WORLD OF THE PRINTED PAGE—INTERNET ADVERTISING

You don't need to have a website to advertise on the Internet, although it can certainly help. You can still pay for listing with your business name and phone number to start having an online presence. Then when you launch your own website, you can contact these advertisers and request that they add your domain name and your URL to your listing.

Many of the print advertising pointers I've listed above also apply to Internet advertising. **Here are a few extra suggestions that pertain only to buying an online listing or a banner advertisement:**

1. **Be willing to pay top dollar for an advertisement on a popular local wedding directory or local chamber of commerce site.** How do you find out which sites are the most

popular? Do a Google search on "Weddings in _____" and fill the blank with the place where you want to perform. You'll immediately see which online wedding directories are most popular by their rankings.

It's worth paying for local Internet advertising, especially if the website advertiser sends qualified leads to your email inbox. You can then turn around and send these brides an email message to introduce yourself. They may just book you! See the **Netiquette for Wedding Musicians** Appendix for information about how to introduce yourself to a bride via email.

2. **With nationwide online wedding directories, negotiate for free reciprocal links instead of paying for advertising.** Chances are that a bride in your local area will not be shopping for your talents on a nationwide wedding website directory, but it's good to be listed on these sites. It will help to improve your website ranking in search engines. Of course, you'll need to have a website to take advantage of free reciprocal links.

3. **Ad exposure varies greatly, and so will the amount you spend for that exposure.** The length of advertising can run anywhere from a 30-day trial offer to a "lifetime" advertisement (meaning the extent of the lifetime of the particular web site directory on the Internet). The lifetime advertisement can work out to be a good deal if you can foresee advertising on that web site for at least a few years. If you aren't sure what kind of response you'll receive from a certain listing, then don't bother with the lifetime deal.

4. **Do not let online advertisers design your banner ad.** Assign the task of creating a banner ad to your webmaster to make sure that the ad reflects the look of your website. If you do not have a website yet, enlist the aid of the graphic designer for your print materials to design a banner ad for you.

I have been shy of using other forms of online advertising, due to the cost of investment. I am particularly wary of pay-per-click, often abbreviated PPC. This is where the advertiser bids on keywords that describe their service. In this instance, maybe some keywords would be "wedding musicians" or "reception musicians". These are words that someone would type into a search engine to find you. You have to pay money only when someone clicks on your listing.

The advantage to PPC advertising on Google, for instance, is that your listing would appear as a "Sponsored Link" next to or above the other listings on that search engine. They may also appear on one of Google's partner sites.

PPC advertising adds up pretty quickly. Consult with your webmaster to make sure this is the right investment for you and is within your budget.

YOUR WEBSITE—THE BEST FORM OF INTERNET ADVERTISING

Around 1998, I was entertaining the thought of getting a computer. I figured I could save time by using a word processor to type up correspondence to brides, rather than relying on my old IBM Selectrix typewriter. The buzz was circulating about the Internet. "What was this .com stuff all about?", I wondered. I needed to see it for myself. So my good friend Reverend David Beronio took some time out of his day to let me experience how to navigate around the worldwide web on his computer. I remember that day very well, because I was blown away by the power of the Internet. Certainly I was impressed by the flashy technology of it all, but there was one big reason why I knew right then and there that I needed to buy a computer and develop my own website: This form of advertising has no spatial limits.

Unlike print advertising, where buying an ad is "buying space" of a certain fixed dimension, a website is like a book that can have as many pages and as much content as I like. The homepage serves as title page and a preface, and the navigational bar lists the table of contents. Each click within the "table of contents" goes to a different "chapter" of material.

I immediately bought a computer and started surfing around to see what other musicians included on their websites. Very few musicians had an online presence back then, and those who did neglected to take advantage of this new technology. Their websites usually contained only one page displaying a big photo, and with a dial-up connection, I could make a cup of tea in the time it took to download. Those musicians didn't understand that a website is the best advertising investment available.

For a wedding musician, the purpose of having a website presence is simply to reach brides and other clients who surf the net and convince them to contact you and book your services. That's it.

I'm not a web designer, but I know what works and what doesn't work. **Here are just a few basics to consider when preparing to launch your own wedding musician website:**

1. **Select a good domain name.** Pick something that is easy to say, easy to spell, easy to read in your print and online advertisements, and easy to remember. It can be your own name, your band name, or what you do (for instance, "LAWeddingJazzBand.com")

2. **Make sure that your website concept and "look" ties in with the rest of your PR materials.**

3. **Create your website as your online wedding press kit for brides.** Take advantage of the fact that you are not limited to having just one page. Definitely include the following sections in your website navigation bar:

   - Your Homepage—A quick overall description of you and what you have to offer. Base this on the information in your brochures and expound on it.
   - A Bio Section—Go into greater detail than on your homepage
   - A Press Section—Photos and downloadable press releases
   - Wedding Gallery of Photos—So brides can see you in action
   - Your Music List
   - Sound Samples and if you have them, Video Samples
   - Testimonials
   - Booking Information—DON'T list your fee schedule. On this page, invite the bride to phone or email you for more information.
   - A Links Page—List the domains of your reciprocal link partners here. Remember: Links on their sites to yours will drive qualified visitors to your site, brides who are interested in what you have to offer.

Other optional pages that you might want to add to your navigation bar include: A public performance calendar, a shopping cart for purchasing your CDs online, additional sound samples for your CDs, an online contest, and . . . be creative. Make your website reflect your individual talents.

4. **Keep your web pages simple.** Avoid the use of Macromedia Flash intros, multicolored backgrounds, icons that quiver on and off, and other things that are difficult for some Internet visitors

to download and view. Even in this age of high-speed innovations, some people are still on dial-up connections or their computers have slow processors. If a bride doesn't want to wait for your website to download, she'll go elsewhere.

5. **Make your website easy to read.** Strange backgrounds and weird fonts can render your website unintelligible.

6. **Let your visitors decide if they want to listen to your sound or video samples or not.** It is incredibly rude to land on a homepage and suddenly hear "We've Only Just Begun" belching through the computer speakers. Forcing your music on a website visitor will make you look less than professional.

Let a bride decide if she wants to hear your music by giving her the option of clicking on a sound or video file icon to begin play. Give information about what kind of file it is (mp3, QuickTime, Windows Media Player, RealAudio, etc.) so that she can download the appropriate player if she doesn't have it yet. This gives her a chance to prepare for what she is about to hear and adjust her computer speakers.

7. **Make your website easy to navigate.** The navigation menu should appear on every page and in the same place. Check that your navigation links work correctly and go to the right pages.

8. **Include your contact information on ALL pages of your website.** Place it at the top of the page and under your navigation bar, too, for good measure. You can even place it within the body of the text of each page.

9. **Avoid long, scrolling pages.** Include HTML files of extensive information that users can print—do this for your online music list and press releases. List the most important information at the top of long pages, so that if a bride doesn't want to bother scrolling to read all of your information, she will not have missed much. Or better yet, if you can break down a page into another category or sub-category on your navigation bar, by all means do so.

10. **Include links to main pages at the footer of all your web pages.** If a bride scrolls to the bottom of a page, don't make her scroll all the way back up to navigate to another page.

11. **If you haven't added any information to a page yet, don't display the words "Under Construction".** Wait until you have

some content for a web page before adding it to the navigation bar of your website. Whenever I see the words "Under Construction" on a website, I think that particular online company is not ready to do business. What must brides think when they see this on a website?

12. **Don't bother with posting questionnaire forms for wedding inquiries.** Invite brides to contact you by email or by phone for a quote. I used to have an inquiry form on my site, where a visitor would enter her wedding information in specific fields of a questionnaire. Very few brides took advantage of this. Most of them opted to send me an email instead.

13. **Have your webmaster create your site so that you can make text changes yourself.** You'll save a lot of money if you can regularly update your performance calendar and add new press releases without having to go through your webmaster for every little change or fix. Have him set you up with a software program that enables you to update your website from your own computer. You'll only need to contact your webmaster to make significant changes.

"Time is money! A nonprofessional who does websites on the side and takes three or four times as long as a pro will end up costing you marketing opportunity and sales as well as money." Jan Zimmerman, Author of "Web Marketing for Dummies"

You don't have a webmaster, your very own web page developer? If you are a do-it-yourselfer, get ready to take some college extension courses for a while on the topic, and then scramble to keep up with the newest technological innovations. Or if you think you'll save a few dollars asking your friends or relatives to create your website, think again. They may dilly-dally, doing it on their own time in their own way. They may not understand the purpose of your site, which is to convince brides to contact you for their wedding music needs. Better yet, leave the creation and maintenance of your website to a professional who has your ultimate goal in mind and is up on all the latest software advancements.

One extraordinary benefit of having your website maintained by a professional webmaster is that they will work to keep your website safe from viruses, spam attacks, and hackers.

They should also be capable of providing you with a weekly or monthly statistical report of the number of visitors to your site, which key words they are using to find your site, which other domains are referring visitors to your site, and so on. Use this information to determine whether to change your key words or Meta tags, and whether you should continue advertising on certain websites if they aren't sending you visitors.

Your webmaster can act as your site host and graphic designer. They may also handle optimizing your site for search engines using Meta tags, key words. And, they may consistently submit your site to search engines. If they are only going to develop your website, you will need to shop for a separate person to work on the graphic design for your site. Maybe you'll have a different web host, too. Regardless of whether the above tasks are handled by just one person or several, they are all necessary to launch and maintain a business presence on the Internet.

Here's how to shop for a great web professional:

1. Approach the creators of the websites that you love.

2. Approach the designers of your competition's websites.

3. Ask other local wedding vendors whom they hired for their webmasters.

4. Make sure that your webmaster and web host have stability.

"I have helped with a number of website transfers and am amazed how lousy some hosts are in supporting their clients and at providing a continuous online presence. One host literally stopped cold with no contact. Here today, gone today."—Stephen Vardy, sound engineer for harpist Alison Vardy

Strive to hire local professionals who have long track records in business. I have heard some dreadful horror stories about web page guardians who suddenly disappeared and went out of business. Their victims were innocent musicians whose pages magically disappeared off of the Internet. Verify that your webmaster and web host have at least two backups of your web site in case anything goes amiss.

With all of these points in mind, do a little surfing on your own. Type in some names of famous and not-so-famous musicians into a search engine and see what comes up. Check out the websites of your competition, those other musicians in your local area. Don't forget to look up the websites of local wedding vendors to see what they do to appeal to brides online. Click through all the pages of each site you visit. List your favorite URLs here:

_____

_____

_____

_____

_____

_____

_____

_____

_____

Give this list to your webmaster candidates and explain to them what you like about these sites. With this list, they'll have a good idea of how to build your website. They will also give you fee quotes and time lines to accomplish the creation of your own site.

A good web professional should be a good communicator with an understanding of what you want to achieve with your website. If you encounter a webmaster who wants to charge you for every single phone discussion, don't hire them. Besides the fact that you'll go broke paying for their services, they probably would rather sit in their cubbyhole staring at a computer screen than talk with you anyway. This doesn't make for a good, long-term business relationship.

When you start receiving quotes, you may find that you'll have to cut back on the grand scheme of your website for now. A good webmaster will be able to give you some less expensive choices for getting an efficient website launched. You can always add new pages and technology to your website at a later date. Regardless of the initial size of your website, take the plunge and invest. You will reach brides you never could have reached before.

A QUIET WORD ABOUT MYSPACE

In a nutshell, it doesn't work, at least right now. In my experience, it is not an efficient marketing tool to reach brides.

Because it is absolutely free to have a MySpace page, I signed up just to see if I could receive any inquiries from brides through this means. Here's the first thing I discovered: there is no way to actually market to brides. If "Wedding Music" were a genre of music in the artist profile setup, then brides would be able to search for wedding musicians. I also checked the forums and found that they were mostly made up of other wedding professionals networking to try to locate brides, too. So, all I could do was launch my MySpace page and wait for brides to find me.

Not ready to give up just yet, I asked fellow wedding colleagues about whether they have a MySpace page or would consider signing up for one. They scoffed at the mere idea of it. They believe that the demographics of MySpace users are too young and do not match those of brides who make financial decisions for their weddings (who are in their late 20's at least). At the time of this writing, I have not received one inquiry from a bride in the six months that my MySpace page has been up and running. My fellow wedding colleagues may be right.

I also asked brides if they used MySpace to look for wedding services. Their response was, "MySpace is for kids". These brides assumed that they can only find touring bands on Myspace, not professional wedding musicians. In my research, clients rely on Google, Yahoo, and other general Internet search engines and wedding directories to start an online search for wedding musicians, not MySpace.

However, Christine Boulton of ThinkLikeABride.com states that currently, 50% of the 89 million members of MySpace are under 18, and more than half of them are female. She encourages wedding professionals to tap into these MySpace users as they mature, inviting them to bridal shows where you may be exhibiting.

If you have absolutely no money to invest in an online presence with your own domain name, you could sign up for a MySpace Artist Account, a musician's page. To get local wedding vendors and brides to visit it, print your MySpace page URL on all of your stationery, business cards, and brochures, just as you would print the address to your official website, if you had one.

Security is one issue to consider about creating a MySpace page. You may have heard that there are crazy people roaming around on MySpace. Well, there are crazy people roaming around the entire Internet, too. But you are safer with an official webpage on the world-wide Web, with your own domain name, where your professional webmaster takes care of placing a force field of security around your site.

"Warning: The Internet may contain traces of nuts."—Unknown Author

When you set up a MySpace Artist Account, you will have to be your own webmaster (unless you get someone to maintain it for you). You'll need to do things yourself to protect your privacy. I like to check the profiles of all those folks who want to be my Friend*, deleting requests from those who have profiles that are offensive to me. I answer each Friend request, asking why that person wants to be added to my Friends list. The whackos don't answer me or reply with something like, "The voices in my head said I should be your Friend". I find that a primary way of filtering out undesirable contacts is to reply to Friend requests regularly, even though it's a time consuming task. Other things you can do to protect your privacy is to change your password regularly. You can also change your profile preferences to tighten up access to your page (which may defeat the whole point of having a MySpace page in the first place).

*A "Friend" on MySpace is someone who is interested in you and your music and wants to keep in touch. This word is capitalized in the text to differentiate it from the broader general meaning of this word.

To be fair, MySpace can be an excellent tool for all musicians. I have successfully referred MySpace users to my website, iTunes, and CDBaby.com, where they can buy my CDs and digital downloads. I have seen a marked increase in sales revenue from MySpace users. I've also successfully used MySpace to increase my fan base and network with other musicians. It just hasn't worked for reaching brides.

If you want to find out more about MySpace, how to set up an Artist Account, HTML codes that you'll need for your profile, and so on, I highly recommend the book "MySpace Maxed Out" by the editors of Bottletree Books LLC. If you're in a band or tour regularly, look for additional information in "MySpace Music Marketing" by Bob Baker.

Since MySpace is an unproven way to reach brides, let's move on to a conclusive way to find them. It's a form of advertising that's so important, it deserves a chapter all its own.

Anne Roos
Celtic Harp Music
P.O. Box 15190
South Lake Tahoe, California 96151 USA
Phone 800-555-1212
http://www.celticharpmusic.com - anne@celticharpmusic.com

Listen to Your Music Requests Performed on the Celtic Harp!

Anne Roos Appears Every Thursday Night at the Fremont Bistro

SOUTH LAKE TAHOE, California—February 16, 2007—Professional Celtic Harpist Anne Roos will play your music favorites at the new Fremont Bistro & Wine Bar every Thursday night, starting this coming Thursday, the 22nd, beginning at 7:30 pm. Anne actively seeks music requests from her audience ahead of the concert, too, so the program for the performances will be a special surprise (even to Anne).

"If you are planning to attend, you are welcome to send your request before the event, and I'll do my best to play it," says Anne. She invites future audience members to visit her website at www.celticharpmusic.com to view her extensive music list and then e-mail her a request.

She can accomplish this because she has over twenty-five years of experience performing on the Celtic harp. Anne's three CD titles will be available for sale at the Fremont Bistro performances, and she will be happy to sign them personally. Additionally, her CDs are available for purchase at www.celticharpmusic.com, where a money-saving gift special is posted. You can also purchase them locally at Neighbor's Bookstore.

For concert, wedding, and special event booking information, contact Anne toll-free at 800-555-1212. If you are planning a wedding or private event, these Fremont Bistro performances are a great way to meet Anne and hear her play live.

Here are the details of this live performance:

DATE: Every Thursday, Starting February 22, 2007
TIME: 7:30-9:30 pm
WHERE: Fremont Bistro & Wine Bar, 1041 Fremont Ave., South Lake Tahoe, California
FOR MORE INFORMATION: Phone (530)541-6603
*Reservations are not required!
*Dine on sumptuous vineyard cuisine presented by award–winning Chef Peter Coleman
*Anne takes your music requests
*Purchase CDs, signed by Anne at these performances

For more concert and for booking information, Anne Roos can be reached at 800-555-1212 or online at http://www.celticharpmusic.com.

*No, I don't need a musician for a wedding
...I was just wondering if you knew where the restroom is.*

CHAPTER 7

Exhibiting at Bridal Fairs: A Ripe Combination of Advertising and Promotion

"Of course I'm ambitious. What's wrong with that? Otherwise you sleep all day."
—Ringo Starr, Beatles drummer

BRIDAL FAIRS ARE NOT FOR THE LAZY

I polled a small sample of wedding musicians across the U.S., and I asked them about their bridal fair experience. There were two sharply divided opinions expressed. In one camp, there were the musicians who said that bridal fairs were an exhaustive waste of their time. The other camp said it was a great way to meet brides who are ready to book. This second group even offered some helpful tips to make bridal fairs a successful experience. Your decision about whether to participate in a bridal fair will hinge on the amount of work you'll be willing to do before, during, and after the show.

The key to being successful at bridal shows is to think in terms of whether your investment (in time and money) will turn a profit. Will you receive enough bookings from the show to more than pay it off?

Personally, I find that if I've done my research and chosen the right bridal fair, I always make a profit. Brides book me at the fair and I come home with deposits in hand. They continue to book me for days and weeks afterwards. I get a chance to meet and network with other local wedding professionals, too. I receive referrals from these new colleagues long after the bridal show has ended. Bridal fairs have proven one of the best ways to promote and advertise my services.

DO YOUR RESEARCH—IS THIS BRIDAL FAIR THE RIGHT ONE FOR YOU?

First and foremost, you have some homework to do if you have never stepped foot onto a bridal show floor (and even if you have, you may want to do this assignment). Attend a show with a note pad. Examine the booths that attract constant attention by visitors to the show. These are booths where the brides will linger to ask questions, not just collect brochures, enter a drawing, and then move along. Take note of:

1. How are these favored booths arranged? Describe them here:

_____
_____
_____
_____
_____
_____

Draw a diagram here:

2. How are they decorated? Flowers? Balloons? Lighting? Carpeting? Is the exhibitor using her own backdrop? Explain:

_____
_____
_____
_____
_____
_____
_____

3. **What materials are provided to brides?** Business cards? Brochures? Candy? Roses? Demo CDs? Explain:

_____
_____
_____
_____
_____
_____

4. **What attitudes do the exhibitors have?**

_____
_____
_____
_____
_____

5. **How are the exhibitors dressed?**

_____
_____
_____
_____
_____

6. **Is there a discount or a raffle being offered?** Describe below:

_____
_____
_____
_____

7. **Is there anything particularly unique about this booth that is drawing brides?**

_____
_____
_____
_____
_____
_____

Buzz and Sue Gallardo, of **Business Network Expositions** in Sacramento, California, suggest another way to measure the success of a booth at a bridal fair: "Look at the exhibits as you would if you were the bride. Is the booth inviting? Do the people look friendly? Is this someone I would want performing at my wedding?"

Your visit to a bridal show will arm you with an arsenal of ideas. It will also give you an idea of the work involved to produce an attractive presentation to brides.

There are no short cuts to exhibiting at a bridal fair. You'll discover that the musicians that gather crowds at their booths are the ones who are performing in their booths. They are dressed as they would look at a wedding and they play music that a bride wants to hear (even if it means playing "Here Comes the Bride" and "Canon in D" over and over again, all day long, ad nauseum). If you expect to participate at a bridal fair by standing behind a table with a boom box and a pair of headphones for brides to sample your music, you won't get any attention. Exhibiting at a bridal fair means exactly that—Exhibiting what musical magic you can offer to a bride for her wedding day.

Finding the Perfect Bridal Fair to Show Off Your Talents
Your introduction to local bridal fairs may arrive as an invitation to purchase booth space from an email message or a postal mailer. Or perhaps other wedding vendors in your area sing the praises about the profitability of an upcoming bridal fair. Spend some time getting to know the company that is producing the show. Speak with the promoter to determine whether you will want to sign a contract with them and what hidden costs may be involved. **Ask the following questions:**

1. **Has the promoter produced any other wedding fairs or is this one of their first events?** If they produce shows on a regular basis, request statistics of how many brides walked through the front door. This way, you will get an idea of how many bookings are possible at the show (but if they quote 1,000, remember that you will only have time to talk with a small percentage of these brides). Keep in mind promoters may quote the number of *people* in attendance, not *brides*. If this is the case, this figure will be inflated, since brides often bring parents and friends along with them to shows.

In addition to requesting statistics, also ask the promoter to send you a program from a previous show. Phone a few of the businesses who are listed in the program to get their take on whether that show was profitable and if they liked working with the promoter.

2. **Where is the show located?** Brides are likely to attend shows that are in the same towns where they plan to get married. If you live in a rural town fifty miles away from where the bridal fair is held, are you willing to drive this distance for each wedding you book at the show?

Is the show being held at a low-end venue or at an upscale establishment? A higher-class location, with a higher entrance fee to the fair, tends to attract brides with healthy wedding budgets. In contrast, a bridal fair with little or no entrance fee in a lower-quality venue will attract bargain-hunting brides who may think they can haggle with you to get you to quote a lower price.

3. **What are the dimensions of the booth?** You'll need to determine if you, your ensemble members, your performance equipment, several chairs, and a table can fit comfortably in the space provided. After your visit to another bridal fair, you should have a good idea of how much space you will need to effectively promote your musical talents to brides.

4. **What's in the contract?** Find out what the promoter guarantees:

- Where will the show be advertised and will your name be included in the advertisements?
- Can you choose your booth location in the floor plan so that you are not adjacent to DJs and other musicians?
- What is the promoter's cancellation policy, and under what circumstances can you get a refund?
- What happens if the promoter cancels the show after you pay for a booth space?

5. **Use your gut feelings to decide if you want to work with a particular promoter.** If they come off like a slimy used car salesman with a hard-sell attitude, run in the other direction. One bad sign is when the promoter quotes huge, inflated numbers for the attendance at past fairs. Another is when it is months before the wedding fair, and they tell you that you have only one day to make a decision. Otherwise, they'll sell the wonderful booth space they had planned for you to another musician or wedding vendor, and they don't have any others for you to choose from. That's just a line to get you to commit to a booth space right away without thinking about it.

6. What is the total fee that the promoter will charge to you? Take into account not only the booth fee, but extras such as electricity, linen rather than plastic tablecloths, and extra chairs or table. Some promoters add on fees for all of these items.

You need to determine if you expect to get enough bookings from the fair to justify the cost of the booth space, and then some. Don't forget your mileage to and from the bridal fair and any other costs you may incur.

When discussing the booth fee, also ask the promoter what they are willing to provide for the cost of the booth. **These questions will determine any hidden costs:**

1. **Will there be curtains and piping provided around your booth?** Some bridal fair promoters do not provide booths with any walls that separate one booth from another. This often happens when the bridal fair is in a small venue (such as in a historical Victorian house). This is not necessarily a bad thing, as you and your group may be able to get away with overflowing into the aisles. However, other vendors who purchase space may overstep their bounds and impinge on your space, so think it over before deciding to buy a booth at one of these fairs.

2. **Will the promoter provide you with a table?** If so, how large will the table be? Calculate how much room will be left over for you and your band members in the booth. Will the table come with a tablecloth or skirting? If not or if the promoter provides plastic tablecloths and skirting, plan to bring your own linens. You may need to rent these yourself if you do not have the right sized table linens at home. The tables that are normally provided at bridal fairs are pretty beaten up.

3. **Will the promoter provide signage for your booth?** Most promoters will only provide a sign for the back wall of your booth. The sign will also contain your booth number, so that brides who are looking through the program can find you on the map of the floor plan. Promoters for smaller bridal fairs may not provide any signs at all. Regardless of what is provided, make a sign for the table in your booth, or have one made for you. A unique sign, which is at eye level, is easily readable across the aisle and helps attract brides to your booth.

4. **Is the floor carpeted?** It's not as ridiculous a question as it may seem. If the bridal fair is held at convention center, for

instance, the floor may be cement or old linoleum. Bring an attractive area rug for your booth if there's no carpeting so that your feet and the brides' feet are comfortable. Besides, carpeting makes a booth look much more inviting.

5. **How many chairs do you get with your booth?** Bring the chairs that you and your ensemble are used to sitting in when you are playing, and ask for extra folding chairs. You'll need at least two chairs for the brides to sit in while they listen to your perform. Certainly, you'll want to make them feel comfortable. However, there is a more important reason for offering them a seat—You need to be at the same eye level to effectively sell your music services. You will be in your chairs, performing or getting ready to perform, and the brides will be sitting in their chairs auditioning you.

6. **Is electricity available in your booth?** Does it cost extra to have electric outlets placed in your booth? You won't want to run any equipment off of batteries at a bridal fair—You may lose juice before the end of the day. Request electricity if you are using an amp or a television monitor.

7. **Do you have enough brochures, business cards, and other printed materials for the bridal fair?** Check the statistics the promoter gave you for the number of attendees. Then check your stock. Bring more materials than you think you'll need, because you'll want to distribute them to other vendors exhibiting at the show, too (networking!). If you need to print more, then factor this into your extra cost, beyond the booth price, for you to participate.

8. **Does the promoter require that you offer a door prize?** Some promoters are very specific about this, denoting the minimum acceptable amount for a product or a gift certificate. If you are required to offer a door prize for your services, either give away something that has your name on it—like a wedding book with a message from you written next to the title page. Or, if you must offer a gift certificate for your services, make sure you include "fine print" on the certificate, such as, "Only good if booked within one year of this bridal fair. Only good for performances that are at least three (3) hours in length. Blackout dates include Saturdays from June through October. Subject to availability. . . ." You get the picture. The restrictions will make it highly unlikely that the gift certificate will get used in the first place, but of course, you'll need to make good on what you promise in the certificate.

9. **Do you plan to hold a raffle at your booth?** This is an outstanding way to generate a mailing list from the entries you receive, but what will be the prize? Keep your costs down—give away something that promotes you. Perfect prizes may be your latest CDs and gift certificates for a dinner for two at a restaurant where you perform. Make sure you display an example of how the bride should fill out her entry, and insist that she write clearly (some brides have gotten wise to all the contests at bridal fairs and bring address stickers with them to the fair stick onto entry forms). Use a lovely glass container, even a clear-colored cookie jar, and bring plenty of index cards for entries.

By the way, skip buying a guest book for brides to sign. You won't generate much of a mailing list from it, since brides won't win anything by taking the time to sign your book. If they do happen to sign your guest book, they'll have no incentive to write legibly.

Of course, contact the winner of your raffle after the bridal fair. But don't forget about everyone else who entered your contest. Send personal email messages to each bride (not as an email blast using bcc). Thank her for entering your raffle at the bridal show, and then re-introduce yourself to her. Remind her of what you can provide for her special day and how to contact you for booking information. You may land a few extra weddings with this kind of personal follow-up.

10. **Place fresh flowers on your display table.** Fresh flowers are in abundance at bridal shows. Most vendors decorate their booths with flowers, even if they aren't florists. Forget about flowers and your table may look empty without them. Before the bridal fair, select a florist and give them the dimensions of your display table. They'll determine the most appropriate size arrangement for your needs.

11. **Offering chocolates or other sweets as an attraction to your booth.** Confections do not necessarily invite brides who are interested in your musical talents—they may just be stopping by your booth to satisfy their sweet tooth. I have frequently heard that there are always a small percentage of brides who attend bridal shows just for the food samples and the fashion show. They may even be done shopping for their wedding services!

That being said, scientists have found that chocolate does contain several organic compounds that produce feelings of well-being in the human brain. Offering a bowl of chocolate Kisses to brides may work magic to increase their levels of elation and happiness. This may be due to the levels of tryptophan and phenylethylamine. Placing science aside, if you are one of the only wedding vendors at the bridal fair offering chocolate to visitors at your booth, brides will definitely be attracted to your booth like bees to honey.

If you would like to offer goodies, refer to the exhibitor rules for your particular bridal fair. Some only allow food to be served in booths that are promoting food service businesses (caterers, restaurants, banquet halls). I've participated in some bridal fairs that insist that if any food is offered in a booth, a trashcan must be available in plain sight for wrappers and partially eaten sweets. If the trashcan is not allowed to hide under the display table, it will be another item that will take up precious space in your booth.

12. Do you need to prepare new materials for the bridal fair?
If you are creating new materials for the bridal fair, not just reprinting, add the cost of the design of these materials to your total cost for the bridal show. Also consider whether you will have these materials ready in time for the bridal fair.

There are several items you might want to place on your display table, besides your business cards and brochures. Brides will want to see your music list at the fair, and you could include this in a binder or scrapbook with your bio, testimonials, and photos from previous weddings.

You may also wish to blow up some of your photos into 8 × 10s and frame them, decorating your display table with them.

Some musicians plug in a TV monitor to show a video of their group in action. The video is usually on a loop, or the DVD is set on repeat, so it is on continuous play. Of course, the sound is off. Or provide headphones so that brides can listen to the video. A looped video comes in handy when you are not performing in your booth and busy chatting with brides, and booking weddings.

Speaking of booking, make sure you have plenty of contracts with you, reprinting them before the fair if necessary. Of course, bring your booking calendar to the fair, along with lots of pens, a credit card slider machine, and anything and everything you need to book weddings right there.

Is your wedding wardrobe in order? Bring everything that you wear when you perform at an upscale wedding. This includes your wedding music equipment and wearing your most formal wedding attire (tuxes for gentlemen and gowns for ladies). If you need to replace equipment, buy new clothing items or accessories, make sure you do so well before the date of the fair.

13. **Will you receive a mailing list or mailing labels of brides who attended the fair?** You can use the list to contact brides after a bridal fair, as a way of reminding them about your wedding music services. Most bridal fair promoters provide these lists as an Excel computer file, but receiving this list may not be automatic. Sometimes, you have to pay an extra fee to receive the list. And then other times, these lists are not part of your contract with the promoter—they may only choose to send you a list if you followed all of their show rules. Which is one reason why you must. . . .

Follow the Rules—Don't be a Maverick

Ask the promoter about their rules and regulations, and get everything in writing. Do not send in your payment for booth space until you receive a contract and rules governing the fair. Take a copy of this contract with you to the bridal fair, in case any disputes arise.

Some examples of the rules may include: Set up and break down times, parking restrictions, whether food is permitted in your booth, and items that can and cannot be displayed. Most promoters have strict rules about subletting your booth to someone else for part of the day, and they are equally strict about observing fire marshal regulations. A few promoters actually fine exhibitors if they break rules, such as tearing down their booths before the bridal fair is over and the last bride has left the building.

If you want to receive a mailing list of brides after the fair, follow the rules. And certainly, if you want to develop a relationship with the promoter and would like to attend their future bridal fairs, you should be on your best behavior.

Get Ready to Negotiate

The point is that you can negotiate with a promoter to make it more reasonable for you to commit to purchasing booth space. **Here are some items to bring up in contract discussions with the promoter:**

1. **Ask if you can get a discount on a booth if you are the only musician interested in purchasing a booth.** Sometimes, a promoter has plenty of other kinds of wedding services

exhibiting at a bridal fair, but no live musicians. They might want to make a deal with you, just to offer brides more variety of exhibitors at the show. They want their show to be successful as much as you do.

2. **As it gets close to the bridal show date, a promoter may be willing to unload booths for a discount that are still empty.** Empty booths at a bridal show look bad.

3. **Some promoters will give you a price break when they know you are not a corporation or a large company.** My rule of thumb is that if I need to book more than three weddings from a fair to cover the entire cost of participation, than I will decline to buy a booth in the first place. I've explained this to promoters when I think the booth price is too high. Sometimes, promoters have come down from their original price quote when they understand this.

4. **You may be able to swing for a free or discounted booth with the promoter if you agree to play for the fashion show at the fair.** It could mean more exposure to more brides at the fair, but personally, I prefer to pay the full booth rate and man my booth all day. I get more bookings when I stay in my booth and talk with brides than leaving my booth to play on a fashion show stage. And staying in my booth means I don't have to move my musical equipment to the stage and back.

5. **You may be able to reduce the booth cost by sharing the space with another compatible vendor.** In this case, you'd be paying for half of a booth. Of course, check the dimensions of a full booth before investigating this possibility.

I caution against sharing a booth at a bridal fair. Buzz and Sue Gallardo explain why this may not be the most profitable decision to make: "Our experience is that sharing booths is usually counterproductive to the exhibitor . . . Unless there is a clear demarcation between the sharing companies, brides are confused as to what the booth is promoting and is it one company or two? Do you have to book both? Most times one company or the other loses visibility or 'presence.'"

However, sharing a booth may work if you perform weddings exclusively at a hotel or chapel, and they are going to be exhibiting at a fair. If you share a booth with the only wedding facility where you will perform, the bride will clearly see that you are part of the package she could get if she books her wedding at that wedding site.

Here are three final questions to ask a promoter before signing on the dotted line:

1. **Are DJs allowed to play loud music or will there be multiple musicians in the same room?** Either avoid these shows or arrive at an agreement that DJs provide headphones and monitors for brides to experience their services.

Some promoters say, "You can rotate with the other two musicians in the room, deciding when each of you will play." This does not work. First of all, there is always a musician who performs far longer than you agreed, and secondly, you'll have brides aching to hear you perform and you won't be able to because it's someone else's turn. What an easy way to disappoint a bride, and I'm not in the business of doing that. Shows that allow only one musician per room will be the most effective for highlighting musicians.

Will the promoter permit you to use amplification? If not, will interested brides be able to hear you perform above the chatter at adjacent booths?

2. **Where will your booth be located?** Normally, a wall location works best for good acoustics. A corner with two walls works best for ensembles and bands. Don't ever agree to a booth space that is adjacent to another musician or a DJ, no matter how much the promoter promises, "We've told them to play quietly." Select a booth on the right of the entrance, because most people walk up the right aisle first. This is at least true in America, but in places like England, where people drive on the left side of the road, maybe the opposite is true.

3. **Will your booth be anywhere near the fashion show stage?** If it is, every time a fashion show is about to start, the brides will vacate your booth and you will have lost their attention. Furthermore, any brides who decide not to attend the fashion show and visit your booth will not be able to hear your music while music is playing for models on the runway. Don't bother exhibiting at a show with this kind of floor plan, because you'll spend a good chunk of your time in your booth all by yourself instead of greeting brides.

The secret to booking weddings at the bridal show: Offer a discount if the bride books you at the show. It shouldn't be a big discount; something like free mileage will do. Make a sign, or have one made professionally, that spells out your discount. Place it prominently on your display table so that a "hard sell" approach from you is unnecessary.

Just remember that whatever discount you are offering is only good when a bride wants to book you at the show. If she really wants to hire you, and her fiancé or parents aren't there to help her make the decision, she'll call them on her cell phone. If she can't reach them, don't worry. There is no reason to believe that she will give up the idea of hiring you. If a bride wants to book you and can't make up her mind at the fair, she will call and book you tomorrow, and you don't need to give her a discount then.

Set up your booth to make yourself approachable. In the **Booth Diagram** at the end of this chapter, you'll see my favorite booth setup. To make a booth approachable, move the display table to one side of the musicians instead of using it as a wall to block brides from entering the booth.

"Go to Bridal Shows AND PLAY!"—Norma Morse Edelman, wedding coordinator and owner of Wedding Casa

Play for brides while they sit comfortably in front of you. They will want to see you and your ensemble in action. Play every song as if you were playing it for that bride's wedding. Get into it. Glue that smile onto your face. You'll move a bride to tears and she'll book on the spot. You are a visual effect in addition to providing wonderful music, and remembering this at a bridal fair will get you booked.

Even if the bridal fair is not well attended, remember the networking opportunity you have with other wedding vendors. Hotel managers, caterers, photographers, and florists will take handfuls of your business cards and refer brides to you if they are impressed with the way your present yourself and perform. Bridal fairs, like other forms of marketing, can be worthwhile investments if you do your homework.

If I've convinced you to take the plunge and buy booth space at an upcoming bridal fair, refer to the **Bridal Fair Worksheet and Checklist** at the end of this chapter. This checklist will help you prepare for a profitable bridal fair experience.

Booth Diagram

Do *This:*

(Back Of Booth)

Musician's Chairs

Place To Stash your Gear

Table

Music Stands

Small Amp

Chairs For Brides

Not *This:*

Musician's Chairs

(Back Of Booth)

Boombox with Headphones

Brides Standing On Opposite Side of Table

Table

Bridal Fair Worksheet and Checklist

Start by drawing a diagram of your booth. Show the placement for you, your ensemble, your instruments, your table, and your chairs within the confines of your booth space.

Now draw a tabletop and include all your items on the table. Include the dimensions of the tabletop so that you can determine if you have enough space for everything you will need.

Take inventory of exactly what the promoter <u>will not</u> provide for you. These are the items you'll need to supply on your own for booth set-up:

❑ A table or an extra table--Table dimensions: _____

❑ A tablecloth or skirting for the table--Measurements: _____

❑ Area rug for booth--Dimensions of rug: _____

❑ Chairs for brides--How many: _____

❑ Floral arrangement for display table, ❑ Balloons, ❑ Confetti for table

❑ Other table decorations:

_____

_____

❑ Sweets? Chocolate?—What kind: _____, ❑ Garbage can for food & wrappers

Electrical Stuff:

❑ Electrical outlets—How many: _____

❑ Amps—How many: _____, ❑ Music stand lights—How many: _____

❑ Television monitor, ❑ Looped video, ❑ DVD, ❑ Headphones,

❑ Additional lighting

❑ Additional electrical equipment:

_____

_____

Signage for the booth:

❑ As a backdrop, ❑ Signage over table skirting, ❑ Sign for display table

Miscellaneous signs for your booth:

❑ Sign displaying bridal fair discount, ❑ Sign displaying how to fill out raffle entry

Materials for in-booth raffle:

❑ Container to hold entries, ❑ Index cards for entries, ❑ Pens

❑ Display of raffle prize

Printed Materials:

❑ Business cards—How many: _____, ❑ Brochures—How many: _____

❑ Contracts, ❑ Gift certificate for bridal fair door prize

Additional Promotional Materials:

❑ Binder, scrapbook, or photo album

Contents:

❑ Bio, ❑ Repertoire list, ❑ Testimonials, ❑ Press clippings,

❑ Photos

❑ Additional contents:

_____

_____

❑ Framed photos for table display—How many: _____

❑ CD demos to be handed out—How many: _____

❑ Other promotional materials to be displayed or handed out:

_____

_____

Important materials necessary for booking, besides blank contracts and extra pens:

❑ Booking calendar, ❑ Calculator, ❑ Credit card slider, ❑ Credit card slips,

❑ 8 X 10 clasp envelope to hold cash deposits, checks, completed credit card slips, & signed contracts

Miscellaneous materials to bring to the bridal fair:

❑ The promoter's rules and regulations

❑ Parking permit

❑ Your bridal fair contract

❑ Your business license

❑ A sack lunch, protein bars, water, snacks, fruit, etc. to keep you going for the day

Sheet music favorites: Bring the most requested music for weddings (see Appendix A for suggestions). List the music you plan to bring here:

_____

_____

_____

_____

_____

_____

_____

_____

_____

Of course, the above items are in addition to the musical equipment you need for a polished performance (your instruments, chairs, music stands, sheet music, etc.). You'll also want to dress the way you do at your most upscale wedding job. The bridal fair is your opportunity to demonstrate to brides what you'll provide for their very special day.

*Well, I think it's safe to say that I **will** be running another ad with you!*

CHAPTER 8

The Cardinal Rule for All Advertising

All advertisements, including bridal fair exhibition and Internet ads, are not about building your ego or your reputation. Their purpose is to book more weddings, which makes your more money, pure and simple.

Certainly, if you don't have the budget to invest in a particular advertising vehicle, then don't even bother considering it. Dig your heels into the sand and refuse to budge when you receive calls from advertising salesmen. Wait until you can consider investing, and then:

ONLY SIGN UP IF YOU THINK YOU'LL BOOK ENOUGH WEDDINGS TO BREAK EVEN.

Think in terms of how many weddings you'll have to book to make an advertisement pay off. Look at the average amount you charge per wedding and then quantify that in terms of the advertisement opportunity.

For example, within a year, I need to book just one wedding from a referral from the Yellow Pages to pay for that ad. If I book two, I've

"Don't spend more on marketing than you can make back. Losing money on every sale is not a good business plan."—Jan Zimmerman, author of "Web Marketing for Dummies"

made a profit. At bridal fairs, I usually need to book at least three weddings from brides who attend in order to break even. I make extra money off of the bridal fair if I book more. If I need to book more than three weddings to pay for an ad, then I usually shy away from committing to that advertising opportunity.

What is the average amount you'll make per wedding? This is the unit that you'll compare against all advertising. In the world of marketing and finance, this is called ROI, or "Return on Investment". It comes equipped with mathematical formulas, too. But all you need to remember is that you'll only want to invest in advertising when you have a reasonable idea that you'll make a profit.

The next time someone calls upon you to commit your hard-earned money in an ad, talk to them in these terms: tell them how many weddings it would take for you to pay for that ad. If the ad is expensive, they will understand why you cannot buy into it. And just maybe, they'll offer you a discount when they realize that you are a working musician. This makes for a positive conversation with the advertising sales rep. You won't feel badgered to sign on the dotted line, and you'll be able to logically explain why you are deciding for or against buying that ad space.

Once you have decided to pay for space in a wedding insert in a newspaper, inside your local Yellow Pages, or on a web site, let the ad run for a while. At the end of each month, review its effectiveness. At the end of the advertising period, review its effectiveness, again.

How can you determine if the brides who saw your ad were driven to book you? If the ad is on a website, check your monthly website stats report. If you see that a significant number of new visitors were referred to your site from the site where your ad sits, your ad is working. And regardless of where your ad is running, when brides phone ask, "How did you hear of me?"

There are many more questions to ask a bride when she shows an interest in booking you for her wedding. A list of these questions, and much more, are included in the next chapter.

Uh, Hello? Yeah...I perform at weddings. Hold on a minute,
let me put down this laundry basket, pick up the baby
and get the dog out of the garbage.

The Nitty Gritty: Selling Your Services to the Bride

"Customers buy for their reasons, not yours."
—Orvel Ray Wilson, coauthor of the Guerrilla Marketing series of books

All of your efforts in marketing and advertising will make your email inbox swell and your phone ring with inquiries. If the inquiry comes by email, instruct the bride to phone you for more information. You can give her a specific quote for her wedding via email, but don't offer your fee schedule. Tell her in your email response:

"When you have decided that you want to book my services, please phone me and we can discuss all the details. When we talk, I may be able to offer you a few options so that you can decide what best fits your budget."

More details about handling email inquiries can be found in the **Netiquette for Wedding Musicians Appendix.** I urge you to review the material found there, because it will offer a litmus test for determining whether an email inquiry is legitimate or spam.

Once you know you've received a true inquiry, the bride will either give you her phone number within the body of the email or she'll just call you out of the blue when she has made up her mind to hire you. You may not even hear from a bride by email at all—she's seen you perform, visited your website, or heard about you from another wedding vendor and is ready to give you a ring.

No matter how you look at it, you'll need to talk with her over the phone to close the sale...

TREAT EACH PHONE CALL WITH GREAT IMPORTANCE

Telephone first impressions can make or break a sale. Your voice speaks for your professionalism.

Clients base their decisions on feelings, not logic. A new form of research, called neuroeconomics, is looking into what the mind sees when it makes decisions. Dan Houser, a professor at George Mason University in Virginia found that, "Emotional guidance plays a sizable role in our decision making."

Success in selling your services and closing the sale over the phone isn't just about sales strategy; it's about reaching the bride's emotions. And you can do this through good customer relations, which can be summed up in one affirmation. This is a direct quote by Christopher Kight, a highly successful Sacramento wedding photographer. Keep this in the back of your mind whenever you are talking with anyone about your musical talents:

"One of the deep secrets of life is that all that is really worth doing is what we do for others."—Lewis Carroll, 19th century author, mathematician, clergyman

"The impression a customer should have of me is of my generosity." When you sincerely convey this virtue of generosity to your clients, they will believe that they'll get more for their money by hiring you. They will believe that you'll treat them more than fairly. If you go beyond their expectations, which in every case you should, you will have no difficulty landing gigs. Your clients will sing your praises. They'll be walking advertisements for your business—You'll be cloning an unsuspecting sales force!

Have you ever phoned a company and felt like the person you were talking to did not want to take the time to meet your needs? I'm sure this left you with a very poor impression. Taking time to work with contacts and inquiries, and more importantly, *sounding* like you're interested in them, is being generous with your time. This translates into bookings. The most effective sales tool you can own is great phone skills.

You can begin by conveying generosity in your phone voice. There are two ways to sound like you are generous, friendly, and trustworthy, and it's not in what you say, but how you say it. I learned the following techniques at a job I held many years ago while dispensing information and handling complaints over the phone at the Hollywood Bowl Box Office. **Whenever you speak on the phone or in person, practice:**

1. **Smiling naturally.** If not forced, smiling will break you away from monotone, boring patterns of speech. Smiling lifts the sound of your voice, actually making you come across as friendlier. You spread contagious cheerfulness with a smile. Even if your client can't see your smile, they can hear it in your voice.

If you have trouble remembering to smile, place a mirror next to the phone so you can make sure you're smiling when you answer it. Or maybe place silly photos or cartoons next to your phone to elicit a grin. These sound like corny suggestions, but they work magic. Your clients will be nicer when they hear you smile.

2. **Lowering your voice at the end of sentences, except when asking a question.** We all know the ditsy sound of a "Valley Girl" accent, popularized by Moon Unit Zappa several decades ago. It is characterized by the rise of the voice at the end of sentences in comments like, "Whatever!" If you practice lowering your voice at the end of sentences, you won't come across as a flakey musician to potential clients. Deeper pitches sound more assertive, convincing the party on the other line to trust what you have to say and not question your talents or your prices.

Try using the above two techniques in your outgoing voicemail message. Also give them a shot when you are phoning clients to leave messages for them.

If you have ever worked at a desk job, the following pointers will be obvious to you, but if not...**Here are some suggestions about how to make the most of our trusty receptionist, the answering machine:**

1. **In your outgoing voicemail message, state your name, the name of your ensemble and the information you wish the caller to leave.** Keep it all down to 30 seconds or less while pronouncing everything very clearly.

Please don't just say, "Leave a message," without identifying yourself to the caller. Sound like you are in business, even if you are picking up wedding jobs part-time to supplement a 9-5, Monday through Friday job. You're wasting a prospective client's time if you force them to figure out if they dialed the correct phone number.

2. **Think twice about using music in your outgoing phone message.** If your machine ever malfunctions, your music can sound terrible. Music played back on an answering machine is a poor way for a bride to audition your talents.

Some cell phones even play music to the caller while your phone is ringing, and it may not necessarily be the music you play. Try to find a way to turn off this function. If the caller doesn't like what they hear, they'll hang up before you ever pick up the phone.

3. **Know when and how to answer the phone.** When a prospective client calls and you don't have at least twenty minutes to talk with them, uninterrupted, kindly say, "I would like to be able to talk with you when I have plenty of time to answer all of your questions. May I take your name and number and call you back at_____," naming a time within 24 hours. If you don't phone them back at the appointed time, you can kiss that wedding job goodbye, because the client will not see you as honest, trustworthy, or punctual.

4. **Sound professional from the moment that you pick up the phone.** Don't believe for a second that a prospective client can put up with your household distractions, even if you're used to talking with your screaming kids, barking dog, and favorite soap opera blaring in the background. Your client will not appreciate it, and she won't be able to hear you very well, either. Talk when your home sounds like an office, like a place of business. Make an appointment to phone your client back when your attention is undivided.

5. **Avoid using a speakerphone.** Since speakerphones have a tendency to amplify extraneous noises in a room, and they can alter the sound of our voices, use the handset of your phone instead. Also, only one party at a time can talk on the speakerphone. This can stifle a dynamic conversation.

If the need arises for you to use the speakerphone during a call, then always ask permission of the person on the other end to switch to the speakerphone.

6. **Don't keep the caller on hold for longer than a minute.** If you need to do so, check back on the line within a minute and give them the choice of continuing to wait or to let you call them back.

7. **Caller ID is useful if your conversation is cut off by a dropped cell signal or a bad connection.** You can easily phone the bride back if the call is interrupted. If your caller ID does not reveal the caller's phone number, kindly request it at the beginning of your phone conversation. This way, if you do get cut off, you can still phone them right back.

An added benefit to using caller ID is that it displays the brides phone number when you receive a voicemail message from a bride who forgets to leave her callback number in her message or you couldn't understand what she said.

8. **Learn to let the phone ring when you cannot talk, and allow your answering machine be your secretary.** Return all phone calls within twenty-four hours. Otherwise, your prospective client will think they are not important enough to warrant a phone call from you and will go shopping for wedding musicians elsewhere.

9. **If you return a phone call and reach an answering machine, be brief.** Don't get long-winded and use up the entire answering machine space, or worse yet, have to phone back and leave a second message because your first message was too long and you were cut off. Reserve the details when you speak with your prospective client in person, and don't unload a sales pitch on their answering machine.

When leaving a voicemail message, state who you are, the name of your ensemble, and why you are calling. Give your name, spelling it out if you have an unusual name. Say your phone number slowly and distinctly. Also explain, "If you reach my answering machine when you return my phone call, please let me know when the best time is to reach you. That way, we won't be playing a lot of phone tag." Close by repeating your name and phone number again. You can easily say all of this in about thirty seconds of time.

GET TO KNOW THE BRIDE—TAKE GOOD NOTES

Your voice conveys volumes about you, but you cannot control a phone conversation with your voice alone. You take control of a conversation by asking questions. You also receive valuable information to make the sale and establish a rapport with the client when you ask questions. It's not about interrogating your client by digging for the information you want to know about the gig—It's about having a friendly chat and inserting your questions in the conversation as you go along.

Often, you'll talk with a bride who is so excited about her upcoming wedding that she has to tell you about all kinds of extraneous wedding details, like her little nieces who are coming all the way from London to be her flower girls or her auntie who made her bridal gown. Just pull the conversation back into your corner by asking a question about her music details. She'll be happy to oblige and let you take control, because your questions will make her feel like she is the center of the universe. Remember, the bride is the star.

If you ask the right questions, the answers you receive will tell you everything you'll need to know to quote the right package to the bride. But you've got to take good notes in order to do this.

You can record the bride's answers on notebook paper in a binder, a simple yellow legal pad, or index cards. You can create a computer file and type in the bride's information while you speak to her on the phone. I prefer using an old-fashioned columnar pad. Use whatever note-taking system suits your taste, as long as you get all the fine details down before hanging up.

In essence, you are really conducting a meeting with a prospective client. The caller is obviously aware that you are taking notes from the very beginning of the call, when you ask how to spell their name. This sends a message to the bride that you are interested enough in her to bother to write down her wedding details. She will already be impressed with your professionalism.

As Stephan Schiffman says in his book "The 25 Sales Habits of Highly Successful Salespeople":

"Taking notes helps you listen. There's something about having an empty sheet of paper in front of you that really tunes you in to what is being said, and makes it more difficult for you to miss important points."

Detailed notes of the bride's wedding specifics will arm you with the ability to supply the bride with just one quote to cover the entire performance job. It will help you to know what course of action to take after the phone call, because you'll be writing down when she wants to hear back from you. And of course, taking notes during the initial phone call will give you an accurate record of her wedding details for future phone meetings.

> *"When you ask questions, you tell people that you care about them, that you're interested in what they have to say. You also send an oh-so-subtle message that you're a bright, inquisitive individual who would like to know more. That's why event the smallest question can have a huge impact..."*—Linda Kaplan Thaler and Robin Koval, authors of "The Power of Nice"

Take out your notebook, legal pad, columnar pad, index cards, or computer, and prepare yourself to receive that first phone call. Refer to the **Sales Call Checklist** at the end of this chapter to set up your notes. Keep it near your phone so that when you get that call, you won't leave out any important information.

During the phone call, you'll go through a specific line of questioning. This will provide you with all the information necessary to provide a quote and close the sale.

THE FLOW OF A SALES CALL

You might find it surprising, but most phone inquiries follow a similar pattern. **This is the order of steps to a typical phone inquiry:**

The caller says, "Hi. I just want to know how much it costs for you to play at my wedding." Notice that there is usually very little information provided to you in the initial statement. Here is where your line of questioning comes in.

The first ten steps are all about gathering information:

Step 1: Your initial response is: "Hi! What is the date of your wedding and where are you getting married? Of course, I need to know if I am available first, before giving you a quote." Take immediate control of the conversation. Write this information down! Also write down the date of the phone call.

It helps a ton when you learn people's names and don't butcher them when trying to pronounce them."—Jerry Yang, co-founder of Yahoo!

Step 2: Now ask, "What is your name?" and get the correct spelling of it.

Step 3: If the phone line is not clear, ask: "It sounds like we don't have a good connection. In case we get cut off, can I have your phone number?" Write it down. Repeat it back to them.

Step 4: This is the research question: Ask, "How did you hear of me?" Find out whether they found your website on a specific wedding directory on the Internet, if you played for their sister's wedding, if the local wedding chapel gave them your name.

Not only will you be able to track the success of any advertisements you have paid for, but you'll also know how much the bride may already know about you. For instance, if she just found you in the Yellow Pages, it's unlikely she has heard your music or knows anything about you at all. Conversely, if she heard you play at the last bridal fair, she knows plenty about what kind of music you play and has even experienced your performance.

By the way, it's perfectly okay if she cannot remember. Brides who are doing a lot of shopping around may not recall where they saw your name or picked up your business card.

Step 5: The next question to ask is "What time will your wedding ceremony take place?" or, if the inquiry is for reception music, "When would you like me to perform for your reception? How many hours?"

Listen and write everything down. Ask further questions to clarify the amount of time you will be needed to perform.

You may find that the bride grossly miscalculates how long she'll need you. For instance, she might say, "Oh, the ceremony is only fifteen minutes long, so I guess I only need you for twenty minutes." You may have a one-hour minimum to perform at any wedding ceremony, even if it is an elopement, because of your set up time involved. Don't tell the bride this right now. You are establishing a relationship with her. Just listen and write down what she says.

Step 6: Check your calendar, and if you are not available, say, "I'm sorry. I'm already booked on that date at that time. Can I give you a referral?" This is where you win points by referring other musicians you know. Guess what? When other musicians find out you are referring them for gigs that you can't do, they'll send you gigs, too. Write down the names of all musicians you refer out.

By the way, it's still important for you to keep records of inquiries you turned down when you are already booked. If you get a cancellation, you can review your notes, phone the bride back, and if she hasn't already booked another musician, you may still be able to land the job.

Even though you are not available, the bride may still ask questions about what you charge, because she wants to know the going rate for other wedding musicians. She's being a savvy shopper. Don't give her your rates. Instead, answer her with a range of fee quotes she may receive from other musicians, and add, "Your final cost will depend upon a number of factors, including the distance the musician will need to drive to get to your wedding and the length of time you want them to play." This will at least offer her an idea of what to expect and whether live music will fit into her budget.

Skip to Step 16 after writing down the names of other musicians you have referred.

Step 7: If the bride hasn't yet set a wedding date and time, you can still continue on with the conversation. Just let her know that you cannot determine your availability and she cannot reserve your services until you have this information.

Skip to Step 16 if the bride doesn't know when she is getting married.

Step 8: If you do not perform at the location where she is getting married, let the bride know this. Give a good reason why you do not perform there. For instance, "I'm sorry, I don't perform at that beach because the parking or loading zone is a quarter mile from the wedding area. This is too much to haul a harp all that way."

If the reason why you do not want to perform at a certain location is for personal reasons, say, "Oh, I just realized I'm booked elsewhere on your wedding day." Then proceed with Step 5.

Take the high road. Be nice. Don't "dis" anyone, because it will come back to haunt you, I guarantee it. For instance, the bride may tell the banquet manager, "The Greek band refuses to play here because you didn't clear out the dance floor in time on a previous wedding." Then that banquet manager will drag your name around town as the worst Greek dance band in the land.

Skip to Step 16 if you don't perform at the bride's wedding location.

Step 9: Sometimes, the bride knows the time and date but has not settled on the exact location for her wedding. Without this piece of information, it's difficult to go on with the conversation, because any quote you give her is so dependent upon how far you'll have to drive and where you'll need to set up.

Ask the bride for some information about the number of guests attending and what she is looking for. Does she want a view? Or perhaps she interested in an evening candle-lit ceremony in a mountain-style lodge. Does she want Italian food served at her reception? Get a feel for the bride's wedding plans and then refer her to some of your favorite performing locations that fit the picture of her perfect wedding. Give her the names of the contacts at these locations, and write down everyone you referred to her.

Skip to Step 16 after you have given her suggestions of where to have her wedding.

Step 10: Next, find out some of the particulars of the performance:

- Approximately how many guests will be attending? (This will help you to determine if you'll need amplification)
- Will it be indoors or outdoors?
- Will you be setting up on carpet, concrete, grass, or sand?
- Will a stage be provided?
- How large is the performance space? What are the approximate dimensions?
- Is power available for amplification, and how far is the electrical outlet from the performance area?
- Will house sound be provided, or do you need to bring your own sound system?
- Will you be provided with shade?
- Is there a loading zone?
- How far is the performance area from the loading zone?
- Are there stairs?
- Will you have to pay for parking?
- Is a changing room available?

If the wedding festivities are outdoors, here's the most important question to ask: Is there a "Plan B" in place for bad weather? If so, where will that be?

At this point in the conversation, refrain from explaining to the bride your opinion of her wedding plans. Even if you think that she is nuts for having her ceremony on the end of a pier, with no sun protection for anyone and a mile away from the parking lot, don't say a word. You are just collecting information right now. Let the bride bubble over with delight while sharing her wedding plans with you. Just listen and write everything down.

The bride is now opening up to you, because she sees that you are showing   interest in her wedding details. She may now ask you question ke, "Can you play, "Everything She Does is Magic" by Sting?" and ". v many songs do I need to select?" These are legitimate question of course, so answer them as briefly as possible. Take notes about he favorite music, and then get back to controlling the path of the conversation with your questions.

Try to avoid answering any questions with the word, "No." Even if you don't know "Everything She Does is Magic", you can offer other suggestions.

Say, "I don't play that tune, but I do play Sting's 'Fields of Gold', and it sounds beautiful." Then get the conversation back into your corner.

Try to answer the bride's questions with the word, "Yes!" every chance you get. Don't give her any reason to continue shopping to find someone else to hire.

Take note: *Any limitations you place on the services you offer will limit your ability to close the sale!*

You should now have everything you need to offer a quote. But don't speak numbers yet . . .

Step 11: The All-Important Sales Presentation. Remember your three packages back in Chapter 2? You created a Highest Cost Package, a Lowest Cost Package, and the Best Value Package? Here is where that all comes in to play.

Since you now have a good feel for the bride's wedding music needs, describe the largest package that you have to offer that fits her needs. If the bride is planning a huge wedding, start explaining your Highest Cost Package offer. If it's a little elopement, start with your Best Value Package. But don't mention the cost of the package yet!!!

Only explain to the bride exactly what the package includes. In sales lingo, this is called the "sales presentation".

For example, explain what the ceremony package you are quoting her includes:

This two-hour package includes:

- 30 minutes of music before the ceremony, while guests are being seated
- Music for the processional, when her bridesmaids walk up the aisle
- Music for her grand entrance
- Music during the ceremony
- Music for the recessional, while everyone walks back down the aisle after she and the groom kiss
- 60 minutes of cocktail hour music
- Amplification is included, along with set-up time and travel

You get the picture. Itemize every little thing you will be doing for the bride on her wedding day. Tell her she gets to select her music, tell her you'll do your best to wear something that will fit into the theme of her wedding, tell her you'll be on time. Tell her all that you can honestly deliver as her wedding musician. Do this without overhyping or promising to deliver something that you cannot possibly do.

The job of a successful sales presentation is simple: To give the bride the impression that you'll bend over backwards to please her, and she cannot receive your kind of music and service from any other wedding musician out there.

Now give her your quote—but only when you have explained all the special items included in the package, when you are truly at the end of your sales presentation. State the price with confidence. Don't sound the least bit unsure of yourself, because the bride will pick up on this cue, think your quote is negotiable, and try to haggle with you to lower the price.

Take notes. Write down what package and fee you quoted to her.

Give your quote a moment to sink in and then ask, "Is this within your budget?"

If the bride doesn't have the budget to afford the package you quoted to her, be prepared to give another sales presentation. If you quoted the Highest Cost Package, now deliver the sales presentation for the Best Value Package, followed by its cost. If you quoted the Best Value Package, then move on down to the sales presentation for the Lowest Cost Package and its cost.

If the bride has no objections and has heard your music, skip to Step 13 and move to close the sale.

If your fee is way out of consideration for the bride, ask another question: "What were you expecting to spend?"

I have explained to the bride that if she only has only $50 to spend, she could go out and buy a few of her favorite CDs to play at her wedding. Maybe she could find a student somewhere who'll play for her wedding, but she won't get a professional musician to play at that price. It's a reality check for the bride to learn the true cost of professional music.

Do not get pulled into her sob story about how she has to pay for her entire wedding on her hourly wage from McDonald's. Don't budge from your quote. It's what you're worth. If you make the mistake of negotiating with her, you'll encounter a bride who now thinks she has you wrapped around her little finger, and she'll behave like it, too. You'll regret that you couldn't stand firm and won't get paid what you're worth for the job. But the worst thing is that the bride will tell her friends that she got a bargain from you. The word will get out about it, and you'll get calls from brides who will ignore your fee and tell you what they want to pay. They'll say, "Well you only charged $_____ to my best friend."

Stick by your quote. Amazingly, the bride may phone you back to tell you that her father or another relative will pay for the performance. If she really wants you to play at her wedding, she'll find a way to pay for your talents.

If she honestly cannot afford your services, it's okay. There will be other brides who'll happily pay to have you perform at their weddings. You can't change her decision, so don't try. If she cannot come up with the money to hire you, skip to Step 16 and end the conversation.

One caution: If you receive too many objections to your prices, you should re-examine what other musicians charge in your geographical area and then adjust your fees accordingly.

Sometimes the objection isn't about money at all...

Step 12: Offer Opportunities for the Bride to Audition Your Talents. The bride may stall because she has never seen or heard you perform. If she hasn't heard you, how can she understand what you are worth?

Give the bride every opportunity to listen to you play. Here are some ideas:

1. **Send her to your website to download and listen to your wedding demo.** Also invite her to take a look at your online music list, so that she can see what you are capable of playing.

2. **Mail her a CD demo.** If you don't have a website, this is the way to get your recorded demo in the hands of the bride. It's a bit antiquated to provide CD demos these days, since most brides have Internet access and are used to downloading mp3 samples from the worldwide web. I'd urge you invest in a website presence instead. You'll save a ton of money in pressing the discs and mailing costs, alone. Brides rarely return the CDs when they're done listening to them, so you can't save money by recycling them.

CD demos do work well when provided to a wedding venue, because they'll be passed out like audio business cards. A bride may receive your demo from the private country club banquet manager, she'll become enchanted with your music, and you'll get a phone call.

By the way, selling a bride one of your full-length CDs is not the same as inviting her to listen to your free demo. Your full-length CD may not be a correct representation of what she'll be hearing at her wedding if she hires you. Also, I am of the opinion that no one should have to pay to audition my talents—It contradicts being generous.

3. **Invite her to your next concert.** Tell her where you are performing, and if you have the power to do so, give her discount tickets to attend. Plan to spend some extra time talking with her during your intermission or after the show, but don't close the sale there. It's just a chance for the bride to experience your performance.

Take notes and mark your calendar, so that you remember that she will be attending your concert. What if she doesn't attend? Give her a phone call and say, "I'm so sorry I didn't see you at my concert. Were you there?" Regardless of her answer, offer another means for her to audition you. The simple act of phoning tells the bride, " I missed you." It makes her feel noticed and important.

4. **Set up an appointment time for her to meet with you and audition you in person.** When you make the appointment, give the bride an assignment. Tell her that before you meet with her, you need to know what tunes she wants you to play. This way, you can practice them before she comes over, and you won't be setting yourself up for failure by playing anything cold for her. I usually instruct the bride to review my online repertoire list and select 6-10 songs that she wants to hear.

When the bride supplies you with her list of music for the appointment, then give her your address. Explain to her that this is a one-hour appointment, so you are only playing snippets of the tunes she wants to hear, not the songs in their entirety. You are not providing a free private concert for her in your living room. (She'll need to hire you if she wants that.)

You also need to play samples of your tunes because you want to have enough time to close the sale. If you take too much time performing for the bride, she'll check her watch, say, "Oops. I have an appointment with my florist in ten minutes. I have to leave," and she'll be out the door before you can get her to commit to hiring you.

Be prepared before the bride knocks on the door. Ask her how many people will be with her. She may just bring her fiancé along for a listen, or she may bring her entire immediate family, including her two-year-old son. Make sure you have enough seats for everyone. Ask the bride to bring something along to keep any little children busy during the appointment.

"Give the public everything you can give them, keep the place as clean as you can keep it, keep it friendly."—Walt Disney, American entrepreneur and filmmaker

Place your brochures, business cards, and your repertoire list on a coffee table in front of where your guests will sit. Also place a pen and note pad on the table, enabling the bride to take notes during the meeting. Remember the power of chocolate, explained back in Chapter 7? Placing some chocolates on a plate or in a bowl may warm your guests to your music. Or better yet, bake some brownies before the appointment. It will give your home a delicious aroma. Be ready to show your hospitality the minute the bride arrives, offering her water, coffee, or soda to make her feel comfortable. Dress appropriately for a business meeting—a formal gown or tux is certainly not necessary, and jeans and a t-shirt are too informal.

Don't waste too much time chatting with the bride. Get right into playing her music selections. You'll know she's sold on hiring you if she begins to weep when you play "Here Comes the Bride" or the song for the bride and groom's first dance. Bring her some tissue, let her enjoy the moment, and allow her to gush about your music.

Here's the secret: With every compliment a bride gives you, she's convincing herself to hire you. So let her go on about your playing. Don't interrupt her and pull back into your sales presentation. Keep the compliments coming!

Next, go into the same sales presentation detailed in Step 5. Even if you already gave this presentation over the phone, she needs to hear it again, to be reminded of what you'll provide for her when she hires you. 90% of the time, the bride will hire you at a personal audition meeting. She'll fall in love with your music.

"Researchers have found that only 7 percent of our communication is verbal—the other 93 percent of expression comes from body language, facial expressions, and tone of voice."—Linda Kaplan Thaler and Robin Koval, authors of "The Power of Nice"

Remember that you want the bride to answer your questions with a resounding "yes!" in order to close the sale. When you meet with her in person, you can express "yes", too, by your body language, as well as through your voice. Do this by nodding or tilting your head to one side to show interest. You can even mirror her body language. She will subconsciously feel that you are listening and receptive to her wedding music ideas.

5. **Set up an appointment for a phone audition.** Playing music to a bride over the phone allows her to have a chance to audition your talents if she cannot meet with you in person. I live in a popular area for destination weddings, and brides travel from all over the world to get married here. It is impossible for most of them to meet with me before the wedding, so a phone audition is the next best thing.

The phone audition is literally the same thing as an in-person audition, where the bride must do her homework and supply you with a short list of music ahead of the appointment. She calls at the arranged time, I ask if she's ready, put her on speakerphone, and then play shortened versions of the songs she requested to hear. I'll pick up the handset, go though the sales presentation, and close the sale.

The only differences between the in-person and phone auditions is that you don't have to prepare your house for guests and you can wear whatever you please in a phone audition.

6. **Sometimes the bride just wants to meet you.** She may have already heard your music online or on a CD and isn't in need of an audition. Some brides feel more comfortable meeting all their wedding vendors in person, before committing to hiring any one of them.

If this is the case, you won't need to play music. You could meet her just about anywhere, but the very best place to meet her will be at her wedding location. For instance, if the bride is getting married at a wedding chapel, plan to meet her there when no weddings are underway. Of course, ask the staff of the chapel for their permission to meet with the bride before you set up an appointment with her.

When you meet, the chapel will be empty, and you'll be able to talk quietly without interruption. But best of all, you'll be creating a presence with the staff of the chapel. Talk up how wonderful it is to get married there, and the chapel will continue to refer your name for live music.

Bring a briefcase filled with the following items for the bride: brochures, business cards, your repertoire list, and a note pad and pen. Include these items for yourself: your booking calendar, a calculator, blank contracts, a pen, and your credit card materials if you take payments with plastic. Plan on being prepared to close the sale at this meeting.

Are you ready to close the sale? Let's do it...

Step 13: Closing the Sale is Not a Hard Sell. There really isn't anything left to have to persuade the bride to hire you. She's heard you perform and she knows what she'll get for her money.

Here's all you have to do: Ask for the sale. Say: "Would you like to go ahead and reserve my services?"

You have now put the wheels into motion. "Yes. How do we go about it?" is the answer you'll want to hear. Then get out your performance agreement and ask all the questions pertinent to filling in the blanks on it. Remind the bride of the deposit needed and when the balance is due. Inform her of when you are sending out the performance agreement and when you expect to receive it back from her, with the deposit. Always use the words "performance agreement" or "confirmation" instead of the word "contract" when talking with the bride. It is a softer approach to finalizing her commitment to hire you.

When you've filled out the contract, go to Step 14. You are almost done with your phone meeting!

If the bride isn't ready, it's okay. Keep that point from Chapter 1 in mind, that the bride may never have planned a big party in her life. She's new at this, and she'll want some other opinions. She may say that she needs to check with her fiancé, her parents, or simply think about it. Don't push her to make a decision.

> *"When you set a deadline, you more than double your ability to 'close the sale.'"*—Doug Hall, author of "Jump Start Your Marketing Brain"

Here is what to say: "When do you plan to make a decision?" If she says, "In two weeks," for instance, write down that date and tell her you'll phone her then. Write down her phone numbers, day, evening, and cell, and repeat them back to her. Find out which phone number she prefers you to use.

If the bride tells you that she doesn't know when she'll make a decision, or that her wedding is too far off and she is still shopping around, pin her down to a date to phone her back. Say: "Do you think you'll have a decision in two weeks?" If the answer is "No," ask if she'll have a decision in a month. Write down the date to call her back, take down her phone numbers and read them back to her.

A non-committal bride may tell you not to phone her at all. "I'll phone you," she'll say, trying to take the control of the sale out of your hands. If this happens, gently explain to her that you work on a first-come, first-serve basis, and if someone else calls to inquire about your services for the same day of her wedding, you'll want to be able to phone her to give her first choice. Most of the time, the bride will thank you for thinking of her and give you her phone numbers.

If a bride still refuses to part with her phone numbers and insists that she will call you if she is interested, it's time to end the conversation. Write her off and don't expect her to hire you. If she does suddenly phone you in a few months, she may spin your wheels and tell you she forgot all about your quote and beg you for another one. She's hoping that you'll give her a lower rate than what you originally quoted. You'll go through your entire sales presentation again, and she'll still refuse to provide you with phone numbers. This bride may be indecisive or she may still be shopping, and what she's <u>really</u> doing is wasting your time.

As Doug Hall says so effectively in his book, "Jump Start Your Marketing Brain",

"An important part of sales and marketing effectiveness is knowing when to stop chasing the prospect who asks lots of questions and uses lots of your energy yet is highly unlikely to buy in a reasonable amount of time."

Step 14: Winning Points—Referring Other Accomplished Wedding Professionals

You're not done after closing the sale. Even if you didn't book the job in the first phone call, you still need to show you're here to help her. Show her you are a nice person, and show her that you an authority when it comes to weddings. In doing so, you also convey that quality of generosity, by giving of your time to refer her to resources that will make the bride have a perfect wedding day.

The way to do all of this is to ask the bride: "Are there any other wedding services I can recommend to you?" If you are a ceremony musician, especially ask, "Have you selected your minister or celebrant yet?" You'd be surprised how many brides have selected all their other services, including their caterers, florists, and photographers, and they still don't know who will be doing their wedding ceremony. To me, it's like placing the cart before the horse, because if she decides on a minister who isn't available for the time that's printed on her invitations, she has to scramble around to find another one.

Be a friend to the bride. Offer her names and phone numbers of other wedding professionals you've worked with. Make sure you have seen them in action. And don't give out just one name; let her do the shopping. For instance, if you give her the name of just one baker and they show up with the wrong cake, it's egg on your face for recommending them. However, if you give her several names, it becomes more of a "buyer beware" situation where you can always retort, "Well, we all make mistakes and that baker may have had a bad day. I did give you other names to call, too."

She will thank you up and down for your referrals. She will tell all wedding professionals she calls that you recommended them. Those wedding pros will thank you by phone, email, and personal card. But best of all, they'll remember to recommend you when they are giving brides referrals. You are not just a friend to the bride; you are a friend to your colleagues, too.

Step 15: Compliment the Bride. Customers hire people they like. Be genuine and boost the morale of your bride. Make her smile and feel good about herself. She may be having a crummy day, and you could be the very person to lift her spirits. Who doesn't like a compliment?

"A compliment is verbal sunshine."—Robert Orben, US magician and comedy writer

Compliment the bride on her wonderful taste in music, her choice of wedding location, her choice of minister. If you meet with her in person, compliment her on her appearance, her pretty dress, you name it. Find something wonderful to say about the bride and say it to her.

Step 16: Time to End the Conversation (For Now). Thank the bride for contacting you.

If she has booked you, tell her how much you are looking forward to performing for her on her special day. Also tell her that you are looking forward to talking with her about her music selections.

If she has not booked you, remind her when you will be phoning her to check on her decision. Let her know that you look forward to talking with her by that date. Repeat her phone numbers back to make sure you have them correct.

If you were not available to perform for her wedding, make sure that you have her phone numbers, and repeat them back to her, just in case you have a cancellation. Do this also if she hasn't yet decided on her wedding date, time or location.

Then, use her name when saying goodbye, such as, "It was wonderful talking with you, Tammy." She'll appreciate that you remembered her name and that she isn't just another bride that you are talking with.

A FEW WORDS ABOUT CALLBACKS

If the bride doesn't book you during your initial conversation, you should have her phone number and a date to call her back to confirm whether she has decided to hire you. When you phone the bride back, tell her that she requested that you phone her at this point to ask her if she has made a decision to hire you to perform at your wedding. If she hasn't decided yet, get another date to phone her again. In the meantime, ask her if she has any questions you can answer about the services you provide. If she says, "No, we are going with someone else," don't waste your time or hers. Simply wish her a wonderful wedding day and close the conversation.

If you reach an answering machine or you need to leave a message with someone for her, of course give your name and number. Then say, "I'm just phoning to see if you have made a decision about hiring me to perform at your wedding. Please return my call, even if you are still deciding or have decided against having me play. Thank you." If you don't hear back from her, try contacting her twice more, and then forget about this prospect. A person who isn't kind enough to return your calls isn't someone whom you want as a client.

And finally, rarely, you may meet with a bride for an in-person audition that doesn't hire you right then and there. She brought everyone who was important with her to that special audition, and if she didn't fall in love with your music there, she isn't going to later on. Assume that she was a time waster and don't pursue her. Let her phone you on her own if she miraculously decides to hire you at a later date.

You now know some of the secrets to selling. But your wedding client will not always be the bride!

Sales Call Checklist

Record all of the following information for each inquiry you receive by phone. Also record this information when you meet with a prospective client in person.

Use a notepad, legal pad, columnar pad, index cards, or computer file to record this information. If you like, you can even photocopy this checklist and place the copies in a binder to keep track of your inquiries.

Preliminary information:

❑ **Date of phone call:** _____

❑ **Wedding Date:** _____, **Day of Wedding:** _____

❑ **Location of Wedding (include address, city, state, and any other pertinent details about ceremony and/or reception location):**

_____

_____

_____

❑ **Are you available?** _____ **If not, record name of caller and phone numbers, then offer referral for another musician.**

Who did you refer to perform in your place?

_____

❑ **Name of caller (get correct spelling):** _____

❑ **Is the caller the bride?** _____

If not, what is the bride's name (get correct spelling): _____

and what is caller's relationship to bride:

❑ Groom,   ❑ Mother of Bride,   ❑ Other relation to Bride: _____

❑ Bride's friend,   ❑ Member of wedding party: _____

❑ Booking agent. Name of agent's company: _____

❑ Wedding coordinator. Name of coordinator's company: _____

❑ Other. How does this person know Bride or Groom? _____

❑ **Caller's phone numbers:**

Number on Caller ID, in case line is cut off: _____

Work: _____ **, Home:** _____ **, Cell:** _____

Additional numbers: _____

REPEAT PHONE NUMBERS BACK TO CALLER

Which number is best to use? _____

❑ **How did caller hear of you?**

_____

_____

❑ **For ceremony music inquiry: Ceremony start time:** _____

❑ **For reception music inquiry: Reception start time:** _____, **End time:** _____

❑ **Check your calendar again. Are you still available? If not, record name of caller and phone numbers, then offer referral for another musician.**

Who did you refer to perform in your place?

_____

❑ **Missing location, date, and or wedding time? If yes, then set a day to phone caller back and gather more information. Caller agrees for you to check in with them by phone on the following date:** _____

WRITE THE ABOVE DATE IN YOUR CALENDAR SO THAT YOU'LL REMEMBER TO PHONE

Collect this additional information before launching into sales presentation:

Approximate number of guests: _____

Indoors or outdoors: _____,
If outdoors, is protection from the elements available and provided? _____
Is there a "Plan B" for bad weather, and what is that plan?

_____

_____

Approximate dimensions of performance area: _____

Will a stage be provided? _____, Dimensions of stage: _____

If no stage, what kind the flooring is at performance area? (concrete, linoleum, gravel, sand, grass, etc.): _____

Is performance area level? _____

If amplification is needed, is power available? _____
How far away is electrical outlet from performance area? _____
Is house sound available? _____

Is there a loading zone? _____
How far away is loading zone from performance area? _____
How far away is parking from performance area? _____
Is there a fee for parking or valet? _____, If so, what is that fee? _____

Are there stairs? _____, If so, how many flights? _____

Any additional information received from caller that influences which package to quote in your sales presentation: (For example, these factors may include needing to learn a new tune, renting a costume to wear in a theme wedding, performing with the bride's uncle, the flutist)

_____
_____
_____
_____
_____
_____
_____
_____
_____

Extra information that doesn't relate to the price you'll quote: (for instance, if the caller tells you their favorite song)

_____
_____
_____
_____
_____
_____
_____
_____
_____

The Sales Presentation:

❑ **Name of the package you initially quoted to the caller:** _____

❑ **Price you quoted to the caller:** _____

❏ **Any additional fees you quoted to the caller:** _____

❏ **Any discount quoted (ONLY APPLIES FOR QUOTES TO BOOKING AGENTS AND WEDDING COORDINATORS):** _____

❏ **Any additional lower cost package options quoted to the caller:**

_____

_____

_____

Ask for the sale!

❏ **Booked today?** _____

❏ **Objections?**

❏ Your quotes are completely outside of the wedding budget. Wish your caller a wonderful wedding day and end the phone call here.

❏ Not ready to book. Needs to talk with others to help her make a final decision. Who else needs to be in on this decision? _____

❏ Not ready to book. Still shopping around.

❏ Wants referrals for your services before committing. List referrals here (offer no more than three):

_____

_____

_____

❏ Needs to see your music list. Give your website address, email or fax your music list to the caller.
Caller's email address: _____
Caller's fax number: _____

❏ Needs to hear your music. Give the caller your website address where they can download sound samples, or mail them a CD demo.
Caller's mailing address:

_____

❏ Needs to audition you in person.
Invite them to your next concert. Concert date, time and location:

_____

WRITE THE ABOVE DATE IN YOUR CALENDAR SO THAT YOU WILL REMEMBER THAT THEY'LL BE ATTENDING

Make an appointment for an audition in person:
Date: _____, Time: _____, Location: _____
How many people will be attending audition? _____
Songs you are to prepare to play for the audition:
1. _____
2. _____
3. _____
4. _____
5. _____
6. _____
7. _____
8. _____
9. _____
10. _____
WRITE THE ABOVE DATE IN YOUR CALENDAR.

Make an appointment for a phone audition:
Date: _____, Time they will phone you: _____
Songs you are to prepare to play for the audition:
1. _____
2. _____
3. _____
4. _____
5. _____
6. _____
7. _____
8. _____
9. _____
10. _____
WRITE THE ABOVE DATE IN YOUR CALENDAR

❏ Caller just wants to meet you in person before they hire you. (No audition necessary)
Make an appointment for meeting:
Date: _____, Time: _____, Location: _____
How many people will be attending meeting? _____

❏ Booking agent or wedding coordinator needs to discuss things with the wedding couple and get back to you. By what date will you have an answer? Date: _____
WRITE THE ABOVE DATE IN YOUR CALENDAR TO REMEMBER TO CALL THE BOOKING AGENT OR COORDINATOR ON THAT DATE

❏ Any other objections and how did you counter them?

_____
_____
_____

Mutually agreed upon dates for follow-up calls:

_____

WRITE THE ABOVE DATES IN YOUR CALENDAR TO REMEMBER TO CALL BACK CLIENT

Win Points:

❏ **What other services does the bride need for her wedding day? List other wedding professionals that you have referred to her:**

_____
_____
_____
_____
_____
_____
_____
_____
_____

❏ **Give the caller a compliment**

❏ **Thank the caller for contacting you**

❏ **Use the caller's name before you end the call (such as, "Thank you for contacting me, Stacy")**

CHAPTER 10

When Your Client Isn't the Bride

"My sole inspiration is a telephone call from a producer."
—Cole Porter

The person who signs your contract is your boss. You know that from back in Chapter 2. It is usually the bride, the woman of honor at the wedding. She knows what she wants and it is more advantageous to talk directly with her, rather than to others working on her behalf.

Of course, the bride may entrust others to handle her wedding details. Perhaps she has no time to devote to her wedding details with job or school commitments. Or maybe she doesn't hold the purse strings to making financial decisions. But many times she simply wants to delegate the task of finding and hiring a musician to someone else.

Understand that if the bride isn't overseeing her wedding music details, you may not have any communication with her at all. You'll have to trust the people whom she has trusted to make decisions for her. People who are taking care of the bride's needs tend to be less emotional than the bride. This can be a blessing if you handle things just right. So keep in mind just one thing:

No matter who signs your contract, you must please the bride to make your client happy. Just because you are not dealing with her directly, don't assume the bride doesn't care as much about your performance and you can slack off. Don't ignore the fact that the bride's wedding is *her* big day. The bride is the star...

There are three categories of clients working on the bride's behalf. Here's the first one:

WHEN YOUR CLIENT IS A BOOKING AGENT

Good booking agents have a handle on their musicians' talents, so that they can make decisions about who to hire at a moment's notice.

There are some booking agents who receive a commission from you to find you work. This is the kind of agent, or producer, Cole Porter was referring to in his quote at the top of this chapter.

"A good booking agent cuts through people's unrealistic expectations and offers them other alternatives that will work and make everyone happy."—Jeff Leep, Entertainment Agent/ Musician, Leep Entertainment

Waiting for the phone to ring from a booking agent who hires talent for weddings may be a long wait. They work for the bride, not for you. The booking agent is hired and paid by the bride. They'll phone, fax, or email you with a job order, simply asking you if you are available. Then they'll supply you with the time, date, location, and all the particulars in order for you to respond quickly with your price and availability.

"Quickly" is the operative word here. A brides will hire a booking agent for the following reasons:

1. She hasn't the time or energy to search for live entertainers on her own.

2. She has a lot of money to spare and is happy to pay someone to take care of hiring entertainment for her wedding.

3. She has looked for entertainers on her own, but has exhausted all the possibilities she knows of. The bride either cannot find the instrumentation she wants, or those musicians are already booked on her wedding day.

4. She needs to hire a musician fast! She suddenly realized she forgot to include music in her wedding plans, and her wedding day is approaching soon. Sometimes, the bride has a friend who promised to perform for her wedding, who at the last minute, bailed out and isn't planning to attend at all.

Whatever the reason may be, the booking agent will need a response from you pronto. They want to close the sale on their end with the bride. The longer it takes for them to get back to the bride with your quote, the greater the chance that they will phone someone else and assume you are not interested.

The booking agent charges a commission to the bride on top of the fee you charge. You stand a better chance of landing the gig if you give them a small discount, because the bride is more likely to book you with a smaller mark-up. Also, a booking agent may be more likely to recommend your services if they know you'll give them a discount. This practice is not the norm, though, so decide for yourself if you are comfortable offering any discount.

Some booking agents have a reputation of being slimy. Their practices can be questionable. In California, it is typical for an agent to add a 10% commission to the bride's invoice, on top of what you charge for your performance. It's completely fair, as they should earn their keep for acting as the middleman to hire musicians for a wedding. What is not fair is when booking agents charge a huge markup over what you charge. Then the poor bride is being swindled. If she finds out, the agent is out of business. Musicians who hear about these unjust practices are right to end their relationships with fraudulent agents.

If a booking agent contacts you about a wedding gig and you have never worked with them before, do some research. Phone other musicians in your area and see if they have had any experience working with the agent. You'll want to find out if they were sent good wedding jobs and if they were paid in a timely manner.

Some states regulate their booking agents with a license and a bond requirement (which is an insurance policy in case they don't pay you). A booking agent will be allowed to charge a fixed percentage above the musician's rate. If your state requires booking agents to be licensed, and someone claiming to be an agent approaches you, check to see if they are indeed licensed.

When a booking agent hires you to play for a wedding, ask them to sign your contract, just as you would with all other clients. They may have their own contract for you to sign, as well. If you are at all unsure about the wording or the contents of their contract, have a legal professional examine it before you sign.

The booking agent will tell you what to play, when to play it, and how to dress. They'll give you directions to the wedding location and describe exactly where you'll set up. They'll even let you know if you will be served a meal at the wedding or not. They are your sole contact for the wedding. You will not be working with the bride.

This can be wonderful if the booking agent is truly on top of all the details and communicates them to you. It is not so wonderful when the agent drops the ball and leaves out some important pieces of information that you'll need to know to do your job properly.

After being booked for just one wedding job through a booking agent, you'll know if you'll ever want to work with them again. If you decide to build a good, solid relationship with them, they will continue to think of you when a bride is seeking just your kind of talent.

Get in touch with the booking agent right after the wedding job, thank them, and report to them how things went. If there were some strange situations that you encountered dealing with the bride and her guests, or with the staff at the wedding site, then they should know what they were to prevent problems in the future. Great booking agents appreciate the follow-up.

Of course, if you blunder on a job that they sent you out on, they may never contact you again. How can you blunder? There is one thing you must never do when a booking agent sends you on a wedding gig:

Never give out your business cards or brochures to a wedding guest when you are hired by a booking agent to perform.

If you do, that guest may phone you for your rates only to turn around and discuss them with the newly-married bride. The bride will think that the booking agent overcharged her when they were only charging their commission. It just gets ugly from there.

Instead, give the guests your booking agent's card. This is the best way to say "Thank you!" to the booking agent who sent you out on that job, and it will cement goodwill into your relationship with them. By doing so, you are once again displaying your generosity of spirit.

"I go through an agent because I am comfortable that if there is any problem with a harpist having to put her harp in the shop, or a band being stuck in another town, or whatever, that agency will take care of the situation. That is their job and I don't want it."—Karen Brown, Master Bridal Consultant, Karen For Your Memories

If you are looking to find good, legitimate booking agents in your area, ask local wedding coordinators whom they've used in the past. Yes, wedding coordinators do rely on booking agents when their brides are requesting a music specialty that the coordinator cannot find (or doesn't want to take the time to find). This is ever more reason to cultivate friendly, long-term relationships with booking agents.

WHEN YOUR CLIENT IS A WEDDING COORDINATOR

Call them wedding coordinators, wedding consultants, wedding planners, and even producers and event planners. They are all the same thing—a person who guides the bride through all the details leading up to her wedding day and on her wedding day.

Most brides turn to independent wedding coordinators when they are overwhelmed with wedding details and don't have the time or energy to deal with it all. Sometimes, the bride is planning a "destination wedding"* and does not know how to contact good wedding professionals. And then, of course, sometimes the bride just wants to delegate wedding decisions to someone in the know.

Wedding coordinators come in all shapes and sizes. Wedding coordinators are not only independent, self-employed businesspeople. If a bride decides to have her wedding at a house of worship, that church or synagogue may include a coordinator for the day of the wedding in addition to pre-marital counseling. If the ceremony is in a wedding chapel, the minister or celebrant may act as the wedding coordinator prior to the wedding day and on the day of the wedding, too. Sometimes, I've even seen banquet managers, caterers, and photographers act as coordinators for wedding receptions!

There are no state regulations governing the practices of wedding coordinators, at least that I know of. However, wedding coordinators should have local business licenses and clean records with the Better Business Bureau. This is the way to check them out to make sure they are legitimate. You can also check with the Association of Bridal Consultants to confirm if the coordinator is a member in good standing.

Here is how Gerard Monaghan, past president of the Association of Bridal Consultants, explains the way independent wedding coordinators typically work with musicians:

"Most bridal consultants recommend at least three musicians to the bride and let her make the final decision and sign the contracts. However, a good consultant also will get a letter of authorization from the bride to act as her agent, so the consultant can make the appropriate decisions, freeing the bride to enjoy the day without handling the details."

---

*A "destination wedding" is a wedding that is not taking place in the bride and groom's hometowns. They and their guests travel to a destination, often a place where they have never visited, to exchange wedding vows.

Most of the independent wedding coordinators I reached prior to writing this book do not contract directly with the musicians. They charge a fee to the bride to give her suggestions or even a list of possibilities. The bride then selects her favorite musician or band among the choices given to her. Then the coordinator contacts the musician about availability and cost. The wedding coordinator forwards your contract to the bride for a signature.

"The client contracts directly with all of the vendors. This helps with my liability. It also helps the client as I do not add anything on to what the vendor charges."—Kathy Vaughan, Wedding Coordinator, A Beautiful Memory

Only after your services have been booked will you be in touch with the bride to get her music selections. And even then, maybe not. There are some coordinators who want total control and will contact you with the bride's music list and any other instructions from the bride.

It's quite a different story when working with wedding chapels. These in-house wedding coordinators do not work for themselves: they draw a salary, and sometimes a bonus or a commission, for booking as many weddings as they possibly can to make rental payments on the chapel. They may request discounts from the wedding services and then charge the bride full price for your service to make a profit. Or, they may want a kickback from you. The coordinator may not use the term "kickback", however that is exactly what they are seeking from you—a payment for booking your services. Most musicians frown upon the practice of paying kickbacks.

I like to offer discounts to chapels and wedding coordinators that book my services frequently. It is just another way for me to say, "Thank you!".

The major difference between booking agents and wedding coordinators is that booking agents send you on wedding jobs while wedding coordinators oversee your work at the wedding. This can be a curse or a blessing, depending upon the amount of experience the wedding coordinator has under their belt.

Here are the marks of the ideal wedding coordinator:

1. They are a good communicator and will be in touch with you well before the wedding day to supply you with all the instructions you need.

2. They understand the terms of your contract, the services you offer, and what you need from them to be able to deliver your services properly.

3. They stay nice under pressure. They smile, speak calmly and politely, and truly enjoy their work.

4. They believe in teamwork to accomplish the bride's vision.

By contrast, bossy or inexperienced coordinators are the most difficult to deal with. As Van Vinikow, the Supreme Being of the String Beings String Quartet/Trio says:

"Wedding coordinators mean well, but the inexperienced ones can screw you up good. They may want you in the church balcony or choir loft because THEY think it may sound better, forgetting you can't see the action during the prelude up there."

He offers the only piece of advice I can offer:

"Just be nice to them, humor them and do your job the best you can."

This means not arguing with them or telling them what to do.

"Wedding coordinators turn over quickly. Cultivate those with longevity."—Stephen Vardy, sound engineer for harpist Alison Vardy

Word spreads among wedding vendors if a coordinator doesn't perform their job properly. You can spend a lot of time building a relationship with a coordinator at a wedding property, for instance, and then next week, they'll be gone. I know of several wedding chapels that have had such a high rate of turnover that I always have to start over, introduce myself, and send out promotional materials every few months.

Finding good wedding coordinators in your area is easy. Contact banquet managers and wedding site owners for recommendations. Also contact celebrants in your area. They are usually tickled to refer their favorite coordinators.

When you work with a wedding coordinator, regardless of whether they are an independent coordinator or an on-site coordinator, talk with them well before the wedding day. What do they expect from you? What is the bride like and what does she expect? You'll find the wedding coordinator opening up and realizing that you want to offer the bride a wonderful wedding experience, too.

WHEN YOUR CLIENT IS THE MOTHER OF THE BRIDE, THE GROOM, OR OTHER FAMILY AND FRIENDS OF THE BRIDE

These people, the bride's loved ones, are emotionally connected to the wedding details, unlike booking agents or wedding coordinators.

Most of the musicians I interviewed had no problems or issues working with the mothers of brides, or any of her family and friends, for that matter. They typically do not hover about musicians on the wedding day, because they are part of the wedding party and busy tending to other activities. As long as they are speaking for the best interests of the bride and groom, family members are a pleasure to work with.

The trouble arises when a loved one, typically the mother of the bride or the mother of the groom, makes decisions about your services without consulting with the bride and groom first. Then she is no longer working for the wedding couple's best interests.

At a wedding I performed in a forest park, I was booked by the mother of the groom. She was my client, and I had no contact with the bride or groom about their wedding selections. When I arrived at the wedding, I understood why. The groom was so young that he was barely shaving, and his friends were all young teenagers, jumping on boulders and kidding around. I think his mother took over the wedding details because he and his bride were too immature to do so.

When I went to set up, there was a guitarist setting up under the tree where I was to perform. The groom told me that the guitarist was his best friend and would be playing for the entire ceremony instead of me. His mother overheard his comment and said, "Oh no he isn't. I am paying for this wedding, and I have hired a harpist. Period." The young teenage guitarist slunk away, and I sat down to play. I was embarrassed for the groom, but his mother was my client and my boss. I later explained to him that I needed to fulfill my agreement with his mother and play at his wedding.

It's rare when a conflict of interest arises between the wedding couple and the person who actually hired me. When it does, I try to be as diplomatic as possible. I listen to the bride's concerns and then explain my situation: Her mother signed my contract, and therefore, I must follow her instructions. Then I ask the bride if she can discuss the issue with her mother and come to a mutual agreement.

The person who signs my contract has "veto power." That's the way it is, legally. So, I take the time to explain this to the bride and groom if differences of opinion come up. Open communication is the key.

I've barely touched the surface of the problems that can arise at weddings and how to solve them. In the next chapter, you'll find out how to prevent many of them from happening in the first place.

This is Fred. He needs you to sing at his and my daughter's wedding...TODAY!

CHAPTER 11

Bride Relations: Avoiding Problems

"No one can drive us crazy unless we give them the keys."
—Doug Horton, science fiction author

Imagine for a moment that you are getting ready to move across country and need to hire a moving company. You contact several companies and make appointments to receive estimates. Each company you reach sends a rep to your home to look over the stuff you have to move and to give you a quote. These reps are actually working to close the sale with you, to get you to hire their moving company. You make your decision based not only on the price they quote, but also on how professional and service-oriented the representatives appear to be. You give one lucky rep a huge deposit and they happily leave your home with another sale.

Moving day arrives, and the movers are four hours late, they're rude, they drop your cherished coffee table, and they fight your damage claim. The service you thought you paid for is nonexistent. As soon as the representative made the sale, their company assumed that was where customer service ends.

Customer service does not end when the sale is closed. It continues throughout your relationship with your client, however long that may last. Going the extra mile with generosity is synonymous with good customer relations, and in this case, good bride relations. However, there are limits to what you can or should to for them.

From the time a bride contacts you, the key to making your relationship run smoothly is a secret that all successful seasoned wedding professionals know. And here it is: **Be honest.**

From your prospective, here is how you draw the line:

THE WEDDING MUSICIAN'S MANTRA: NEVER TAKE A JOB YOU THINK YOU'LL REGRET!

Many musicians will take any stupid gig that comes along. If you are that hungry, get yourself a full-time job that pays well so that you won't be so worried about your income. As Jeff Leep, entertainment agent and musician says:

"You have to have enough money in the bank so that if a job comes along that you don't want to take, you won't feel like you have to take it. This way, if you have a weekend off, you're not going to die."

This notion of viewing each job as a paycheck is actually the monster of greed at work. Greed will sabotage your ability to be kind and patient with your clients. Greed will make you sound desperate for work, and your clients will haggle with you to lower your price.

"Desire for the fruits of work must never be your motive in working."—From the ancient Vedic text, the Bhagavad-Gita.

If you are performing only for the money, not because you enjoy playing and want to share your music with others, you'll become resentful because you'll never feel like you were paid enough. With this attitude, you will resent your client for putting you through the rigors of doing a job you didn't want to do in the first place.

The opposite of greed is generosity. From your first contact with the bride, through closing the sale, through your performance and beyond, always present the very best attitude that you have to offer. There is no room for generosity when you view a bride as a meal ticket.

Here's what Timothy Goldsmith, musician with the Red Davidson Trio, has to say on this subject:

"I have occasionally worked with musicians who seem to feel that brides are cash cows who exist only for musicians to milk dry.

Obviously, this attitude creates conflict and bad feelings all around. I have had very few problems with brides because I see them as people, not as contracts. (Besides, who wants to play for a cow anyway?)"

So, if you really don't want to take a job, don't take it just because you need the money. If you do, you'll live to regret it.

Every single experienced working musician that I know can relay stories about jobs they should have turned down. They learn from those gigs and then listen to the voice of intuition that says, "Do I really want to do this?" when a job sounds like a nightmare they once experienced. The trick is to hear and obey this voice of intuition before contracts are signed.

The litmus test is different for every musician. Here are some of the wedding jobs musicians who were interviewed for this book won't consider:

"Gigs where there are shuttles to a wedding site are dicey. The musicians will ALWAYS be the last to leave, and if you are on a tight schedule, oy."—Van Vinikow, The "Supreme Being" of "The String Beings" string quartet/trio.

"I'm a little leery of last minute weddings [so I] use common sense and intuition. 'Is it in extreme conditions? Do I feel safe? Do I have a reasonable expectation of getting paid?'"—Seán Cummings, eighth generation professional bagpiper.

"Brides who seem very indecisive and anxious, and don't want to commit to a booking or keep making changes in the arrangements. They may well be having doubts about the whole marriage thing and expressing those doubts by fretting about the music."—Gwyneth Evans, concert and Celtic harpist.

"No nudist weddings, Please!"—Destiny, Harper from the Hood.

Amen to Destiny's litmus test!

(I'll have to admit that I once played for a dinner party at a nudist colony. I was permitted to wear clothes, because it was a "clothing optional club". It was weird to see my audience in various stages of undress, and a bit unnerving when I looked up from my music stand from time to time. It's not something you'll want to do, unless you are a practicing nudist yourself. But I digress!)

Your decisions for turning down gigs can be very personal:

1. Do you trust the bride?

Sometimes you won't hit it off with the bride. She'll be difficult from the beginning, even before you decide to commit to perform for her. It's not that she is behaving irrationally. You just get a bad feeling whenever you speak with her. Think twice about taking this job.

It takes time to develop your intuition for knowing when to turn down jobs. Maybe you don't trust the bride or don't believe that she is being honest with you.

If you have this feeling in your gut, don't be afraid to refer her to a booking agent or wedding coordinator to help her find another musician. Please don't send her to other musicians in your area if a dark cloud appears above your head whenever you talk with her. If you don't want her as a client, do you think other musicians will?

In truth, this turn-and-run-and-don't-look-back feeling is pretty rare. There was one bride who inquired about my services by email. She finally phoned me, months after her initial email inquiry to ask for a quote. I knew, just from talking with her, that she wasn't being straight with me. Something wasn't right. So, I chose not to follow up with her.

Several months passed again, then she called me to say that she decided to hire me. By that point, someone else had booked my services and I was no longer available to perform for her. She responded by yelling four-letter words and promising she was going to sue me. "Fine," I said. "We have no contract, so I don't know how that will happen." Of course, I never heard from her again, but I talked with several other harpists in my area with similar stories to share about her. Apparently, when this bride didn't get her way, she spouted swear words and threatened to sue. That was her mode of communication.

I'm *not* suggesting that you should turn down gigs from every nervous, high-strung bride who contacts you, or you will have no work. Many brides will be emotionally wound up. Show some compassion. Remember, each bride has many details to iron out before her big day and must figure her own family and future in-laws into her plans. It's particularly normal for a bride to be nervous a week or two before her wedding day. Be helpful and recommend the names and phone numbers of a few good massage therapists to calm her last-minute jitters.

2. Can you deal with the bride's emotions?

Some nervousness is normal; fear is not. When a bride is in extreme panic, especially when her wedding day is months away, this is a red flag. Rather than assuming it is none of my business, I find it best to say, "You really need to think about what has you in such a panic." This usually has an effect of calming her down, diffusing her emotions so that I can talk with her easier.

It's very difficult to get performance details out of a person who is overwhelmed with her wedding plans. Help the bride by suggesting the names of a few reputable wedding coordinators in your area.

If none of this works, you need to decide for yourself if you want to work with a client who is emotionally high-strung and probably exhausts everyone with whom she comes in contact. The wedding professionals I know use the phrase "high maintenance" to describe these kinds of brides, because they need a lot of handholding. They can be very sweet but they will sap you of your energy and time. If you take a job from high maintenance bride, take it all in stride when you need extra time to communicate with her.

3. Can you deal with the staff at the bride's wedding venue?

Sometimes personal reasons for turning down a gig may not involve your client at all. Maybe the employees at the bride's wedding site are the problem. Perhaps you shudder at the mere thought of performing where the staff barks orders at you, complains that they have to move tables to accommodate you and your instrument, refuses to communicate to you when you have questions, and generally treats you like dirt.

This leads me to my own personal litmus test for turning down certain jobs:

Don't perform where you are not welcome.

When the staff at a wedding site does not consider me as part of the bride's team for her wedding day, then my job becomes impossible. I can't offer my best performance because I don't feel welcome. I'm not treated like a wedding professional.

If a bride is inquiring about your availability to perform at a wedding in a venue that you have blacklisted, never speak badly about the staff there. For thoughts about how to handle your response, refer back to Chapter 9.

4. Is the bride expecting you to do something that you cannot do?

Sometimes, you'll take a job you know you shouldn't take because the client seems so nice, and you are getting along just peachy with her. You'll want to bend over backwards to please her, which is wonderful, except when she asks you to do things you are not capable of doing. You'll be in a quandary, wanting to do a great job but knowing you cannot meet her expectations. What should you do?

"Being honest about your weaknesses will often gain more customer support. When you are honest about a weakness, you increase your credibility. When you admit that 'No, we don't,' you actually increase customers' desire to purchase from you."—Doug Hall, author of "Jump Start Your Marketing Brain"

Be honest. Know your limitations and don't be embarrassed to communicate them. If you are a classically trained violinist and the bride wants you to play a few bluegrass tunes after the recessional, it's okay to say that you are not comfortable with her request. If you are only a few days away from the wedding day, and the bride wants you to learn some new tunes, it's okay to say that you don't have the time to get those tunes down. And if the latest hip-hop tunes sound unintelligible when played by your string quartet, it's okay to admit that your ensemble can't do justice to those songs.

As a Celtic harpist, it's not unusual for me to get requests to perform entire symphonic movements on the harp. That's the job of a concert harpist, not me. Instead of pretending that I can fulfill this request, I'm honest. "You'll need an experienced orchestra harpist to play that selection, and I'm not the person to do it," I explain. If the bride hasn't booked me yet, I give her the names and phone numbers of some good orchestra harpists. Everyone is happy: my harpist friends, the bride, and most importantly, me. If she's already hired me to play for her wedding, I offer other choices that are in my repertoire, shorter classical pieces by the same composer, for instance.

The one way to avoid problems with brides who expect too much of you is:

EXPLAIN YOUR REQUIREMENTS AND KNOW WHEN TO SAY "NO"

Most difficulties with brides stem from miscommunication or non-communication. Keep in mind that your job is to educate your clients about your services. Remember, the bride is likely to never have thrown a big party. She probably doesn't understand why you need to be seated in the shade or why you need to receive her music requests prior to the wedding day.

Educate the bride about what you need to do your job well. Explain your set requirements when she books your services, and remind her of your needs again before the wedding day. If she wants you to do the impossible, gently and firmly say, "No". Always explain why you are denying her request. If you cannot play a concert harp in an open horse-driven sleigh in twenty-degree temperatures, explain why. Give the bride options. Maybe you can still perform back at the lodge during the reception, where your harp can stay in tune, be protected from the cold, and fit into the space provided.

And if the bride insists that you perform in a sleigh, put it in writing that you have not agreed to do so. Write it down and initial it on your contract. If you have already signed contracts, then send a letter by postal mail restating your position on her request. Putting things in writing means that if the bride still begs you to do the impossible on her wedding day, you have every right to deny doing so (and she will still be obligated to pay you).

Turn any negative statements that you make into a positive. You must reinforce what you *can* offer the bride. Provide alternatives to the bride's impractical request. Turn your "no, I cannot do that" into a "yes, I'll be happy to do that for you."

Recently, I was asked by a bride to perform on a beach, at the water's edge. I have a policy of not performing on soft beach sand, because my chair sinks, my harp sinks, and then I have to visit the chiropractor the next day. There is also no shade at the water's edge, and the harp will not stay in tune with the sun beating down upon it. I explained all of this to the bride. I offered her an alternative, to allow me to perform inside the beach pavilion, a covered area with a cement floor above the beach. I could always use an amp to get the sound to carry down to the water.

Several months pass, and I assume this bride has decided against having me perform for her wedding. Then, the phone rings and I hear from her again. She asks me the same question, whether I would play at the water's edge. She had forgotten that I would not, or maybe thought I would give her the answer she wanted to hear this time around. I went through my entire explanation again. She then countered that she didn't think anyone would hear the harp down by the water if I sat up at the pavilion. I stuck by my policy and concluded the call with, "Maybe I'm not the right musician for you. That's a decision you'll need to make."

She immediately phoned back and said that she discussed the issue with her fiancé. She decided to move her entire wedding party up to the pavilion so that everyone would hear the harp and people could sit in the shade. "I can always have my pictures taken down by the water," she said. She finally understood my requirements, and because I stuck by my guns, I didn't lose the job at all. The bride was willing to compromise to make it work. She wasn't stupid or stubborn—All she needed was to be patiently educated about my needs.

BE A CLASS ACT—KEEP YOUR REPUTATION INTACT

You obviously know now what you need to do to build a good reputation: honesty, integrity, professionalism, flexibility, and generosity.

If you realize you have stepped into a relationship with a difficult bride, and your intuition didn't kick in before contracts were signed, put yourself in the bride's shoes. The bride, your customer, is always first. She expects this from you. She thinks her wedding is special to you, as if it is the only wedding you have on your books.

If, for any reason, she becomes dissatisfied, it will quickly become frustration and anger if the issue is not handled quickly and with care. She needs to know that helping her is your top priority. Don't take it personally, because she may be upset with something very trivial to begin with.

It's okay to admit your mistakes. Sometimes, just letting the bride know you goofed and that you're sorry is enough to satisfy rational brides.

Support your band members and your assistants. If they made a mistake, stand behind them when they are faced with an irritated bride. Don't take the bride's side in front of them. If the bride is correct in her claim that someone on your watch messed up, tell her you'll talk with them privately about the issue and that you will take care of it. If you are not the bandleader and the bride is complaining to you, ask her to take up the issue with the leader of your group.

In his book, "Success in Dealing With Difficult People", Ken Lawson reminds us that our clients are not our friends. "Try to understand their viewpoint and do your best to help. Remain detached, and you can proceed with attending to the customer's issues, not your own

"When you treat people like idiots, they will often meet your expectations. But if you treat them like the smartest, most talented people in the world, you'll be amazed by what they accomplish."—Linda Kaplan Thaler and Robin Koval, authors of "The Power of Nice"

"Speed of response reduces the potential for damage...and also communicates your concern and commitment to customers."—Doug Hall, author, of "Jump Start Your Marketing Brain

"The secret of a man's success resides in his insight into the moods of people, and his tact in dealing with them."—J.G. Holland, 19th century American novelist and poet

feelings." Mr. Lawson also offers a seven-point plan of action when dealing with clients' feelings. **I've adapted this plan for our topic of bride relations:**

1. Listen.
a) Don't interrupt the bride when she wants to discuss an issue with you, unless you need to verify what she is talking about.

b) Repeat what she is saying to you in your own words to make sure you've got it right.

c) Don't let the bride air her complaints in front of others. Tell her that you'll be happy to talk with her in private.

d) Don't answer any other calls when you are on the phone with a bride who is upset. Don't put the bride on hold; she expects your immediate attention.

e) Take notes to make sense of her complaint. Recording the date that the complaint was made will help you keep a reference if you could not solve the problem immediately or need to talk with another wedding professional regarding her complaint. I like to use the blank box on my contracts to keep a record of dates that I spoke with the bride.

2. Acknowledge
a) Try to understand where she is coming from. Say supportive phrases like, "I understand," to show you are making the effort to see the situation from her point of view.

b) Showing sympathy does not mean that you are agreeing with the bride or accepting that she is right. The main objective is to take the heat out of the moment by showing that you care.

3. Stay neutral
a) Don't start defending yourself or talk about yourself in any way. The bride will think you are not interested in her issue. She'll also think you are trying to steer away from her concern.

b) Don't give the bride the false impression that you are going to resolve the issue immediately when you can't promise that. Wait until you have all the facts before answering her concern.

4. Clarify

a) When the bride has finished her complaint, summarize what you heard back to her for clarification.

b) To make sure you haven't misunderstood what you have been told, use phrases like, "Do I have my facts correct?" and "Have I missed anything?"

5. Find a solution

a) Make the bride feel like she was helpful in the solution-finding process. Ask open questions like: "What would you like me to do to resolve this?" and "How can I help you?"

b) You can apologize. This doesn't mean that you are admitting wrongdoing. This shows empathy on your part. Say something neutral, "I am sorry this has happened to you." But if you honestly made a mistake, take ownership of it.

c) Provide her with alternative ways to resolve the issue.

d) If you cannot offer the bride an immediate solution, don't tell her you can't help her. Instead, explain that you are trying to do the best you can for her, you have taken down all the details, and you will keep her informed. Say something like, "I know that this is very important to you, so I want to put some time into coming up with some solutions."

6. Follow through

a) This is the most important stage of dealing with complaints, because it is what the bride will remember the most about you. You have to deliver what you promised, even if you have to give her the bad news that you can't resolve her issue or that the matter takes more time to resolve.

b) If you cannot offer the resolution the bride is seeking, again, be honest. Ask her, "What can I do for you?"

The worse case scenario is when a bride is unhappy with a performance. Let's say you forgot to bring the sheet music for her walk down the aisle, you had to wing it, and you butchered the song. You cannot go back and correct that moment. There is nothing you can personally do to fix it.

The best thing to offer is a partial refund, or if she is really enraged, a full refund. Amazingly, a reasonable bride will calm down and maybe even say, "No, that's okay. I'll live with it. Maybe I'll laugh about it all in a few years." Offering monetary compensation on a job you cannot fix makes you look professional, because you are standing by your service 100%. And if other wedding vendors get wind of this, they'll tell you, "You did the right thing to offer her a refund."

7. Check back

    a) Make sure that the bride is satisfied with the resolution. When you check back with her, it demonstrates that you care about her. Customer care is what makes you stand out among your colleagues.

    b) Once a bride verifies that she is now a happy camper, it makes it more difficult for her to come back to you with any other complaints.

If the bride comes at you with difficult behavior, never, ever mirror her. Instead, use these ways to diffuse it:

1. **If the bride screams at you in public, invite her to talk with you in a private setting.** Don't continue to attempt to carry on a conversation with her in front of her guests, her family, and other wedding vendors.

2. **If the bride screams at you on the phone and she won't let you get a word in edgewise, don't hang up.** When you can interrupt, remain calm and say something like, "You are obviously unhappy. What can I do to help?" Hanging up on an enraged bride is the worse thing you could do, so bear with it.

3. **If the bride is rude, ignores your questions, says rude things to you, don't retaliate.** Ask her, "What can I do to help?" Some brides don't understand proper behavior, and it isn't your job to teach them.

One wedding coordinator I know worked with a bride who never bathed. She was dirty in her language and her habits. The wedding coordinator informed the bride that she needed to bathe on the day of her wedding or she wouldn't work with her. She also recommended a make-up artist and a hair stylist for the wedding day. The wedding coordinator explained proper etiquette to the bride, and I'm sure she charged quite a bit for all the extra attention she showered on this bride. But the bride didn't complain at all, taking the wedding coordinator as an authority on the subject.

The slovenly woman was transformed into a gorgeous bride, and she behaved much more appropriately for the occasion. So if you have a bride as a client who is not schooled in the art of being a gracious, you may want to recommend a few good wedding coordinators to help her.

4. If the bride uses four-letter words, point out that you'll be glad to help her when she stops swearing. Although some people use these words in their regular, everyday conversation, it has no place in business. And it certainly has no place at a wedding.

Ask the bride to refrain from using that language when speaking with you. Sometimes a bride who talks in this manner doesn't even realize it!

I played at a wedding where the bride expressed her stress by swearing at anything and everything in sight. Before the wedding she saw my roadie arrive and set up my equipment. The bride didn't know who my roadie was and marched out of the bridal changing room to yell at my roadie. She shouted, "Who do you think you are, you _____? You weren't invited to this wedding, so get your _____ out of this wedding and out of my sight!" My poor roadie was flabbergasted and stood there like a statue with her mouth gaping wide open.

I went over to the bride and quietly introduced myself. I explained that the person she was yelling at was my assistant, my roadie, and I would appreciate it if she would not direct that kind of language at my assistant or me. Then I asked the bride, "Is there anything I can help you with before I set up?" She answered, "No." and returned back to the dressing room. The bride eventually apologized for her behavior after the ceremony, saying, "I'm sorry. I talk that way when I'm nervous."

5. If a bride refuses to take "no" for an answer, remain calm. Repeat your answer over and over again to her, using a phrase like, "I understand what you are saying, but that is not my policy." Try to provide alternatives if the bride is being reasonable. If she is not, continue parroting the same answer until you get through to her.

"It takes twenty years to build a reputation and five minutes to lose it."—Warren Buffett, American investor, businessman, and philanthropist

We all make mistakes. But if one client is unhappy with your performance, or unhappy with your service in general, and you don't take immediate action to resolve the problem, your delicate reputation will be sullied. An enraged bride can be very vocal about her dissatisfaction, telling anyone who'll listen about her sob story. Other wedding professionals in your area may get wind of it, and the gossip will spread like wildfire. She may contact the local Chamber of Commerce and the Better Business Bureau with a complaint. With the onset of

Internet reviews and wedding blogs, a simple mistake on your part can be broadcast all over the worldwide web, far beyond the radar of fellow local wedding colleagues, from only one angry bride.

It is very rare, but you may work with a bride who you cannot please no matter what you do. Accept this fact.

Here is an example: A wedding coordinator hired me to perform for a wedding at a beautiful lakeside resort. When I talked with the bride, she said that my harp didn't fit into the "look" she wanted for her wedding. I informed the wedding coordinator that I wouldn't be able to make this bride happy. I suggested that the coordinator look for another musician to take my place.

As it turned out, she could not be satisfied with other wedding details, either. The bride phoned the wedding coordinator every other day, asking numerous questions and changing her plans at a whim. The coordinator gently explained to the bride that it was not necessary for her to phone every other day.

The final straw was when the bride asked, "What is the temperature of the fruit punch?" That was it. The wedding coordinator went to her boss, the director of the resort, and said, "We've got to fire this bride. I can't please her." The director of the resort phoned the bride, explained that it was obvious that he and his staff could not satisfy her wishes, so he was terminating the contract with her and would refund her deposit. The bride was dumbfounded and had no understanding of how she brought this on.

When things escalate to a point that you can do nothing in your power to satisfy the bride's wishes, it is time to consider asking her to terminate the contract. Refund all her money and move on. For the record, this happens very rarely, and you may never need to ask a bride to mutually terminate a contract.

It will also be very rare to work with a bride who is in such a tizzy that she won't allow you to help find a solution to her problem. If she is creating a bad buzz about you, you've got to act fast to nip it in the bud.

"Next to doing the right thing, the most important thing is to let people know you are doing the right thing."—John D. Rockefeller, American industrialist and philanthropist

If the bride reports her problems to your wedding colleagues and local business groups, respond by explaining to them exactly what steps you took to resolve the problem and that the bride would not accept any of those resolutions. Most likely, other businesses will view you as behaving in a professional manner, because you attempted to take logical steps to avoid a dispute.

It is more difficult to fix blogs, chats, and reviews about your services that a furious bride spreads around the Internet. It's viral. If a negative comment is on the homepage of a large wedding or bridal site, email the webmaster of the site and ask him to post your letter as a reply to the bride's complaint. Let your letter explain how you attempted to resolve the situation. If your letter is posted, it will make you sound utterly professional.

Or, you could pay a service to do the dirty work of destroying a bad rap about you on the Net. A new website called ReputationDefender. com is now offering a service to dig up every possible piece of information about you and report it to you on a monthly basis. If anything shows up in a report that you find offensive, they work to correct or remove that information. I have not personally subscribed to their service, but it may be a useful way to combat negative online rants from an irate bride.

Another way of combating bad press about you is to increase your own publicity on the websites and blogs where the negative comments appear. Post free articles, take out short-term advertising space, and do whatever you can to make that bad comment about you appear extremely insignificant.

In the end, once you have publicized the actions you took to try to rectify the situation, the passage of time will cause the bride's rant to fade in everyone's memory.

Of course, if you have failed to respond or not responded professionally, wedding colleagues will remember your mistake forever. And I do mean forever.

Case in point: I was finished performing and was packing up at a wedding ceremony when the baker delivered the cake for the reception. It was lopsided. It leaned to one side precariously. The bride was outside, having her photos shot, so she didn't see the cake, but the wedding coordinator took immediate notice of it. She quietly instructed the baker to fix the cake before he left. Instead of saying, "I'm right on it," he looked her in the eye and said, "You want me to fix the cake? Alright." And with that, he pushed the entire cake into a nearby trashcan and stormed out. I asked the coordinator what she was going to do. "I'll have to order a cake from the grocery store."

I'll never forget that vision of the cake flying across the table into the trashcan. I'll never forget the look on the wedding coordinator's face. I'll never forget that incident. Think I'd ever recommend that baker (who, incidentally, is still in business)? No way, even if he gave the bride a full refund. That story is now a legend among wedding professionals in my town. It doesn't go away.

Again, be honest, professional, flexible, and generous, and you will save face in the worst predicaments.

Once a bride has signed your contract, the way to keep her happy is to recognize that she is your boss.

ONLY TAKE DIRECTIONS FROM YOUR CLIENT, THE PERSON WHO SIGNS YOUR CONTRACT

Wedding decisions are often made by committee. The bride discusses her plans with her fiancé, her parents, her future in-laws, the celebrant, and even her best friends, the bridesmaids. Things can get pretty messy if they all try to give you instructions. Legally, as well as ethically, whoever signs your contract is your boss. That is the one person you answer to, because that is the one person who is responsible for paying you.

You'll avoid a lot of headaches if you make sure that the person who signs your contract knows that you answer to them alone. Explain this to them. If they want you to receive your music list from someone else in the wedding party, make a note of this in the contract and initial it. Your client has now given you permission to receive your music instructions from someone else.

Another story for you: A bride who booked me for her wedding sent me her music list plenty of time before her wedding day. She wanted to walk down the aisle to Canon in D and loved that piece.

One evening, I received a phone call from her future mother-in-law, the groom's mom. She wanted to know what the bride chose for her music selections. I told her, and she said, "Oh no. The bride will walk down to Here Comes the Bride, not Canon in D." I said something like, "Oh, I see," not choosing to argue with her.

As soon as I was off the phone with the groom's mother, I phoned the bride. I informed her of my conversation with her future mother-in-law and gave her details of what was discussed. The bride began crying and whined, "I want Canon in D, not Here Comes the Bride!" I clarified that she alone was my boss, because she signed my contract. "I promise you will walk down to Canon in D."

I didn't phone the bride to upset her, only to tell her of my conversation with her future mother-in-law. I thought that she should be aware of it, just in case she had changed her mind about her music selections and I was not informed. And I explained this to her.

The bride calmed down and thanked me. A few hours later, I received a phone call from the groom who apologized for his mother's behavior.

If you are not straight about who is your boss, these communication entanglements will occur. If someone other than the bride signs your contract, you are obligated to answer to that person. But you still need to please the bride, because if the bride is happy with your work, your client will be, too.

HOW TO GET PAID—ASK FOR WHAT IS RIGHTFULLY YOURS

From the time that you book with your client, you need to be very open about when the deposit is due, when the final balance is due, and the amounts of these payments. Perhaps no other issue is more irksome to a musician than trying to get paid on time. Review Chapter 2 if you haven't established a payment policy. When you have a policy in place, don't waver from it.

To prevent late payments, remain in constant communication with your client. Remind them about money that is due to you. **Supply your client with plenty of information about your payment policy and gently enforce the rules of your contract:**

1. **Prepare by making your contract watertight.** See Chapter 3 about these details.

2. **At the time of booking, explain what payment is needed to secure the date.** Tell your new client about the amount of the deposit required, the form in which it is required (check, money order, cashier's check, credit card), and when it is due.

3. **If you are sending out your contract by postal mail, enclose a self-addressed, stamped envelope with the contract.** This gesture will help the bride to get the contract back to you on time—It makes it that much easier for her to get it into the mailbox.

4. **Never reserve a date without a contract in hand.** Some clients will ask you to "pencil them in" and reserve a date for

them. When a client decides to hire you, state that you do not consider an event booked until you receive a signed agreement with the deposit. Don't even think about holding a date without a signed agreement in your hand. What if you turn down other jobs for one that doesn't come through?

5. **Educate your clients with helpful consumer advice.** Sometimes brides will say, "I'll send you a check and you don't have to bother with the paperwork." Tell them, "Never send money to any service you are hiring without first signing a written agreement. A person could walk off with your deposit and you'll never see them again." Your clients will inherently trust you when you offer this kind of advice, making it more likely that they will pay you on time themselves.

6. **Try to be flexible with payment arrangements.** Some clients may request unusual financial arrangements. When you are working out special financial arrangements with any client, spell them out on the contract. Include the dates when deposits are due and the date when final payment is due.

For instance, wedding coordinators may not send you a deposit and instead, they'll insist on paying you in full upon the completion of your performance. They may even insist on mailing you a check after the big event is over, in which case you may not see your final payment for two weeks after you've played. Booking agents also like to pay in full rather than cutting separate checks for deposits, but some will send you your payment by mail ahead of the wedding date. And then, some brides are financially strapped but really want to have you play at their wedding. They may request to make several smaller payments instead of one big deposit check.

By the way, never accept a post-dated check. If you ever need to file a claim in a bad check restitution program because the check bounced, it may not be enforceable. (I'll address bad check restitution later in this chapter).

7. **Never, ever, send your contracts out "on speculation."** In other words, don't send out blank contract forms. What would you do if you received two contracts, with deposits, in one day for events occurring on the same date and at the same time? This presents a real moral and ethical dilemma. Who booked you first? Besides, how can you plan your calendar ahead of time if you send out your contracts on speculation?

This is ever more reason to insist upon receiving the deposit on time. Include the date when the deposit is due on every completed contract.

8. **Be honest about inquiries for the same date.** If you are waiting to receive the deposit and signed contract from a bride, and another bride phones to request you for that same date and time, advise her of the situation. Let her know that you are awaiting confirmation on a previous inquiry for that date, but you'll be happy to give her a quote in case the other inquiry doesn't come through. Keep your options open, because it isn't booked until you have that deposit and signed contract.

9. **Remind the client about overdue payments.** What if you don't receive the deposit and signed contract by the due date on the contract? Pick up the phone and tell the bride, "I haven't heard from you and wanted to make sure you received the agreement." If she doesn't have it, maybe you didn't have the bride's correct mailing address, email address, or fax number. Double-check and send off a duplicate with a new deadline for return.

If she did receive the agreement, and she gives you some excuse of why she didn't send it to you with the deposit, ask her when you can expect to receive the deposit and contract. Remind her that you do not consider the event booked until you receive these materials from her.

If you still don't receive the contract and deposit by the new due date, you might be right to give up. Some musicians won't bother wasting time on someone who does not honor deadlines.

I prefer to phone the client to ask if they still intend to hire me. I like to know why they procrastinated. Sometimes, I'll find out that I never received the contract and payment because the bride decided not to hire me after all. She plainly didn't to bother to inform me of her decision. It's just as well, because I don't need to work for inconsiderate clients, anyway.

No contract and deposit means the job is a figment of your imagination. Send the bride a letter, keeping a copy for your own records, explaining that you will now leave the date open for another client because you did not receive the deposit and contract from her. She can contact you if she's interested. Don't hold your breath, though.

10. **Gently enforce your rules of cancellation.** If the bride phones to tell you that she wants to cancel your services, she'll probably also ask you to return her deposit. Ask her why the wedding is cancelled, and then refer to your contract. You should have at least one clause that explains what happens in case of cancellation. Refer the bride to the clause number that applies to her situation, and then read it to her verbatim.

Be firm. Don't refund the deposit if you get to keep it according to your written policy. Charge a cancellation fee if your contract deems it appropriate. Don't roll over and forget about what you have coming to you. If your client begins to argue with you, remind them that by signing the contract, they agreed to the terms of cancellation.

11. **Remind your client about final payment deadlines.** If your client has returned the deposit and contract within the allotted time, you're booked! Now make sure you'll get paid your balance. Here's what to do: phone your client one week before the balance is due and remind them of that fact. Explain, "I'm just calling to confirm all your wedding details and that there are no last-minute changes that I need to know about." They will be so happy you called, because they won't have to worry about whether you are going to show up or not. Your client will think you are really on the ball.

Go over all the details in the contract, making sure there are no time changes, repertoire changes, etc. This is also the time to clear up questions you may have about pieces of information that were not provided when you first booked the gig.

Ask how the bride is doing and show that you sincerely care. Now's the time to recommend that massage therapist if they tell you that the bride's a nervous wreck.

Studies show that people remember the first and last points of a conversation best, so leave the discussion of payment to the end of the conversation. If your client has already paid you in full, say, "Thank you!" and that you look forward to seeing them on the big day. If not, remind them that a balance is due, when it is due, and what method of payment you'll accept.

If you are expecting a payment on the wedding day, offer your client a wonderful suggestion: "Place my payment in an envelope the day before your wedding. Write my name on the outside of the envelope and hand it to your maid of honor or best man to give to me when I arrive." Find out the name of the person who will be giving you your payment, and write that person's name down in your notes—This will make it easier to hunt down your payment upon your arrival.

Also suggest that she can place payments in envelopes for all her wedding vendors that are expecting payment on her wedding day. Tell her, "You won't even have to take out your pocketbook to write checks on your wedding day!" Your client will thank you for the suggestion.

The best reason for offering this advice is to avoid having to walk up to the bride and ask for your balance due during all her wedding festivities. Of course, you'll perform far better knowing that you won't be left wondering, while you are playing, when you will be paid.

12. **Insist on payment up-front when the need arises.** What if a client calls to book you within days of the wedding? If you are available, you can email or fax the contract in plenty of time, but what about the deposit? Unless you take credit card payments or expect the bride to overnight your payment to you, your regular payment policy may not fit the situation.

When I am hired to play on short notice, I agree to let my client pay me in full at the wedding, but as mentioned in Chapter 2, she must hand me my payment before I unload my car and begin setting up. I indicate this on the contract that I fax off to the bride to sign.

13. **Don't leave the wedding site without final payment.** If the client forgets to have your payment ready for you at the wedding, follow the client around until you receive your payment. Yes, this sounds idiotic, but it works. She'll realize that she can't get rid of you until she pays up. (It doesn't work so well when you have another wedding gig to run to, though. You won't want to be late.)

How do I know this method works? For one of my first wedding jobs, I phoned the bride a week before her wedding day to remind her that payment would be due on her big day. She understood, or so I thought.

This turned out to be a biker wedding at a public botanical park. The men all cycled in, wearing their black leather and helmets. The women were in more festive wear, except the bride, who wore a white leather dress and go-go boots. Payment was due at the end of my performance, at the end of the ceremony, but none was forthcoming. So, I approached the bride and asked, "Who is handling my payment?"

Her answer was, "I thought I could just mail it to you." She was trying to weasel out of paying me. She *knew* that she owed me money on her wedding day.

"No. Payment is due now."

"Well, I don't have my purse with me." She asked her new husband to pay me, and he only had credit cards. I didn't take payment in plastic. So, I continued to tail her everywhere at the wedding. I shadowed her through her photo shoot. I was quietly obnoxious about it. As far as I was concerned, I had done my job, and I wasn't going to let her stiff me. I was worried that she and the guys in black leather would hop on their motorcycles, drive off into the sunset, and I'd never see my money.

The bride ended up taking a collection from the wedding guests. I was paid in lots of loose one-dollar bills and coins, but I was paid. I felt embarrassed about the situation, but for the bride, not for me.

If you do not get paid your balance due when you have fulfilled your obligation to perform, you've got to take things a step further.

MAKING COLLECTIONS—THE TO-DO LIST

If you must leave the wedding without payment, it will be a lot harder for you to collect. Here are some steps to take if you leave empty-handed:

1. You can try running the client's credit card, even if they insisted on paying you with a check or cash. Advise them that you will be doing this, since the payment is due now. This is the easiest way to receive money that is still due to you.

2. If you do not have a way of accepting credit card payments, check with other wedding vendors who worked at the same wedding. Maybe they received a credit card payment from the client and will be willing to run the payment through on their merchant account and pay you out. Of course, you need to do this with the client's approval.

3. If your client is the bride, phoning or emailing her right after her nuptials will be futile, because she has probably gone off on her honeymoon to parts unknown. Send the bride a hand-written note, thanking her for inviting you to perform at her wedding *and* reminding her of the overdue balance and the amount immediately due.

4. Wait about a month, because by this time, she will have returned from her honeymoon. Then phone her. Ask if she received your card and when you can expect to receive your overdue fee. Make her commit to a date and write that date down. Also record the date of your phone call to her.

5. If that date comes and goes without payment, get out your formal letterhead stationary and send her a letter detailing the amount of days the balance is overdue and the dates of the calls you have made. Even quote from your contract about when the balance was due.

Add to end of your letter, "If I do not receive payment within ten days, I will pursue legal action." Keep a copy of the letter for your own records and send it by certified mail with a receipt, or some other method that makes the client have to sign for the letter. You will receive notice of the date it was received.

Usually, this is enough to get the client to pay up. If not, don't be afraid to seek legal advice or file in small claims court. If you have to go this far, you will have all the dates of the efforts you made to collect, and you will have a written contract making the client obligated to pay, because you fulfilled your obligation to perform.

6. If you are paid with a bad check or insufficient funds, I don't suggest putting the check through your bank again without doing some research.

Phone the bank where the account was drawn and ask if there are presently enough funds to put the check through again. Some banks will not offer you any information if you don't personally hold an account with them, and they certainly won't tell you how much is actually in the account. But other banks may tell you if there is enough money in the account to cover for the check. If there is, make a beeline to your bank and put the check through immediately. It should clear without a problem.

7. If the bank tells you that the account is closed, you need to phone the client right away. Unless you can accept a credit card payment, tell them that they must pay you with a money order or a cashier's check, and you must receive it within ten days or else you will take legal action. Follow up this phone call with a letter stating this same information, sent by a method that forces the client to sign for the letter.

Make sure to charge the client for any bank charges you received and any extra late payment fees that you have stipulated in your contract.

8. If the client does not pay you within ten days, or if they skipped town and you cannot find them, it is time to fill out and submit a crime report with the bad check authorities in your jurisdiction. In the county where I live, there is a bad check restitution program where bad checks are reported to the district attorney's office. If the client won't pay you what you deserve for your job, then they should at least have to pay with bad karma.

Things rarely go this far. Only once have I ever threatened a bride with legal action for neglecting to pay me. She paid up pretty quickly once she knew I wasn't about to go away and forget about it.

You deserve what is rightfully yours. I have heard numerous stories from wedding musicians who did not ask for what was due to them. They regret it, have never forgotten it, and they carry around that grudge as extra baggage to every gig. Because one bride "screwed" them, they think all brides are the same and badmouth weddings in general. Maybe they should stick with playing in the bar scene if they have such a poor opinion of brides. No one benefits from this kind of attitude.

Be strong, confident, and never give yourself any reason to resent anyone. Ask for your payment, and you shall receive.

*Duuude...your Daughter's wedding **can't** be over already. I was <hic> supposed to perform there, **silly!***

CHAPTER 12

The Wedding Day Part I: Preparation

"Two important rules: a wedding needs to be elegant and fun (and no cheesy DJs!)"
—Jeff Leep, entertainment agent and musician

I'll admit it. I have a bit of a hidden agenda for this book. My concern is that the poor behaviors of a few musicians cause the rest of us to be negatively stereotyped. We're losing work to DJs.

This fact was proven in the responses I received while interviewing wedding professionals for this book. Fully 20% of the wedding coordinators said, "I don't like having live music at the reception. I prefer to recommend DJs." And there is evidence that more DJs are being hired to provide music for the ceremony, as well. Brides figure that if they've hired a DJ for the reception, they could save money and have the DJ take over for the ceremony, too.

Some of my favorite wedding colleagues are wedding DJs. The professional ones who make a good living at it know what to play, when to play it, follow directions from coordinators about when to make announcements, keep up on all the newest technology, and keep the party going while behaving professionally. I've learned a few things from them—I've even quoted a few of them in this book.

Sadly, musicians are losing work to DJs because of the problems that coordinators, celebrants, and banquet managers have experienced. What behaviors lead them to recommend DJs instead?

To find out, I polled wedding professionals with at least ten years experience in the US and Canada to uncover their pet peeves about hiring live musicians. These pros include wedding coordinators, celebrants, booking agents, and musicians (because working musicians see a lot of unacceptable things happening, too).

You can view the results of my research at the end of this chapter, **The Top Seven Unacceptable and Unprofessional Wedding Musician Behaviors**. I'll go through each of them here, offering examples of how to correct them so that we can all be better prepared for the wedding day.

1. **Substance abuse.** If there is a number one reason why some wedding professionals refuse to recommend live musicians for weddings, this is it. Almost a quarter of the pros interviewed found alcohol and drug use the top unacceptable behavior. This problem is much more pervasive among reception musicians than ceremony musicians, because access to alcohol is more available after the ceremony.

You need to be clear-headed to prepare, play well, and act professionally. Even if you are taking medication, if it makes you feel fuzzy in the head, curtail it when you are performing at a wedding. People who work regular 9-5 jobs are not allowed to drink or take drugs when they are working. Musicians shouldn't either.

This means:

a) **Arrive sober and leave sober.** Everyone knows when you've already had one or two drinks when they meet you. It isn't just your behavior—they can smell it on your breath. Don't start off with a bad first impression.

b) **Avoid drinking during your performance and when taking breaks.** Sometimes, well-meaning guests will buy you drinks while you are performing. To prevent this, order a tall glass of water, juice, or soda from the bar when you're setting up. When guests see that you already have a beverage, they usually will not try to buy you one. And if they insist, politely say, "Thank you, but I do not drink while I am on the job."

c) Don't arrive high or disappear to take drugs when on breaks. You may not think anyone notices, but they do. Case in point: Norma Morse Edelman, wedding coordinator, shares:

"An expensive top local band were bombed, snorting, and drinking heavily from the bar. They were obnoxious in front of a large Philipino/Latino wedding with Seventh Day Adventists. They were so shocking. Cost the couple $7,000. I was horrified and sick that the couple chose them."

2. Being late. Your car breaks down, you get lost, there is road construction. These sound like plausible excuses, but for a wedding, there is no viable excuse for missing the wedding or holding it up. "It surprises me how many people think being late plus a good excuse equals being on time. It doesn't count for weddings," says Seán Cummings, eighth generation bagpiper.

You cannot start setting up at a ceremony after guests have arrived. Moving equipment between guests looks bad (and it's a hassle, because people are often too busy socializing to move out of your way).

You'll also need to arrive in plenty of time to allow time to go over the ceremony cues with the celebrant or wedding coordinator. The same goes for wedding receptions. If you are a bandleader, make sure you arrive in enough time to check in with the banquet captain and the wedding coordinator to review your timeline and list of announcements to make.

Important information about running a sound check: Whether you're setting up to play at the ceremony or reception, your client, the celebrant, and the coordinator expect you to be done testing sound when guests begin filing in.

If you are in a reception band, and you test sound or rehearse within earshot of the guests at the ceremony, you're in trouble. It's extremely disruptive to hear the band rehearse "Old Time Rock 'n' Roll" while the mothers are being seated to "Ave Maria". Gwyneth Evans, concert and Celtic harpist, adds:

"The one thing that upsets me when I'm playing harp during the reception is when the dance band arrives and starts doing a sound check while I'm playing! This has happened a number of times, not just once, and it makes me furious."

This complaint is common among solo acoustic wedding musicians. If you want other musicians to recommend you, never upstage them. So, here is a suggestion to reception bands about running sound checks from Jeff Leep:

"A great band doesn't need a sound check, not with small gear that you know very well and have used often. Sure, if you're playing at a big outdoor concert using a big PA system, you need an hour for a sound check, but not at a wedding. Just a tap on the mic once and playing one note on the guitar and you're ready to roll. To me, having a really loud sound check at a wedding shows unprofessionalism."

The only way to be able to have enough time to load in, tune up, test sound, and talk over your timing and cues with other wedding professionals is to arrive early. Give yourself a LOT more time than you think you'll need. This way, even if you are ten minutes off your scheduled arrival time, you can hustle and still be ready in time to begin playing.

Including the arrival time in your contract will help you to be punctual. When you make a promise in writing, it has a way of making you adhere by your words.

When you do run a few minutes late, phone the wedding coordinator and let them know when you're expecting to arrive. They'll be grateful to hear from you, because they know you are on your way. You don't want them to think you aren't going to show up.

If setting up and breaking down is exhausting for you, I strongly suggest hiring a roadie to help. About seven years ago, I was in a car accident and injured my lower back. Whenever I lifted my equipment, my back went into spasm and I ended up in the chiropractor's office. One day, my doctor said, "You know, you could pay an assistant to help you at your gigs instead of paying me to fix you afterwards. And you wouldn't be in any pain."

I started hiring roadies and haven't looked back since. I train them to unload my car and set up equipment. This leaves me free time to talk with the wedding coordinator and celebrant about my cues and tune up. This way, I'm ready in half the time it takes me when I am on my own. At minimum wage, it's a small price to pay to make performing less exhausting and more enjoyable. To learn more about this, check out the **How to Hire a Roadie** supplement at the end of this chapter.

Bandleaders may not need roadies if they assign unloading, set up, and break down tasks to different musicians. You'll all work like a

"Seventy percent of success in life is showing up."—Woody Allen, Academy Award-Winning film director, comedian, and actor

well-oiled machine. When each person has a job, no one is stuck with the entire chore. It makes your band look productive and you'll be ready to play on time.

> **3. Ignoring the elements of a wedding.** Remember: You are on the job and not an invited guest. You are supposed to be working, which means that the guests shouldn't be hearing you chatting with the other musicians in your band. If you need to spend a lot of time talking about what tunes you'll playing, then maybe you should have reviewed or rehearsed the order of songs before the wedding day. Set up quietly.

Since you are on the clock, you can't perform and socialize with guests at the same time. Of course, it's fine to talk with them when you are on a break or answer a question or two from guests when you are between songs, but not to the point that it cuts into your performance. Everyone will notice when there are long pauses between songs, or "dead air". "Dead air is so unattractive—you can actually see it hanging there," says Karen Brown, Master Bridal Consultant.

"Pay attention to what's going on around you."—Reverend David Beronio

The number one pet peeve from celebrants about musicians is that they don't look up from their music to see the ceremony cues. Play smoothly between the music for the seating of mothers, to the processional of the wedding party, to the bride's entrance without long gaps between each song. Play the bride's processional as long as it takes for her to arrive at the altar and then stop when she gets there. Stay alert and watch for cues during the ceremony. Start right up with the recessional when the ceremony ends.

If you haven't developed the peripheral vision to see what's happening while you looking at your sheet music, then hire a roadie to be your second pair of eyes if you are a soloist. If you are in an ensemble, select one musician to be in charge of looking up and giving the rest of the group their cues, even if they have to drop a few notes to do so.

To know when to look up, you'll need to review your cues with the celebrant. Sometimes when I've talked with the wedding minister, I discover that there is an addition to the ceremony that was never part of my pre-wedding discussions with the bride. Suddenly, I realize that I'll have to play behind a unity candle or a reading. It's even more disconcerting when the minister finds out that I am supposed to play behind a ceremony element, such as a reading, and he doesn't even have a reading as part of the ceremony! For these reasons, if the bride hired a wedding coordinator, review the wedding program with them, too. Make sure that you all have the same information.

For the reception, you'll also need to go through the bride's agenda with the wedding coordinator. Therefore, you cannot take breaks whenever you want to. You'll also need to watch the length of your breaks. Karen Brown explains,

"Since we sequence reception activities by order, not time, it is sometimes tricky to make things go smoothly if the musicians are not flexible about breaks. For instance, we may have the couple's cake cutting scheduled to happen at the point when it can be served for dessert after the meal. While the staff is cutting and serving the cake, we prefer all eyes focused on the dance floor, since destruction of the cake is not a pretty sight. If, however, the band has disappeared for a break at that time, the party will really go dead. Another reception problem is when the musicians decide to create their own agenda rather than following ours. When a certain activity is about to happen, we let the bandleader know so he can work into it and announce it. You can see how things would not go smoothly if all are not playing by the same book."

Keep the music continuous, even when you are on a break. You can accomplish this by rotating out certain band members on a break, or you can bring some CDs to play while the entire band takes ten.

4. **Rudeness.** Proper etiquette happens when you intuitively understand that the bride's day is perhaps the most important day in her life. Treat her like a queen, the guests like her royal subjects, and the other wedding professionals like co-members of the queen's appointed court. Sounds silly, but anything less is simply not acceptable. "Musicians, like any other business people, need to treat all clients professionally and with a smile (and perhaps gritting their teeth)," says Lora Ward, wedding coordinator.

If you don't know what it means to be rude at a wedding, then take another look at **The Top Seven Unacceptable and Unprofessional Wedding Musician Behaviors.** Here are some additional specifics about which wedding behaviors will brand you as boorish and disrespectful:

a) **Don't eat when you haven't been specifically invited to do so.** The bride delivers an exact guest count to the banquet manager prior to the wedding reception, and based on this count, the manager knows how much food to prepare and how much to charge the bride for the meal service. If you have not been included in the count, you are adding an extra, unexpected cost onto the bride's bill. And if it is a buffet service, the food may actually run out if the banquet manager ordered only enough food to feed the guests.

Eat well before you leave for a wedding, even if you are only playing for the ceremony. Performing on an empty stomach is no fun, especially if people are eating gourmet entrees right in front of you. My performance is never 100% when I'm thinking about food instead of music.

If you have a tendency to get hungry on the job, or if you have low blood sugar problems, bring some snacks to eat on your break: protein or energy bars, string cheese, apples, bananas, nuts, sandwiches, and other easy-to-eat finger foods that keep hands relatively clean. Make sure to eat any snacks out of sight from wedding attendees.

b) **When you have been invited to dine, don't dine with guests.** When you arrive for set up at the reception, inform the banquet manager that you have been invited to dine. If you have any dietary restrictions, now is the time to mention them. Ask them when food will be ready for you and where you and your band will be seated.

Let the wedding coordinator know that you will be served a meal and when it will be ready. Always clear reception breaks with the wedding coordinator. If there is no coordinator, clear this with the best man or maid of honor. Bands and ensembles may be able to efficiently rotate out one member at a time when meals are served, and the rest of the group can continue performing. If your band only performs as an entire unit, or if you are a soloist, you will need to have the wedding party approve any breaks that you take. If possible, take a meal break during the toast, when no music should be played.

The banquet captain may set up a table in the back of the room for the musicians. Other wedding vendors, including the photographer and the videographer, may join you. Sometimes, you'll be seated in a different area, away from where the reception is taking place. Or, you may even be seated in the kitchen. Don't be insulted by this. The meal is simply to provide you nourishment to keep you going, nothing more.

c) **Don't fraternize with the guests.** Sitting with guests, telling off-color jokes to them, hitting on them, and dancing with them is out of the question. So is using vulgar language. You are on the job and not invited to party.

Avoid sharing your religious or political views with guests, too. This can get into some pretty heated discussions, and some may dislike you for your particular slant on life. You want everyone at the wedding to like you.

d) **Be nice to other wedding professionals, even if they don't treat you with the respect you deserve.** Coordinators, celebrants, banquet captains, and all wedding vendors are working hard to make the bride's day special. Sometimes, they are under stress to get things done or have to deal with an emergency and cannot give you a moment. So, they may be curt or even ignore you.

Instead of getting angry, ask them if there is anything you can do to help. They will soften up a bit. Even if you can't help, they will recognize that you are on the same team and that you want to make the bride's day unforgettable, too. "I prefer to work with those who work well as a "team" member. If someone respects your job and your abilities as much as you respect theirs, it is always a better team," mentions Karen Brown.

Whatever you do, listen to other wedding vendors when they have information to give to you. In particular, pay attention to the wedding coordinator, because in most cases, they are in charge of the wedding details. The bride has given them specific instructions to follow and it's their job to carry out those instructions exactly.

e) **Don't wait around to receive a tip after you are off the clock.** Are you so hungry for money that you need to follow the coordinator or bride around, waiting to receive an additional morsel? If you need money that badly, charge more for your services to begin with. Then, you won't worry about whether you'll receive a tip or not.

5. **Don't Expect the VIP Treatment and Act Like a "Drama Queen".** Only the bride gets the VIP treatment on her wedding day. Don't expect anyone else to help you with your equipment. Hire a roadie if you need help to be completely self-sufficient.

When things don't go your way, and that will happen from time to time, just smile and continue. Complaining on the job, especially in front of guests, will only make you look ungrateful. If you have viable issues to bring up with another wedding vendor, please do so in private. Preferably, wait a few days after the wedding to contact the wedding vendor to discuss things rationally. Leave emotion out of your discussion and stick to the facts.

If something makes you want to lash out in anger, think twice about it. By putting your impatient behavior on display, you'll ruin your reputation, and you'll lose referrals over it.

Thankfully, I rarely have issues with my wedding teammates. Here's an exception: I performed at a wedding where the minister was particularly rude to me. While all the guests were getting seated, he shouted to me "I heard you double-booked a wedding next weekend and Mary has to fill in for you!" Then, he laughed out loud. I was fuming.

First of all, I didn't double book. He didn't have his facts straight. But I was angrier that he turned something that wasn't his business into everyone's business at that wedding ceremony.

I had to speak my mind before I began playing, otherwise, I felt like I would explode in rage in the middle of the ceremony. My roadie could see steam coming out of my ears!

As soon as all the guests were seated, I got up from my harp and told the minister that I needed to speak to him, motioning him to the alcove between the outdoor ceremony area and the reception room. There, in privacy, I quietly told him that I work very hard to keep my reputation intact, and I didn't appreciate him shouting at me in front of wedding guests. He apologized, though it took me a while to forgive him, because he placed my reputation on the line that day.

I would have been seen as a crazy lady if I complained loudly and picked an argument with him in front of the seated guests. As Pastor Rob Orr says, "Never argue with anyone. If you react in anger, you can hurt not only your own reputation, but also the wedding business in your area in general." Guests will go home afterwards and describe the poor conduct they witnessed, discouraging others from coming to your town to get married.

Complaining, being argumentative, and acting in anger is the stuff of "drama queens", not professional wedding musicians.

6. Poor Appearance or Hygiene. The first impression that you make is how you look, not how you sound. This was covered back in Chapter 1, but it goes beyond your dress or cleanliness.

Habits such as chewing gum or smoking while performing make you look less than professional. Depending upon where you live, you may not be allowed to smoke indoors anyway. But if you are, it impinges upon others who may be sensitive to smoke. Do it outside on a break, and eat a breath mint afterwards. The smell of tobacco, even on your breath, can be offensive.

Guests can be equally offended by strong perfume or cologne. Many are chemically sensitive to it. Especially during the summer, you won't want to wear any scents, unless you want to attract bugs.

Other turn-offs are visible tattoos, facial piercings, and extreme hairdos. Even if you are in a punk band and this is part of your look, ask when you book the gig if body art will offend the bride, her wedding party, or her guests.

7. **Improper Set Up Display.** Hide any equipment that is not essential to your performance. This includes gig bags and street clothes. Photos will be taken, and you don't want a bunch of junk at your feet to ruin the shots.

Ask the wedding coordinator or banquet staff where things can be stored until it is time for you to pack up and leave. Rooms that can be locked or are off-limits to wedding guests are the best places to store your equipment. If you are at an outdoor venue, areas behind trees or bushes work well (but zip up all bags so that you won't be taking home ants, spiders, sand, and leaves).

If you cannot find anywhere to store unneeded equipment, put it all back into your car. However, I caution against storing anything of great importance there. Of course, there's the possibility of theft, but you may not want to lock sensitive equipment in your car when temperatures are scorching or below freezing.

When setting up, keep in mind that weddings are private affairs where only the people who are near and dear to the bride and groom are invited to attend. They aren't public promotional events. Therefore, any overt efforts you make to promote yourself, your band, or your ensemble are frowned upon.

You aren't allowed to advertise at a wedding, and your performance area isn't a billboard. This means no huge band signs on equipment, no display of business cards or brochures, and don't exhibit your latest CDs for sale. And no tip jars! (Yes, I've actually seen a few tip jars at receptions, as if the band wasn't collecting enough money from the bride).

By the way, I routinely see the big band name displays at weddings, but after receiving feedback from coordinators, I've discovered that this is frowned upon. Perhaps the best solution is to check with the wedding coordinator or client if it permissible to display your band name boldly.

If a guest wants to contact you after the wedding for their own private party, then you can certainly hand them a business card discreetly. And remember that if a booking agent landed you the wedding gig, hand the guest your booking agent's card instead.

A guest may want to buy one of your CDs as a souvenir of the event. When you are finished performing, ask them to meet you outside and handle the transaction there. If the timing is bad, give them your business card and ask them to contact you later to purchase a CD. If you don't hear from them, oh well. Losing a sale is better than overtly promoting yourself at a wedding and putting your reputation at risk.

If an important member of the bride's wedding party wants to buy a CD, just give the CD as a gift. You'll be remembered forever for this nice gesture.

I was invited to perform at a very intimate wedding gathering where an American groom married his bride from South Korea. She barely spoke English, and her parents spoke none at all. Her parents were enamored with the harp music and didn't know how to express their thanks. So at the end of the main course, the groom asked me to sell him a couple of CDs for his new in-laws to bring home to South Korea. I gave them the CDs, refusing to be paid. They were so happy that they started feeding me forkfuls of dessert while I was still performing!

I've covered the major wedding musician pitfalls to avoid. Now it's time to...

PREPARE FOR THE BIG DAY!

As soon as you have a signed contract, you've got to get ready for the gig, even though the wedding is probably months away. Here's what you'll need to accomplish:

1. **Contact the on-site wedding coordinator or banquet captain.** When a bride books your services, get in touch with the wedding or reception site sales staff and let them know that you'll be there. Ask if there are any particular details you should know about the wedding, and share what you have learned about the bride. They will be very grateful that you

gave them a heads up, because they will be able to plan for where you'll be setting up. If you have any questions about the venue that the bride cannot answer, such as where the electrical outlets are located, this is the time to ask.

"If the wedding is at a venue unfamiliar to the musicians, one of the ensemble or band members needs to do a site inspection prior to the wedding in order to avoid any surprises. Thirty minutes before the wedding is not the best time to discover that there is insufficient power or that the stage area the bride had in mind is inadequate."—Jean Picard, Master Bridal Consultant and California State Coordinator for the Association of Bridal Consultants

If you have never performed at the bride's wedding site, make an appointment with the coordinator or the banquet manager for a site inspection (make sure to bring your promo package along to the site inspection, too). Check it out and take notes about where to load in, stairways, service elevators, available electricity, lighting, and the dimensions of the performance area. If you'll be performing outdoors, is there protection from the elements? Is shade available? Are heater lamps available? Is there a backup location in case of threatening weather?

If the on-site coordinator cannot answer your questions, or if you have any concerns, share these with your client immediately. You client has plenty of time to address your questions when you present them months in advance, instead of days before the wedding. For example, if you will be performing outside in April, and the weather is usually iffy at that time of year, you've got to talk to your client about it if the on-site coordinator doesn't have an indoor option for you. Let your client know that they need to have an alternative "Plan B" for bad weather, or else you may not be able to perform.

2. **Say "Thank You!"** Make sure to thank the person who referred your new client to you. Give them a phone call or send a little handwritten note of thanks. But the best way to say "Thank you!" is to return the favor—send them referrals, too!

3. **Music selection.** Immediately after a bride has hired you, provide her with guidance about how to select the music that you'll be performing. It's your job to educate her about when and where music can be used at her ceremony and reception.

Let the bride know how many tunes she'll need for the prelude, her cocktail hour, during dinner service, or for dancing. Give her the option of selecting the type of music she wants or actually providing you with an itemized music list, chosen from your repertoire list.

As covered in Chaper 1, the most important selections that the bride needs to make are her entrance and her first dance song. She'll remember these tunes for the rest of her life, so leave the decision up to her. I usually ask for specific titles for each element of the ceremony and reception, and most brides comply. However, some will want to leave it all up to you, and if that is the case, just go with it. It will make your job easier.

Post your repertoire list on your website, or email or fax the list to your client. I like to email instructions for selecting music as a follow-up to initial phone conversations with the bride.

For religious weddings, instruct the bride to contact her priest, rabbi, or pastor to approve any specific ceremony selections. Some churches or houses of worship do not permit non-religious music or certain selections to be played. It is the bride's job to check with her celebrant well in advance of her wedding day so that she can make an informed decision about her music.

Here are some other specifics to ask the bride when having the music discussion: Find out which selections the bride does not want played, under any circumstances. And if you are a reception bandleader and your group is capable of playing some CDs when they take a break, ask if the bride has any favorite CDs she wants played, too.

Advise the bride of when you'll need to receive her music list. Write that due date on your contract, and include it in all email correspondence and phone conversations until you receive the list. Explain that you must have her song list in advance so that you'll have plenty of time to rehearse for her big day.

If you are within a week of the deadline that you have given the bride, then phone and remind her that you need her music list. I've warned brides, "If you don't tell me what to play, I'll play whatever I want." This fact is also part of my contracts, but when brides hear me say this live and in person, 99% of the time they will jump on the task right away. Most brides want to be in charge of making all of their wedding decisions.

The few brides who don't bother choosing their music will trust your abilities and be happy with whatever you play. The only music question you must have all brides answer is, "Do you want to walk to 'Here Comes the Bride' for your grand entrance, or do you want me to play something else? You'll remember your entrance song for the rest of your life, so please let me know what to play."

If the bride has hired a wedding coordinator, ask her permission for you to share her music decisions with the coordinator. Most coordinators appreciate receiving this information prior to the wedding,

"All ceremonies are different and unique, so working to coordinate with the couple and the person officiating become vital keys to success. The more open and easy the musician, the better."—Rabbi Jonathan Freirich

"Make it as easy as possible for brides to select what they want, but don't overwhelm them... Keep it simple. I get four specific things from them (mom's seating, bridesmaids, bride, and recessional), and tell them to trust us to do our job well."—Van Vinikow, the String Beings string trio/quartet

and they may use it during the wedding rehearsal itself to confirm the bride's choices of music.

It is completely up to the bride what she wants to have played at her wedding. Comply as best as possible. Sometimes she'll make ridiculous requests. Even if she wants funeral music at her wedding, then ultimately, that is her choice. But if she wants you to play a song that is completely inappropriate, tell her why you have reservations about playing it.

The bride will look at you as a wedding music authority, so it's fine to offer your personal opinion about whether her choices will work at her wedding. However, never tell the bride what kind of music to select. Don't boss her into making certain music decisions based on what you do or do not like playing. Here's Pastor Rob Orr's view on this topic:

"The biggest no-no for a wedding musician is to tell a bride what she must have played. What this really points to is a musician who doesn't know how to play many selections and is forcing his meager song list onto a bride. Instead, the bride should be telling you what she'd like to have played, and you should be offering her supportive advice."

4. **Schedule band members and roadies.** Bandleaders: Get your personnel to commit to the date immediately, as soon as you know the requested instrumentation and the bride's choice of music. Schedule rehearsals far in advance, because you'll want to have plenty of time left to add extra rehearsals if someone can't make it. Or you may just want to add another pick-up rehearsal to tighten up your band a bit more before the date.

If you hire assistants, sound techs, or roadies, make sure they also commit in advance. I find that usually one month's notice works well for scheduling.

5. **Reception bandleaders: Devise a timeline with the bride.** Include your start and finish times, when to make certain announcements, proposed time of food service, important key songs to play and when to play them, and the names and correct pronunciations of the wedding party's names. Share this list with the wedding coordinator or hotel contact so that you are all on the same page. This will keep you in the loop when they get wind of changes well before the wedding day. If there are important changes to your song list, you'll have plenty of time to include them in your rehearsals.

"I was asked years ago to sing for a wedding. I did not know the couple in question. I was simply hired to provide two solos. One was from the Faure Requiem!! That's what the bride wanted and that's what she got."—Joanne Barnes, agent and manager, speaking about singing a piece appropriate for a Mass for the repose of the souls of the dead

6. **Rehearsing for the bride.** If the bride wants you to perform with her friend or relative, and you have agreed to do so, arrange a rehearsal as far in advance as possible. Charge the bride a fee for this rehearsal, because, in essence, you are rehearsing for the bride; you are performing with her friend as a favor. Schedule this practice session far enough in advance. Then if you decide after the rehearsal that it's best for everyone that you don't perform with her friend, the bride will have time to decide what to do instead—She can opt to ask her friend to perform solo, with a karaoke tape, or not at all.

Find out the particulars of the music and the performer before you rehearse. What song will be performed? In what key? Do you both have the same version of sheet music?

When you get together to rehearse, if the other musician or vocalist is too nervous, can't hold a pitch, can't count a beat, or simply stinks, don't agree to work with them. Make sure there is a clause in your contract that states that the client can't cancel your agreement because you won't perform with the bride's friends. Review Chapter 3 if you want to consider adding this to your contract.

For receptions, if your band is fine with winging it when someone wants to get up and sing into the mic, then that's okay. Everyone is having fun, and they have no expectations of performance quality when you are acting as a karaoke band. But for a ceremony, don't play with anyone without a rehearsal. If you perform with a bad amateur, they could make you look bad, too. No wonder many musicians refuse to perform with people they don't know.

7. **Rehearsing for yourself.** I'm not going to tell you to practice. You know that. But what I will suggest is a way of preparing your wedding performances that may be different than preparing for other gigs.

Determine the song order as soon as you have received the bride's music list. Make sure to ask about the music she wants you to avoid, as well as the songs she wants you to include.

Bands and ensembles will want to set rehearsal dates in advance, where the music can be distributed to each member to discuss a game plan of which tunes are used for each wedding element. Even if everyone in your group has all the tunes memorized, each member should write down the order of tunes. Practice the music in this sequence. By doing so, you'll limit the amount of discussion needed between songs, avoiding dead air.

As a soloist, it's up to me to decide when I have to start working on the tunes. If the bride has chosen particularly challenging pieces, then I'll give myself more lead-time to get to work. Then, as the wedding day approaches and it's time to run through all the music, I photocopy the sheet music needed for the wedding day and place it in a binder, in the bride's music list order. This way, I won't have to sort through a bunch of loose sheet music at the wedding, wasting time trying to find the tune.

I also make frequent use of sticky notes, labeling sheet music so that I know which tune is for the seating of mothers, the processional, the bride, during the ceremony, and the recessional. I also write notes to indicate how many bridesmaids, flower girls, and ring bearers will be part of the processional.

If you are a ceremony musician, develop your peripheral vision by looking up from your sheet music from time to time as you run through the processional and bride's entrance music. Learn to wind down music in various places, before the last measure, in case you have to bring the music to a close because the wedding party has already arrived at the altar.

"I played at a wedding in a campground where they dropped the rings and spent forever looking for them. I got to go through my entire repertoire and practice some long forgotten tunes."—Seán Cummings, eighth generation bagpiper

Take one piece of music, say the processional, and practice improvising around the melody. Take it slow, removing the tempo so it just floats freeform. Practice noodling (review Chapter 1 if you don't have any idea what I'm talking about). Be prepared with extra music, running through a few extra tunes that are in the same style and genre of the rest of the bride's music list. Prepare and bring along more music than you'll need for the gig—you never know when you might need to play overtime.

Reception bandleaders also need to develop peripheral vision, knowing where the bride is in the room and keeping an eye on food service. It will be up to you to make announcements for the father/daughter dance, additional family dances, the cutting of the cake, the bouquet and garter toss, and so on. You may also need to invite different tables of guests up to the buffet table to avoid long lines of people snaking around the reception hall.

Even if you have your act down solid, practice anyway. And definitely do a quick run-through of the material, in order, on the day of the wedding before you leave—this has a mysterious ability to cement into your mind the fact that you know your act. When you start to play, your brain will say, "Oh yeah, I know this stuff. I just played it before coming here," and you'll sail through all the music.

Here's a fabulous quote regarding the results of practice by conductor and pianist Vladimir Ashkenazy:

"Working hard at practice is also the best defense I know against pre-concert nervousness, which can never be entirely eliminated but can be psychologically prepared for by convincing oneself that one has done all the homework necessary for a solid performance and everything will work out all right."

There is more to a wedding musician's homework than just practice . . .

8. **Fill in the blanks.** When you contracted with the bride, there might have been a lot of information missing, information that she didn't know about months before her wedding day. Don't leave for the wedding without having this information in your grasp. This may include any or all of the following:

- An event-day phone number
- An on-site contact person
- A map or directions to the location
- Wedding colors or theme for any particular dress requirements
- The name of the celebrant
- The name of the banquet captain
- The name of the wedding coordinator
- The name of the person who will be paying your balance upon your arrival

"I always check in on Monday or Tuesday of the week of the wedding and talk over the details quickly one last time. About every 12ᵗʰ wedding or so, no one ever called to tell the band about a last minute time change!"—Jeff Leep, entertainment agent and musician

Phone the bride one week before her wedding day and get any missing information, along with a final guest count (so you will know how loud to set up your sound system before the guests assemble). Also review anything that she has promised to supply for you, such as a meal, a stage, a certain number of electrical outlets, a loading zone, or house sound.

Ask the bride to remind her celebrant to take a moment to talk with you about your cues on the day of the wedding, before the ceremony begins. If the bride is having a wedding rehearsal, suggest to her to remind her celebrant then.

Review all the wedding details with your client to confirm that nothing has changed. This is also the time to remind them of any balance due on the day of the wedding.

9. Decide what to bring. Each wedding is different. The equipment that will be needed for one may be unnecessary for another. So, if you are a bandleader, discuss with your band what equipment will be loaded in and what equipment your musicians need to be responsible for taking to the gig. You can discuss this at rehearsal or just prior to the wedding day.

I used to forget many important items for weddings—everything from my microphone and amp to my music stand and sheet music. Find a system that works for you so that you don't leave anything at home.

Here is the system I now employ: I pull all my equipment that's needed the night before the wedding gig and put it near the front door. And if my amp needs recharging, I do that overnight, too. I lay out my clothes for the gig, including my street clothes for loading and unloading.

On the day of the gig, I place the amp with the other equipment and then start loading the car. I always load it the same way, putting equipment in the same location in the car for every gig. That way, if I forget something, there is a "hole" in the back of my car, where that piece of equipment belongs. I also do this when I'm packing up to go home at the end of a gig to avoid leaving an important piece of equipment at a wedding venue.

It's a major inconvenience to have to drive back to a venue to retrieve a piece of equipment. I've learned this the hard way. Once, I left my rolling gig bag at the curb when loading up my car after a wedding. When I arrived home, I noticed the hole in the back of my car where the bag belonged, and I immediately phoned the country club where I performed. The banquet captain didn't know where the bag was. I freaked out and began counting up the hundreds of dollars it would take to replace all the microphones inside that bag.

I jumped into my car and sped back to the country club. It turned out that a caddy found my gig bag and locked it up in the golfers' lost-and-found, a place where the banquet captain wouldn't have looked. That episode forced me to be much more careful of the location of my equipment at all times.

YOU'VE ARRIVED!

From here on, the key to your success is being flexible. You can be fully prepared, having checked and double-checked every minute detail about the wedding. You'll think you know exactly what to expect. Then, something changes in front of your eyes and you'll need

"There are a million things that can happen at a wedding, and if you think you've seen it all, you're wrong."—Pastor Rob Orr

to be on your toes to make adjustments. To me, this is part of the fun of playing at weddings. No two weddings are alike and it's never a dull moment. Going with the flow of things is what every expert wedding professional knows how to do best.

With this understanding, find out about any last-minute changes upon your arrival. **Here is a set sequence of things to do so that you'll be aware of any last-minute changes:**

1. **Meet your on-site contact.** This may be the wedding coordinator, the banquet captain, or even the bride's mother. They will know exactly where you'll set up and may even have your final payment, too.

If you're a soloist or the bandleader, enter the wedding site and introduce yourself to your on-site contact before you unload anything. If you have been on the wedding site before, confirm where you will be setting up. If there is a question about where to set up, now is the time to ask. Sometimes, even if you think you know where you'll be performing, the wedding coordinator will pull a fast one on you and tell you that during the wedding rehearsal, the bride decided that she wants you seated elsewhere.

If you are playing for the ceremony and the reception, ask about where you'll be performing for both wedding activities when you arrive. This way, you'll be prepared to make the transition to the reception without having to hunt down your contact later on to find out where to set up at the reception.

If your contact asks you to review the wedding itinerary upon your arrival, gently request that you would rather wait until you have unloaded all of your equipment. Focus on one task at a time, and if possible, avoid interruptions while on task. I have found that mistakes are more easily made at weddings when I try to multitask.

Special note: If you are a member of a band or ensemble and are not the leader, wait until the leader arrives and have the leader handle all contact with the client, the on-site contact, and all other wedding professionals. Your job is to follow the instructions of your bandleader, the person paying you.

2. **Survey your performance area before settling in.** Make sure of the following when you arrive to inspect the performance area before setting up:

a) **Do you have a clear line of sight?** Ask your contact where the celebrant, the wedding party, and the bride will be entering. Sometimes the bride will enter from a different direction than the rest of the wedding party. You need to be able to see where they will walk from, so that you can be on top of your cues.

Can you see the altar, where the celebrant and the bride and groom will be standing? If not, you won't know when the bride has arrived at the altar and when to start playing for the recessional. You certainly won't be able to see any cues from the celebrant during the ceremony, either.

If you cannot see the action, have a roadie be your extra set of eyes to give you cues. Or ask the on-site coordinator to assign someone to stand in your line of sight to give you cues. Or, find another place to set up where you can see everything, and tell your on-site contact that you'll need to sit where you can see what's happening.

Keep in mind: The congregation usually stands up when the bride enters and takes her walk down the aisle. This will happen regardless of whether the celebrant directs the guests to rise or not. Even if you have an unobstructed view of the altar when you are setting up, if you are seated behind the guests, expect them to be standing in front of you when the bride enters. Have your roadie or another instrumentalist in your group stand up and give a cue when the bride arrives at the altar. Otherwise, tap the shoulder of a guest in front of you and ask them to give you a cue when the bride has finished her walk. They'll be happy to oblige, and the celebrant will be happy that you stopped playing so that the ceremony can proceed.

If you are performing for the reception, a clear line of sight is helpful, too. When you can see what's happening in the room, from the food service to the toast to the guests on the dance floor, you'll have a handle on how the party is flowing. If you don't have a good vantage point, stay in constant touch with the banquet captain, wedding coordinator, and on-site contact to make sure that you are on the ball with the itinerary.

b) **Does the performance area meet your expectations?** If you've been provided a performance area that does not meet the requirements in your contract, you have every reason to inform the on-site contact that you'll need to set up elsewhere.

Check for these requirements: Is the performance area large enough? Do you have electrical power available? Do you have suitable protection from the elements? Are you on solid, level ground? Is there enough lighting?

When outside, make sure you do not face the sun when you are setting up. Position yourself and your band so that the sun is at your backs, even if this means moving to a place at the wedding site where you were not intended to set up. If the sun is in your eyes, you cannot see your cues and you cannot play. Explain this to your on-site contact.

If the wind is blowing from a direction that plays havoc with your sheet music, move to a place where the air is calmer. Explain your move to your contact, too. If the entire area is exposed to the wind, then just positioning yourself in a different direction may alleviate the problem.

Most importantly, check for safety hazards. Sometimes, I have been asked to set up in the line of foot traffic, under a large candelabrum during a ceremony, or in front of the buffet table during food service. The client obviously wanted me to be the focal point, but safety warrants that I don't sit where people will trip over me, candles will drip on me, or food will be spilled on me. And I also try to sit where I can avoid running long cords that guests can trip over.

When it comes to safety, you have the final say over where you can set up. When you arrive, speak up if you are at all concerned about the safety of yourself or others. Don't allow anyone to get hurt by your negligence—brides and their guests can and will sue over these things.

Once I was performing at a country club with an outdoor ceremony setting and an adjoining banquet room. The guest count was over 200, maxing out the available space outside. I was left with very few options of where to set up.

I confirmed with the mother of the bride that it was fine to set up in the only area free to me. Then the photographer's wife approached me. She said that I would be in the way of the stationary camera on the tripod and ordered me to set up in front of the doorway. "That would be a safety hazard for everyone," I said. She retorted, "I'm coordinating this wedding and I'm in charge." She insisted and began raising her voice to me.

I chose to seek a higher authority, the owner of the facility. Fortunately, he was in the banquet room, overseeing the set up for the reception. I approached him and asked where I should perform. He answered, "Set up where you always set up."

"Well, the photographer's wife told me to set up in front of the doorway, which would be a safety hazard. What should I do? She told me that she is in charge."

A funny look came over his face as he said to me, "Oh, she did, did she? Until she owns the keys to this place, she isn't in charge. Set up where you normally play and I'll straighten this up." With that, he went over to talk with her as I left to unload my car. Of course, the photographer's wife was angry with me for the duration of that wedding, but being safe and avoiding a lawsuit was more important to me than ruffling the feathers of one wedding vendor.

Call it an executive decision. You'll be making a lot of these...

c) **What if the performance area is unfit for your requirements?** Sometimes, you will encounter situations where there has been no effort at all to meet your needs. It's odd, but you can phone and confirm all you want, and then when you arrive, nothing is as discussed.

You can opt to be flexible and do the best you can. Reverend David Beronio relays an interesting story. He officiated a wedding at a natural scenic overlook, a vista point overlooking Lake Tahoe. The wedding site is hard-packed sand and boulders with a few pine trees—nothing more. A violinist was hired to perform for the wedding, and he arrived without a chair or music stand. Perhaps he was expecting someone to provide these for him. He actually taped all his music together, yards and yards of it, and draped it over the boulders. As he played, he walked from one boulder to another to read his music. What would he have done if the wind started blowing? What would he have done if the bride and groom chose to exchange vows at an area of the point that was void of boulders? Certainly, this was "thinking on one's feet", quite literally!

However, if you really cannot be that flexible about where you perform, and the requirements stated in your contract are not met by your client, you are under no obligation to unload your car and set up. As hard-nosed as this sounds, by signing that contract, the client has agreed to provide you with a proper performance area. You don't have to accept anything less.

I have heard stories of brides who cajoled musicians into playing in some of the worst places. I personally know harpists who have been asked to play on a diving board platform, in a tree house, and even in a restaurant restroom when the bride didn't plan on the space that the harpist needed to set up. And I've heard about bands being asked to perform on rubber rafts and gravel driveways. It's all nonsense. Don't let them twist your arm to do these ridiculous things when you have clearly stated your needs in your contract.

When it is obvious that my performance area needs are not met, I explain to my on-site contact, "You have to provide me with a proper place to play. When the baker arrives with the wedding cake, if you don't provide them with a table, they won't deliver the cake. It's the same with your music. If you have nowhere that I can play music, then I cannot deliver."

Expect the bride to make a fuss, but stand your ground. You have your contract on your side. If she can't provide you with a place to play, then you are still owed your balance. You set aside the date to perform and met your part of the deal in the contract.

At this same vista point, Reverend Beronio was scheduled to perform a wedding when a furious storm was coming off the Lake. Dark clouds were forming and thunder could be heard. It was about to pour any minute. I arrived at the ceremony and greeted the bride, who expected me to set up and perform anyway. "I will be happy to perform for you if you move your wedding indoors. I can't perform in this weather and risk ruining my equipment," I explained.

She said, "I'll pay for any damages."

With his hair standing on end from the electricity in the air, Reverend Beronio chimed in, "Oh no you won't. You aren't going to make the harpist risk ruining her equipment. She isn't going to play outside in this weather. Are you going to get married right now out here, or do you want to choose an indoor location?"

Forced to make an immediate decision, she chose to get married during the approaching storm. They popped up their umbrellas and went ahead with it all as I drove home, paid in full. Amazingly, I received a phone call from the bride two weeks later. She apologized for asking me to risk ruining my equipment for her wedding.

3. **Time to unload.** Once you know exactly where to set up and have the lay of the land, so to speak, park you car as close to your performance area as possible and begin unloading. Don't unpack your gear until you have completed unloaded your car, especially if you are in a loading zone or parked temporarily in an unauthorized area. You'll want to unload and park as

quickly as possible in case another vendor needs that parking area, too.

If you are performing at a public area, such as a public park or beach, don't unload until you can get another band member, another wedding vendor, or your site contact to commit to watching your gear as you go back and forth from your vehicle. Make sure that appointed person is also standing by when you park your car after unloading. When no one is babysitting your equipment at a public venue, you could drop it off, park your car, and return to find your equipment gone.

Do not allow anyone to carry your equipment, other than your roadie and band members. You can have a huge liability problem if people hurt their backs or trip over something while carrying your things. Never ask well-intentioned wedding guests or unfamiliar vendors to help you carry your stuff. Sometimes when well-meaning vendors that I know and trust will ask to help me, I might break this rule. If I know them, it's okay. By the way, if you can't lift your equipment and always need help, it's time to hire a roadie.

4. **Checking your cues.** Let your roadie and band members do all the packing and set up. Ask the wedding coordinator or banquet captain where to stash your empty bags. Is there a closet or spare room where they can be hidden from view?

Soloists and bandleaders: While your roadies and band members unpack, use this time to check in with the people in charge of your cues.

If there is a wedding coordinator, find out:

a) Where the wedding party enters and where the bride enters (your on-site contact may have given you this information, but double-check this with the coordinator)

b) What is your cue if you have a special song to play for the seating of the mothers and grandparents?

c) What is your cue if you have a special song to play for the mothers lighting the unity candle?

d) How will you know when to start playing for the processional? Will the celebrant walk down the aisle first? Or will they already be standing at the altar, so you'll need another cue to know when the bridesmaids begin their walk?

e) Check to make sure you have the correct number of brides-maids, flower girls, and ring bearers walking down the aisle before the bride. Sometimes, the number of people in the processional changes because a bridesmaid didn't make it to the wedding or a flower girl or ring bearer couldn't handle walking down the aisle during rehearsal.

f) Confirm all song choices for the seating of the mothers, the processional, the bride's entrance, and the recessional.

Ceremony musicians must always check in with the celebrant, too. Even if they aren't coordinating the ceremony, they know their ceremony better than the coordinator (with the exception of wedding coordinators in some churches—they are part of the congregation and know the celebrant's ceremony practically by heart).

The celebrant may be very hard to track down before the ceremony begins. If they are nowhere in sight, they're most likely off checking in with the wedding party or they simply haven't arrived yet. Tell the wedding coordinator, mother of the bride, groomsmen, or anyone who appears to be in the wedding party that you must speak with the celebrant before the ceremony begins. If you don't, you'll be at a loss to know when to start playing the recessional and when to play during the ceremony.

If there is no wedding coordinator, review the above items with the celebrant. Then collect this additional information:

g) When will the celebrant be walking in? (The coordinator may have already answered this question, but make sure her information is correct.)

h) Will the celebrant be asking the congregation to rise when the bride enters? Will the celebrant say anything between the processional and the bride's entrance? If so, pause between music selections so that the announcement can be heard clearly.

i) What are your music cues for traditions during the ceremony?

j) Does the celebrant want you to play for any other traditions that the bride and coordinator neglected to mention to you?

Do you need to jump in and noodle if a wedding ceremony tradition was added without your knowledge?

k) How does the ceremony end? How will you know when to start playing the recessional music? Does the celebrant end the ceremony with the kiss, pronouncing the couple as man and wife, or by reciting a poem or prayer?

l) Will the celebrant be making any announcements during the recessional? Sometimes, they may instruct the congregation about where the cocktails are being served or information about getting to the reception hall. If they plan to make announcements while you play the recessional music, then pull back on your volume when they begin to speak. This way, the announcements will be heard.

Additionally, go over your music notes with the celebrant, too. As I've mentioned previously, sometimes the bride will tell you to play behind a tradition that the celebrant hasn't planned. They'll need to advise you if the bride eliminated this tradition since you last talked with her or if she forgot to tell them that she wanted to include it in the first place.

Ceremony musicians: If the ceremony and reception are in the same room, find out when the reception band or DJ is supposed to start. If they are contracted to start playing before you are finished performing, don't pick an argument with the reception entertainers. Don't pick an argument with the wedding coordinator, either. Instead, wait until after the ceremony is over and inform the bride or your client that your time overlaps with the reception entertainer. Let them decide if they want you to continue playing or not.

Reception musicians: If the reception is in the same place as the ceremony, or if the ceremony musicians are contracted to play into the cocktail hour, check to see when they are off the clock. Just because their instrumentation is quieter than yours, it doesn't mean that you can upstage them if the bride fully intends for them to play through cocktail or dinner service. Ask the bride or your client whether you should start or let the other performers continue playing.

Wedding coordinators may review the reception itinerary with you when you arrive to set up. However, they may only stay until the beginning of the reception, at the grand entrance of the newlyweds and the wedding party. Then it's up to the bandleader to guide the progress of the reception, making announcements and staying within the timeline. Make sure you do the following:

A. Review your timeline of announcements and key songs to be played with the wedding coordinator and banquet captain. Make sure that you have the correct start and finish times for your performance. Verify that you will be done playing the last dance prior to the finish time, so that the bride doesn't run into paying for overtime at the venue.

B. Review that you have the correct pronunciation of the names of the wedding party, and you know their relation to the bride and groom. This is important for announcing their entry into the reception hall as well as calling them up to the floor for family dances.

C. Also review when no music is to be played at all, such as during the toast, during a prayer before the meal, and when the bride and groom cut the cake. These are times when the guests want to hear every word uttered by the bride and groom, and they are often suitable times to take breaks or eat your meal.

D. Double check with the banquet captain about when food will be served, because this is the fulcrum point of the reception. If there is a buffet service, ask if they have a preference about the order of when you call the guests up to the buffet line. (Note: Always call the bride, groom, and wedding party up to the buffet table first)

E. Confirm any meals to be served to you and your group and when those will be available. Find out where you will be seated.

F. Keep the photographer posted about your agenda, too. "I won't do anything at the mic without checking with him first, so that he doesn't miss any pictures," says Jeff Leep.

Important note: Do not go to the bride's room to ask her questions before the ceremony. She expects you to have everything under control. Besides, she might be in a high emotional state before she walks down the aisle. There is only one exception to this rule: If the bride asked you to stop by her room and say, "Hello," when you arrive. Maybe she just wants you to put her mind at ease that you have arrived and everything is going as planned.

Sometimes, the wedding coordinator and the celebrant have different instructions from the bride about where you'll sit and what you'll play. Or sometimes, a bossy maid of honor or mother of the bride will tell you to do things that were not indicated in your contract. Certainly clear up mixed signals with your client, the bride. If you need to get things straight before the ceremony begins, kindly ask the celebrant or the wedding coordinator to talk to the bride on your behalf and inform you of her final decisions.

5. **Before the first guest arrives,**—Here are a few extra things to do after you have checked in with everyone:

a) Change into your formal attire. Find out where the restrooms are and use them before you perform. I always change into my formal attire first, because if an unusually early guest arrives on the scene, I'll make a good impression even while setting up. Reception bands often elect to set up very early and change just before the guests arrive en masse from the ceremony.

b) Order water, juice or soda from the bar. Keep yourself hydrated and prevent guests from buying you drinks. If you are hungry, eat a quick snack before guests arrive.

c) Quietly tune up and run a quick sound check. It should take no more than fifteen minutes to accomplish these tasks.

d) Store away all non-essential performance items

e) Send your roadie out of the room, unless they are helping you turn sheet music pages or adjusting sound during your performance. They can also watch your equipment if you need to make a run to the restroom (never leave your equipment unattended). Any of your employees who are not essential to your performance should take a break after set up.

You have prepared, and now it is time to start the party.

The Top Seven Unacceptable and Unprofessional Wedding Musician Behaviors

Based on 85 responses from wedding professionals in the US and Canada with a minimum of ten years of experience

1. Substance Abuse—24%

• Drinking alcohol during performance and on breaks at the reception
• Arriving intoxicated or high
• Doing drugs or snorting on breaks

2. Being Late—20% Not arriving at the time stipulated in the contract, or with enough time to set up properly. This includes:

• Neglecting to check in with the minister, the wedding coordinator, or the banquet manager about timing and cues.
• Tuning and testing sound after the time you are contracted to start playing
• Setting up after guests have begun congregating at the ceremony
• Setting up after guests have begun arriving at the reception and testing sound while guests are present
• Moving equipment in front of guests

When ceremony and reception are at the same wedding site:

• Running a sound check for the reception while the ceremony musician is trying to tune up or has begun playing
• Running a sound check for the reception while the ceremony is underway, and the guests can hear you

3. Ignoring the Elements of a Wedding—18%

• Chatting, joking, and laughing in front of seated guests at a ceremony
• Mingling with guests instead of playing
• Refusing to look up from the sheet music to see the ceremony cues from the celebrant or the wedding coordinator
• "Dead Air"*—Not playing to the complete entry of the bride or having long gaps between songs
• Taking long breaks or not checking in with the wedding coordinator about when to take a break
• Ignoring instructions from the wedding coordinator, celebrant, or banquet manager

4. Rudeness—14%

• Eating when not invited to do so
• Eating with seated guests

- Telling off-color jokes in front of guests
- Vulgar or inappropriate language—Being crude, using four-letter-words, expressing political or religious views
- Hitting on guests
- Dancing with guests
- Treating other wedding professionals with a lack of respect
- Waiting around after the performance to receive a gratuity

5. Expecting the VIP Treatment and Acting Like a "Drama Queen"—11%

- Expecting the wedding coordinator or the staff at a wedding site to help carry musical equipment
- Expecting to have your own changing room
- Openly complaining on the job

6. Poor Appearance or Hygiene—9%

- Outright sloppiness.
- Showing up wearing inappropriate clothes
- Wearing dark glasses during performance
- Smoking while performing.
- Chewing gum while performing

7. Improper Set Up Display—5%

- Placing signage on equipment
- Displaying business cards and promotional materials
- Leaving non-essential equipment in plain view (such as gig bags)

* "Dead air" is an unintended period of silence. This term is borrowed from a broadcasting term meaning an interruption in a radio broadcast where there is no sound heard.

How to Hire a Roadie

A roadie can be an indispensable employee. He (or she) can do any one of the following for you, or even more, if you need them to do so:

- Load equipment in your vehicle
- Drive your vehicle or park your vehicle (if they have a valid license)
- Help navigate to the wedding destination as a passenger in your vehicle
- Unload your vehicle at the wedding site
- Carry your equipment to the performance site
- Set up your equipment
- Tape down exposed cords to the floor
- Test sound equipment
- Watch for wedding cues that you cannot see
- Turn sheet music pages
- Hold down music stands or umbrellas in windy conditions
- Fetch you water or something out of your car while you are performing
- Guard your equipment when you go on break
- Break down and pack up equipment, including rolling cords
- Carry your equipment back to your vehicle for loading

When hiring a roadie, the first thing to consider is the job skills they should have for specifically what you need them to do. How much weight will they need to lift? Do they need to be at least a certain height so that they can clear the ground efficiently when carrying your equipment? Do they need to have a good ear to test sound equipment? Can they read sheet music so that they'll know when to turn your pages? Do they need to be bilingual, (in the event that you regularly perform at cross-cultural weddings? Consider these questions when determining the job requirements for your roadie.

Remember, we're talking about wedding gigs here, not bar or concert gigs. This means that:

1. It is important how the roadie looks, because the people attending the wedding will see them. Furthermore, your employees represent you—If they don't look good, you don't look good.

Sometimes, if a candidate doesn't own the proper clothes for the job (or refuses to dress conservatively), it isn't the job for them. So you'll need to explain your dress requirements at the outset, before you decide to hire them.

Your roadies should dress conservatively. I instruct mine to wear nice, comfortable casual pants and a button-down shirt—no grubby jeans hanging below the waist and old t-shirts. Women can wear casual pants or a dress or skirt, but a dress or skirt should be below the knees, since they'll be bending over a lot. Of course, jeans that show off thongs or belly buttons are out.

For safety reasons, roadies should always wear comfy closed-toed shoes, like tennis shoes, and no ties for guys (which can get caught while carrying equipment).

A clean appearance is also a must, and I don't just mean hygiene. Weddings are attended by several generations of people, and we need to cater to the most conservative in the way we dress. Older or more conservative wedding attendees will stare daggers at roadies who show up with visible tattoos, face piercings, and extreme hairdos. The attention should be on the bride, not on your roadie.

2. Your roadie will need to possess a responsible manner and proper behavior for wedding gigs. They must have a mature social demeanor. You'll know right away when you interview them, either by phone or in person, if they are socially mature—They'll be able to hold a good conversation with you. You also need to feel a bit of personal chemistry with your new hire. You should feel like you can get along with them.

3. They'll need to be able to keep themselves occupied for long periods while you're performing. They shouldn't pester guests or stand around with nothing to do. I insist that my roadies bring a good book or homework to the job. I require a good GPA from students who apply, because I know they are interested in quietly doing their homework. They also tend to be more socially mature than people who don't care much about school.

My roadies have also brought along knitting and magazines to keep busy, which is quite acceptable, too. What aren't acceptable are mp3 players, or any contraption that requires the use of headphones or ear buds—roadies get too absorbed listening to respond when you need them.

I permit my roadies to bring along a sack lunch with snacks, food, and water. When they are on a break, they can eat and do their homework, as long as are out of sight of wedding attendees.

The next step is to decide how much you'll offer as pay. Minimum wage is appropriate, but perhaps it is too low in your region. That's your call. Make the starting pay a low enough figure so that you can offer raises and bonuses for a job well done.

Finding the proper candidate for your job opening is the most difficult task. I hire primarily teenagers and young adults, but retired people who are in good condition have also done a good job for me. Here's where to look for roadies:

1. If you teach music lessons, ask your students if they are interested in working for you. It will help them to see what performing is all about. They will make the finest roadies, because they are truly interested in what you're doing, they will take exceptional care of your equipment, and simply want to please you. They may even work for you in exchange for lessons, and no money has to change hands!

2. Ask your neighbors, friends and family if they know someone who would fit your criteria for your open position. A referral from them means that the potential roadie comes with recommendations.

3. If you are a member of a religious congregation, you could ask your pastor, priest, or rabbi to make announcements at meetings about your job opening. People who regularly attend church will know how to behave at sacred formal gatherings, such as weddings.

4. Speak to the band and orchestra teachers at nearby high schools or colleges in your area. Let them get the word out among their high achieving music students that you have a job available for them.

5. Create a flier and post your job opening at your local highs school and colleges. Post it at your local gym, too, where people who can lift weights are also capable of lifting your equipment. Post the flier at your local house of worship. In fact, post it anywhere you think a person with the right talents will see it. This is the more blanket approach, so you may sift through a lot of unsuitable candidates before you find the right person.

Once you've found the best worker for the job, explain all your requirements, when you pay, and what hours you will pay them for. Will you pay them from the time they arrive at the gig to the time they leave? Will you deduct food breaks? Again, this is up to you.

You may wish to consider buying a plastic nametag for your new roadie. The nametag will prevent other vendors and invited guests from questioning whether your roadie belongs at the wedding when they're setting up your gear.

There are some legal housekeeping matters to take care of before they ever work their first job for you. They include:

1. Filling out the necessary tax forms. I hire my roadies as private contractors, so they fill out a W9 form for me. I won't need to take out for Social Security and the like. Currently, I'll only need to notify the IRS if any particular roadie makes more than $600 from me in one year.

Don't avoid this step by paying "cash under the table" to your roadies. Making it legal by having your roadie fill out a W9 form makes it legal for you to take a tax deduction for paying them.

If you do not live in the U.S., there may be other simple tax forms that your roadies need to complete. Consult an accountant to find out.

2. Create a form that will release you from liability if your roadie gets hurt while on the job. Make it a short, simple, and easy to understand document. Don't fill it with legal rhetoric. If your roadie is a minor, you will need to have their parents co-sign the liability release form, too. Consult a legal advisor to make sure your liability release form contains the correct information.

*Did anyone else know that the bride was
entering by parachute?!*

CHAPTER 13

The Wedding Day Part II: Have Fun! (Despite the Unexpected)

"We see our customers as invited guests to a party, and we are the hosts. It's our job every day to make every important aspect of the customer experience a little bit better."—Jeff Bezos, founder of Amazon.com

Yes, this is a job. But why not have fun? Love what you are doing and do it well. Your attitude, blended with your stage presence will get you recommended over and over again. Your infectious charisma will create a buzz among the wedding guests, and it will spread to their friends and loved ones.

Reflect upon these words of wisdom from Phillippe Etter, violist with the Purcell String Quartet:

"Love the work you're playing so you're like a person who enjoys telling jokes and who has an especially good joke to share. You look forward to the audience's pleasure. You have an enjoyable thing to share with them."

When you approach playing with this attitude, a few wrong notes will go unnoticed. I've even broken strings during the processional, and no one noticed. Everyone's attention is really on the bride and groom and not on the musician. So relax!

You can't have fun performing if you don't have some confidence when you play. Efficient practice and rehearsal allays nervousness and will give you the support to get through the gig with ease. "If performers focus on the wedding couple, all focus is removed from themselves, therefore removing any nerves or jitters before or during one's performance," suggests Reverend Janice Midkiff.

WHEN THINGS GET OUT OF CONTROL—THE LAUNDRY LIST

"Chaos is a friend of mine."—Bob Dylan, award-winning American singer-songwriter

If you watch enough TV or are a regular visitor to YouTube.com, you've seen plenty of whacky things at weddings that defy imagination. There is just so much planning you can do, and then the unexpected and unintended will unfold in front of your eyes.

What should you do when something happens that is out of your control? Be flexible and be professional. And above all, remember that you are a performer and "the show must go on"*. Weather through it all with a smile and don't let anything bring you down.

Here are some of the more typical wedding horror stories with a few suggestions on how to get through them:

1. **Inebriated wedding couple, wedding party, or guests.** It is my educated opinion that most problems at weddings are caused by too much alcohol. The majority of the stupid behaviors come after people are too drunk to act with any common sense.

Most bridezilla stories involve at least one person who has had too much to drink. There's the bride who got so drunk that when her groom smashed wedding cake in her face, she got mad, said the party was over, and ordered her guests to get off the docked paddle wheeler. Then, she stormed into the boat's head (or bathroom) and tore it apart, ripping off the curtains and yanking the seat and the handle off the toilet. She was billed for the damage, and I understand that she paid without disputing the charges.

Okay, this is an extreme example, but you get the picture. Heavy drinking and weddings don't mix. Expect the strange and bizarre when your wedding group is drunk.

---

* "The show must go on" is a theatrical credo dating back to the 1800s meaning that the audience is counting on us to perform and we cannot let them down.

No musicians were involved in that story, but here are some stories that demonstrate that the musician needs to be flexible and keep the music going...

Kerry Ann Hawk, a wedding coordinator, shares this story: "A bride had to hold her father up to walk *him* down the aisle because he was so intoxicated. During the reception, he laid out three napkins in front of the buffet line, laid down on them and took a nap." You can bet the reception band had to make adjustments to the timing of the dancing if the father of the bride was snoozing on the dance floor.

I once arrived at a wedding where the groomsmen were passing the flask before the ceremony began. They were so plastered that they swayed as they walked. First, they started hitting on my roadie, a shy, awkward sixteen-year-old who was embarrassed by their bold suggestions. I asked the men to leave her alone and let her do her job.

So, they wandered off with the groom and I began playing music for the seating of the guests. All was well, or so I thought...

The groom was fitted with a lavaliere mic on his lapel and inadvertently turned it on. Everything he said and did was heard over the P.A. system while I was still performing seating music. And what were the guests treated to? Fart noises. The guys were off somewhere making rude sounds by putting the palms of their hands into their armpits and flapping their arms up and down wildly.

For fear that the guests would think that those noises were emanating from their harpist, I had my roadie find the groom and tell him his mic was on. The last thing I heard through the P.A. was her voice telling him to turn off his mic, and his response, which was, "Huh? Oh. Me? What? Oh. Okay," and then a few four-letter words. Would you believe he forgot to turn his mic back on during the ceremony?

Then, there was the maid of honor who decided to take the bride out drinking before the wedding. They both arrived over an hour late. By the time they arrived, my time was up and I had another gig to get to. I asked the minister what to do, and he said, "Just play the bride down the aisle and pack up and leave." I did exactly this. Fortunately, I was seated behind the guests, so no one witnessed my fast departure.

I heard later that the bride was so drunk that she got sick after the ceremony, and neither the bride nor groom attended their reception.

2. Weddings or receptions starting late. As you can see from the previous example, weddings can and do start late. Sometimes, it's due to heavy drinking, but there can be many other causes.

A late start to a wedding isn't necessarily a bad thing, as you'll read in the next story...

I was booked to perform at a lovely outdoor location. The bride was a full hour late. Why? Because she didn't like the way her hair looked and figured the groom could wait. When she finally arrived, the minister said, "I have another wedding to perform. I'll return in a few hours, if you still want to get married here today." The bride agreed to this. She also agreed to have me continue playing the prelude music. For me, this meant several hours of overtime and getting some practice in on the extra songs I brought along. The only people who didn't benefit from this arrangement were the poor guests and the groom, who stood outside in the heat for several hours (no chairs were provided for anyone).

Weddings can start late for many reasons, such as:

- The bride locking her wedding gown in the trunk of her car, along with her car keys
- The groom leaving his rented tux at home
- The maid of honor running her pantyhose before the ceremony
- The minister is late because he couldn't find the church, his last ceremony ran late, or he forgot about it completely.
- The divorced parents of the bride hate each other and can't make up their minds if they'll attend the wedding at all.

And the list goes on. In all of these situations, the musician's job is to keep playing music. Bring plenty of extra music and realize that if the ceremony runs too late, you can receive overtime payment—not a bad thing at all.

A wedding that runs ten minutes late isn't unusual, and most weddings don't start right on time, anyway. When the guests start looking restless, you know the wedding is seriously late.

Late weddings become problems for you when you don't have enough music to play. Your only choice will be to play the same material over and over again. You know your guests have heard it all once through, and they may be left wondering if you know how to play anything else.

Late weddings become a real problem when you have another gig to go to afterwards. You'll need to speak up to find out what is happening. It is uncomfortable to be in this position, and for this reason, I know some wedding ceremony musicians who will only book one wedding per day. They don't like worrying about getting to another gig on time if the first gig runs late.

Talk with the celebrant. Find out what's holding things up. Let them know that you have another gig to get to and you cannot go into overtime. Talk with them directly, not just with the wedding coordinator, because the celebrant has the power to push the bridal party along and to shorten the actual length of the ceremony. Explain that you may need to leave before the ceremony ends if it doesn't get started soon.

Even when there is a wedding coordinator hired for the day, if the celebrant is standing around before the ceremony, chatting with the guests, it's an almost certain sign that the ceremony will start late. If the celebrant is waiting for someone to tell them when the bride and her wedding party are ready to walk instead of actually checking in with the bridal party to get them all down the aisle on time, this is a problem. So, in a number of instances, late weddings have actually been the fault of lazy celebrants.

The show must go on, and you must play until they all get down the aisle, no matter how late that may be (unless, of course, you are off the clock and no one will anti up for overtime).

3. **Unexpected mishaps.** The show must also go on when something unexpected happens in the course of the wedding or reception. Keep playing as if nothing went wrong, or even start to play to divert the guests' attention away from the mishap.

If you are a health professional and can help the injured or hurt, then of course, you should break away from your music and be of assistance. Otherwise, keep on playing.

I once played at a small, intimate ceremony and reception where there were about fifteen people in attendance. It was a backyard wedding on a very warm day. One gentleman was having difficulties standing up during the ceremony, and at the beginning of the reception, he tripped, fell, and couldn't get up. He complained of dizziness. The paramedics were called, and it turned out that the man had forgotten to bring his heart medication from home, many miles away.

He was taken to the hospital. During the hubbub, the bride instructed me to continue playing. I think it actually calmed down the guests, who were all aware of the emergency, and they were very complimentary of the soothing music.

Sometimes, the bride, groom, and all who are standing up throughout the ceremony cannot handle it. They faint, have nosebleeds, throw up, you name it. If this happens during the processional, keep on playing. Guests will run to the rescue to help out. And if it happens during the ceremony when you are not playing, watch the celebrant for cues to start playing something. Anything. You'll know when the celebrant looks over at you helplessly to start playing. Stay alert during the ceremony!

Watch for the celebrant's cue when other surprising things happen during the ceremony, too. For example, it's more common than you might think to see wedding rings left in the hotel room, forgotten at home a plane flight away, or dropped into beach sand by the ring bearer. The bride and groom may be incapable of lighting the unity candle—the wick is too small, the wind or air conditioning is blowing it out, or the matches won't light. And there has been more than one occasion where photographers will draw attention to themselves by backing up into candles or walking into great vases of flowers.

There will be times that you'll be the victim of miscommunication. Just play. Don't worry about it. I thought I had all my cues down solid at one wedding, where there were supposed to be three bridesmaids followed by the bride. I played the processional for the bridesmaids, and then, when the last one was in place at the altar, I switched over to Wagner's "Bridal March" or "Here Comes the Bride". Up the aisle the groom came, sheepishly walking to the bride's entrance music! He was red-faced and everyone laughed. The minister laughed his head off, too.

The guests were all standing, so I couldn't see why they were laughing until I peeked between the heads of two guests and noticed the embarrassed groom. I wound down the tune, and when the groom arrived at the altar, the minister announced, "NOW here comes the bride!" I quickly went right back into the Bridal March. I had to be flexible with the music I was playing.

I was very concerned that the bride and groom would be angry with me, but they were as happy as could be and said that they'll have a wonderful story to tell their children about their wedding day. I asked the minister why the groom followed the processional, which is uncommon. He said, "I told the groom to follow me up to the altar when I walked in, but he didn't listen to me. He remained back, chatting with the bridesmaids. What was I to do? I was already at the altar."

There will be other unknown challenges for the wedding musician, something so rare that it may happen to you and no one else. Stay alert and be on the look out for something out of the ordinary. Remember in Chapter 1, where I mentioned wedding the bride who decided to dress all her bridesmaids in matching white gowns? I couldn't tell who was the bride and who was a bridesmaid during the processional, especially since I was sitting about 200 feet away from them at a beachfront park. I finally figured out that the bride would be the one walking with her father, since all the other ladies walked up the aisle unescorted.

Beware of practical jokes. Not that you will be a victim of them. It's more probable that the bride and groom will be the butt of a joke, since they are the special honorees at their wedding.

If you have seen the "The Wedding Crashers" reality TV program or "America's Funniest Home Videos", you know that practical jokes are increasingly popular at weddings. As hired musicians, we usually witness the spoof unfold along with all the guests. It will be rare that you'll be in on the joke, because your clients figure you can just go with the flow. This is ever more reason to stay acutely aware of the wedding as it proceeds.

Ed Miller, wedding officiant, suggests that all wedding professionals should be ready to expect anything. He offers this example:

"The bride arrived by boat. As she waved, seated on the transom, she flipped overboard. Only the bride's mother and I knew it was a stand-in. The groom may have soiled his rented tux!"

Imagine the groom's, the guests', and the ceremony musician's utter surprise as they saw the bride walking down the aisle in pristine condition after falling into the water! Things like this can't stop you. It is the wedding professional's job to pretend like it's just another normal wedding and go on with the show.

Mother Nature may have a hand in things. Play on, unless the entire wedding party runs for shelter, the wedding screeches to a halt, or if you cannot possibly continue. Here are some examples of outdoor tricks that Mother Nature plays: She can dump rain, hail or snow unexpectedly or send a dust devil into the vicinity of the wedding.

More commonly, she'll send gusts of wind to topple over arches and makeshift gazebos.

For instance, I was playing softly in the middle of a ceremony while the father of the bride was in the middle of a reading. Suddenly, a gust of wind made the umbrella I was sitting under airborne. It came to land on my back while I was still playing! I screamed and then looked up from the harp. Everyone was staring at me with their mouths wide open. I turned to the minister and said, "Please continue the ceremony. I'm okay." Actually, I wasn't. I was pretty bruised up, but I didn't want my accident to spoil the bride and groom's special day.

Mother Nature may have another effect on the wedding festivities: Derek Tarpey, a seasoned DJ, shared with me that the bride and groom were missing when he was ready to announce their grand entrance into the reception hall. He came to find out that the bride's water broke and she was off to the hospital to deliver her baby. The reception went on without the bride and groom, and a general announcement was made to satisfy the guests' curiosity.

Although they aren't really a fault of Mother Nature, I have heard more than one story about automated lawn sprinklers suddenly switching on and drenching all those in attendance at garden receptions. Fortunately, this has not yet happened to me. I am understandably leery of weddings in public parks, where the sprinklers are on timers. I usually ask the bride about automatic sprinkler timers early on, when I learn of the wedding location.

And just one more example of the unexpected: Bugs. It's particularly terrible when they are the kinds that bite. (Although many a flutist complains about gnats and flies that travel into their mouths or noses while they are playing, and they spend the next five minutes coughing uncontrollably to avoid swallowing the critters.)

Mosquitoes have stung me through my dress, black flies have attacked my feet, and wasps have traveled up my gown, stinging me in places I don't care to mention. And guess what? I kept on playing.

If you personally have any major medical problems on the job, speak up. Once I performed at a wedding on the edge of the Sacramento River, just after mosquito abatement procedures had been completed. The mosquitoes went crazy and feasted on me before their ultimate demise. I had a severe allergic reaction from the vast number of stings I received. So after the ceremony, I told the mother of the bride that I needed to leave immediately or she'd have to escort me to the hospital. I was sick for several days afterwards, but I can proudly say that I made it through the wedding ceremony without anyone noticing my misery.

>   **4. Children.** You can put older kids to work, giving them things to do that make them feel wanted and helpful at the wedding. They can hold music stands so they won't fall over in the wind, they can help turn your pages, and they can get you some water if you're thirsty. Harpist Natalie Cox tells this story:

"One beautiful summer's day, I was playing at a wedding in the bucolic Marin County forest, home of bountiful wildlife...Once I began the music, huge, fuzzy caterpillars began dropping onto my arms and shoulders from the towering trees! Creeped-out but knowing I was not in any danger, I calmly elicited the help of two darling children sitting nearby to gently pluck the insects away while I faithfully kept the processional music going."

Unfortunately, most of the stories about children at weddings aren't so delightful. For instance, kids can be a cause of delays down the aisle. At one lovely public beach park, the 3-year-old ring bearer panicked when it was his turn to walk down the aisle. He stood frozen for a moment, with all the guests' eyes staring at him. Then he ran off. The minister motioned to me to stop the processional music while the adults formed a search party to find the little boy. The processional resumed fifteen minutes later, with the ring bearer quietly seated with the guests.

Children left to their own devices can cause havoc. Especially during the reception, unattended children will chase each other, running dangerously close to you and your precious equipment.

The one word that works with children of all ages is, "No!" Use this if you are in the middle of performing and kids are running loose nearby. Use this word if they come up to you and want to put their fingers all over you and your instrument (their fingers may have previously been in their mouths or in the icing of the wedding cake).

If they are so uncontrollable that the word, "No!" has no affect on them whatsoever, it's time to take other measures. If you are a bandleader, instruct your group to continue playing while you locate the child's parents or another adult who can keep children under a watchful eye. If you are a soloist, you have no choice but to ask a nearby adult to help control the kids. Usually, a few sympathetic adult guests will help guide the children away from your performance area.

I have had a few instances where guests were upset with me because they claimed I yelled at their kids, even though I only firmly used the word, "No!" My response has always been, "I don't want your children to get hurt playing around my equipment." If guests know I am thinking about the safety of their kids, they calm down (but I'm also thinking about my own safety and avoiding property damage).

Smiling at little children and acting like their friends can invite trouble. Harpist Gwyneth Evans tells this story:

"Two sweet little girls in fluffy dresses were hovering nearby, and I made the error of smiling. Oh dear. During the signing of the register, I was playing something a bit complex on my concert harp, when one of the little darlings not only came up and put her hands on the strings, but also stepped up onto the base of the harp as it was tilted in towards me! While I believe the show must go on, in this case there was nothing to be done but stop and ask the parents who were sitting in the front row to remove their daughter from my harp so I could play it. They seemed rather puzzled: what was my problem? Since then, I don't smile at either little boys or little girls, until the crucial part of the wedding is over."

If you don't already have something in your contract to cover damages to your equipment or person by the client and her guests, then go back to Chapter 3 and consider adding this kind of clause.

5. **Ask for help when you need it.** In the instances above, where you have children running amok, when you or a guest requires medical attention, or when things are so out of hand that it is beyond your ability to make a decision about what to do next, don't be afraid to seek help. Toby Dodge, wedding planner, explains:

"I think it depends on what the problem is . . . If it's with a crazy guest that is obnoxious then the both of us may need to speak to the guest and let them know that the host would not want the band to be harassed and would he kindly go back to his seat. If the person becomes belligerent, then you have to get security to assist in taking any threat of violence or an embarrassing situation out of the area."

Wait until it is obvious that you really need some assistance with a problem, because as Jeff Leep, entertainment agent and musician says, "I need to know when I send a band or musician out that they will be able to handle anything that comes up. If I can't trust them to have the proper judgment to make decisions that are appropriate, then I can't trust them to handle a wedding."

6. **Handling critics.** This is something that any musician should be able to manage with finesse. Keep in mind that people may have had a bit to drink and are having a grand old time at a wedding, so they can be outspoken.

"Critics can't make music even by rubbing their back legs together."—Mel Brooks, Academy Award-winning comic actor, writer, producer, and director

If any guest complains about the volume of your music, the selections the bride requested, or the way that you perform, let it roll off your back. You can check with the bride to make sure the volume is fine, and you can remind guests that your boss is the bride and that you were hired to play her requests. Your client and the bride are the only people you must please. It's just icing on the cake when everyone else loves your performance, too.

7. **Making executive decisions.** There will be times when you've got to go against instructions and act on what you know best. One example is my earlier story about the photographer that insisted I set up in the middle of foot traffic. Another example: Be ready to play something during a ceremony when the priest suddenly motions you to play, and you haven't been given any selections from the bride.

Reception musicians may be called upon to make their own executive decisions, too.

Here's another example, relayed by Jeff Leep:

"I was once contracted to play at a wedding reception where the bride was incredibly dominating, wanting everything to be exactly so. She was very uptight. She said to me, 'I hired you guys as a swing band and I don't want to hear anything but swing. Do you understand? No rock 'n' roll. I want you guys to swing all night. That's all I want. That's what elegance is, and I want elegance for my wedding.'

So at the reception, we're doing the Frank Sinatra and the big band music, and for about a half hour, people were into it. And then all of a sudden, the dance floor died. And the dance floor was dead for half an hour, and I'm looking around for the bride and groom, and they were gone! The party popped. There was nothing going on. I got the vibe from the guests, 'This isn't a fun party. Come on, band, what are you going to do?' The party was desperate, like everybody was going to leave and walk out.

So I took it onto myself and thought, 'I don't care what the bride says, we're gonna rock.' We played some rock tunes, and the dance floor packed and it turned into the greatest party. Finally, the bride came back into the room and said nothing. At the end of the party, she came up to me and with tears in her eyes, she said, 'I was wrong. The party was boring, you took over, you did it, and you saved my party. Thank you for saving my party.' And I thought I was going to get grief from her and was ready to take the responsibility for that. But it was entirely the opposite, and I was surprised."

When things are in trouble, go with your gut feeling. Often, your intuition is right on.

> **8. Handling unwelcome advances from guests.** Speaking of intuition, we all know when someone takes a special liking to us. We also know when they are crossing a line and simple words of flattery are turning into a come-on. People loosen up at parties, regardless of whether they have been drinking, and weddings are no exception.

For the Ladies: You are a beautiful, smiling entertainer, and you are a perfect target. If a guest is obviously hitting on you, and you're afraid to offend him by telling him you're not interested, things can escalate. Kindly turn him down, making sure he gets the message.

You also need to be tactful when a guy doesn't listen and continues to harass you. When he looks you up and down, winks at you, and asks to meet you in the parking lot after the wedding, you can't tell him what you <u>really</u> think about him. He may tell the client that you were rude or not a good sport. Simply say, "No thank you," and tell him that you have a husband waiting for you at home (even if you are single). Of course, if he is blatantly drunk and lunging at you, it's time to call security.

For the Guys: Here is the number one thing that guys should never do if a lady guest wants to see you after the wedding festivities: Never laugh at her. I know, you probably think it's a hoot that a girl is asking for your phone number at a wedding. But if you laugh, you'll risk hurting her feelings, and she's bound to tell someone in the wedding party that you were mean to her. Instead, tell her she's lovely but you have an adoring wife and kids (even if you are a bachelor).

What if the woman who is showering you with lots of attention is drop-dead-gorgeous? You'll want to think twice about responding to her advances. Word may get back to the client, the coordinator, the booking agent, the banquet manager, or even the celebrant. They might think you were the one hitting on her when she was the one who initiated it all. This could deal a devastating blow to your reputation and end referrals from some vendors.

9. **Learn from your mistakes.** We all make mistakes. When they happen, ask yourself, "What can I do to prevent that from happening again?" Prevention is part of the preparation for future wedding gigs.

For instance, one time someone closed a heavy door on the cord that ran from my equalizer to my amp. The cord was severed. The groomsmen spliced the cord together, and we got the sound system to work for the duration of the ceremony. I learned from that experience not to close any doors on cords. And I always carry extra cords with me (remember the Noah's Ark rule from Chapter 1: Bring two of everything).

Pastor Rob Orr recalls a time when a vocalist was singing during a beach wedding. "The cord for the mic came off and landed in the sand. Her eyes were closed and she was so into her song, she didn't even notice it. There she was, singing 'Wind Beneath My Wings,' and she just looked like a mime because no one could hear her. When she did notice the missing cord, she turned red and tried to belt out the song louder. She handled it well. She was professional about it, even though she stumbled through the end of the song when she realized no one could hear her. She probably learned that the next time she performs, she should check the mic and the cord connection before she starts singing. Some musicians tape the mic to the cord because they've had this happen to them in the past and they don't want it to happen again."

He adds, "All musicians are going to have their stories, when they are starting out, when they are learning, or wherever they are in their career. Take those stories, learn from them, and treasure them. Don't let them discourage you. Grow from it. Learn little techniques to save you the next time around."

Make your mistakes, crack a few bad notes, and recover like the wedding performance athlete that you are.

When you've made it through the gig, there are a few things still left to do . . .

BEFORE YOU LEAVE, SAY "THANK YOU"

You'll want to leave a lasting impression on your client and her guests:

Here are some ideas:

1. Boost the morale of those around you. Compliment them on their lovely dress and appearance. And when it comes to the bride, you cannot go wrong by telling her that she looks gorgeous. Don't wait until the end of your performance to tell the bride how lovely she looks—anytime during the festivities is a fine time. Be honest and sincere in your flattery. Be kind and not phony.

2. You don't necessarily have to pack up and leave as soon as you are off the clock (unless the banquet staff wants to clean up right away or you have another gig to rush off to). It's very gracious to play an encore of one of the bride's favorite songs before you say your good-byes. Be generous with your time.

3. Don't appear to rush off after the last tune is played. Thank everyone by name with a smile, a handshake, or even a hug. Of course, thank the bride and groom for inviting you to perform. Then:

   • Thank the person who wrote your check for their generosity.
   • Thank the other wedding vendors for being so easy to work with.
   • Thank the banquet captain for the wonderful meal if you were served food.
   • Thank the other musicians who performed with you, followed your performance, or performed before you began playing.
   • Thank the celebrant for a beautiful wedding service.
   • Thank the wedding coordinator for their patience and solid organization.
   • Thank the people who referred you to the wedding, if you haven't already done so.

   Spread the words, "Thank you!" far and wide. Express your gratitude.

4. When you congratulate the bride, give her a gift to remember you by. She will be unexpectedly surprised. Make it something small that can be easily tucked into the groom's jacket pocket or the maid of honor's purse.

As a musician, the best gift you can give is your music—a CD is not only a souvenir of your performance, it is also an audio calling card. Sign the CD as you would sign a gift card. The bride will share your CD with others who attended her wedding and those who missed it. You may create new fans who'll buy digital downloads of your music, purchase other CDs, attend your concerts, and hire you for future gigs.

If you don't have a CD to give, think of some other inexpensive gift that will help the bride remember you long after her wedding day passes. How about free tickets to an upcoming concert of yours? Or perhaps you can offer free drink coupons at the club where you perform? Remember, a gift is free, so don't give discount tickets where the bride still must pay something to redeem her gift. This gift has to have a direct connection with your music—giving the bride a bottle of wine isn't going to make her remember your music.

A gift not only helps the bride remember you, it helps the bride to feel satisfied about hiring you in the first place. "Studies have shown that customers who were given a present after making a major purchase...reported more satisfaction with the product than customers who were not given a gift," claims Linda Kaplan Thaler and Robin Koval in their book, "The Power of Nice."

HOW TO MAKE YOUR EXIT

When you are done performing and have said your thank-yous and good-byes:

1. Move all your equipment out of the guest's view if you played for the ceremony and the party is still going on when you are off the clock. Once it is safely in a lobby, alcove, or other out-of-the-way place, then begin packing.

2. If you cannot move into another area to pack, then work quickly and efficiently to pack things up, without bringing attention to yourself. Do this with the help of your roadie and other band members. Everyone on your crew should have a job and know exactly what duty they are responsible for.

3. Change into your street clothes after you've packed up, in case there are guests who are lingering. It is okay to remove ties or change into more comfortable shoes in order to have more movement when packing, but don't dress down yet. Wait until

everything is packed and out of view, and then change into your street clothes.

4. Bring around your car after everything is packed. Load equipment into your car in the same places that you loaded it when you came to the wedding.

5. Return to your performance area and do a quick walk-through to make sure you haven't left any equipment. Leave the performance area the same way that you found it, only cleaner. Return any empty beverage glasses to the bar and pick up any trash from the area.

6. If you want to have a drink after you perform, it's best to stop somewhere on your way home rather than overstaying your welcome at the wedding venue. Don't let anyone—guests, banquet staff, or other wedding professionals—see you having a drink, even if you are done. They may think that you fit into the negative stereotype of a musician who gets drunk on the job. Then, a rumor could begin floating around that you like to drink and you'll stop getting work.

As you can see, weddings can be mine fields of concern. To help you avoid major mishaps, use the **Wedding Day Timeline and Checklist** at the end of this chapter for review. You are welcome to make copies of the list to use for each wedding.

The Wedding Day Timeline and Checklist

"I remind [my band] that it's a new crowd out there, it's a new audience, and they haven't seen us before. So it's got to be like the first time we go on."—Elvis Presley, American Singer, Musician, and Undisputed 'King of Rock 'n' Roll'"

Each wedding is a new experience, with a bride and client with unique wants and tastes. Prepare and execute your job using this timeline and checklist.

Prepare for the Big Day!

Immediately after receiving a signed contract:

❑ **Contact the on-site wedding coordinator or banquet staff:**

❑ Inform them of when you will be arriving and how long you will be performing
❑ For receptions, when must the wedding party clear the room? _____
❑ Are there any particular details you should know about the wedding, the client, or the bride? :

_____
_____
_____
_____
_____
_____

❑ Do you have any questions about the venue that the bride cannot answer readily? (location of electrical outlets, house sound available, etc.):

_____
_____
_____
_____
_____
_____

❑ Do you need to make an appointment for a site inspection? If so, write that appointment here:

Date: _____ Day: _____ Time: _____

Notes about site inspection (take note of where to load in, stairways, service elevators, available electricity, lighting, dimensions of performance area. If performing outdoors, take note of protection from elements, availability of shade, availability of heater lamps, and if there is a bad weather back-up plan):

_____
_____
_____

_____
_____
_____
_____
_____
_____
_____
_____
_____
_____
_____
_____

❏ **Thank the person who referred your new client to you:**

❏ Phone them, or ❏ Send them a handwritten thank-you note

And:

❏ Return the favor by sending a referral to them

❏ **Guide the bride through music selection:**

❏ Let her know how many tunes she needs to choose and for which wedding activities. In your preliminary discussion, which tunes has the bride selected?

_____
_____
_____
_____
_____
_____

❏ Advise the bride of when you'll need to receive her music list. The due date for receiving her music list is _____

❏ **Schedule band members and roadies for the wedding gig.**

❏ Who are you hiring? Include details below:

_____
_____
_____
_____
_____

❏ What dates are scheduled for rehearsal?

_____
_____
_____

❑ What equipment is each band member responsible for bringing to the wedding?

_____
_____
_____
_____
_____
_____

❑ What equipment is each band member responsible for setting up and breaking down?

_____
_____
_____
_____
_____
_____

❑ **Reception bandleaders: Devise a wedding day timeline with the bride.**

What date was the timeline approved? _____

❑ **Are you accompanying the bride's friend or relative?**

❑ Who will you be accompanying? Include their name(s), contact information, and instrumentation below:

_____
_____
_____

❑ What song(s) will you be playing? Include title(s), composers, key(s), and any other information below:

_____
_____
_____

❑ When and where is the rehearsal scheduled?

Date: _____, Day: _____, Time: _____

Location of rehearsal: _____

One week before the bride's final music list is due to you:

❏ **Phone the bride and remind her to supply you with her final music selections**

Date final music list is received: _____

Final music list, in performance order:

_____
_____
_____
_____
_____
_____
_____
_____
_____
_____
_____
_____
_____
_____
_____
_____
_____
_____

Songs the client does not want you to play:

_____
_____
_____

CDs that the client wants you to play when your band goes on a break:

_____
_____
_____

❏ **Share final music list with wedding coordinator.**

❏ **Review itinerary with wedding coordinator**

❏ **Preliminary Rehearsal of Music List**

Practice suggestions:

❏ Practice music in the order that it will be performed
❏ Improve peripheral vision by looking up from the sheet music from time to time.
❏ Practice noodling around a melody and making up theme and variations to lengthen short tunes

❑ Throw in extra tunes to practice. Plan to bring this music along with you to the wedding, in case you need to play overtime. What music will you bring?

_____

_____

_____

_____

_____

_____

<u>One week before your final payment is due:</u>

❑ **Phone the bride and remind her that her payment is due to you. Also remind her of the amount due: _____**

<u>One week before the wedding day:</u>

❑ **Fill in the missing blanks:**

❑ What are the event-day phone number(s)? : _____

❑ Who is the on-site contact? : _____

❑ Is there a map to the venue? Include driving directions below:

_____

_____

_____

_____

_____

_____

❑ What are the colors or theme for the wedding? Are there any particular dress requirements?

_____

❑ Who is the celebrant? _____

❑ Who is the banquet captain? _____

❑ Who is the wedding coordinator? _____

List their phone number and email address: _____

❑ Who will be paying the balance due upon arrival? _____

❑ What is the final guest count? _____

❑ **Review with bride all other particulars about the wedding.**

List any changes to your preliminary notes here:

_____

_____

_____

❑ Remind the bride to advise her celebrant to take a moment to talk with you about cues on the wedding day, before the ceremony begins.

❑ Remind the bride of any balance due on the day of the wedding. Amt. due: _____

The Day Before the Wedding:

❑ Decide what equipment to bring. Put these items out by the front door to be packed into the car the day of the wedding:

_____
_____
_____
_____
_____
_____
_____
_____
_____
_____
_____
_____
_____
_____
_____
_____
_____

❑ Charge up any battery-powered equipment overnight, including:

_____
_____
_____

❑ Lay out or pack performance clothes to wear at the wedding:

_____
_____
_____

The Morning of the Wedding:

❑ Do a final run-through of the music, in the order it is to be played

❑ Pack all of the above equipment, including your performance wardrobe, into your car

Upon Your Arrival at the Wedding:

❑ Introduce yourself to your on-site contact, before you unload any equipment:

❏ Collect any balance due to you
❏ Find out where you will be setting up for the ceremony
❏ Find out where you will be setting up for the reception

❏ **Survey the performance areas(s)**

❏ Is there a clear line of sight to the altar and where the bride and her wedding party enter?
❏ Does the performance area meet your expectations?

❏ **Unload all necessary equipment**

❏ **Park car**

❏ **Set up all equipment, tune up, run a quick sound check**

❏ **Change into your formal performance clothes**

❏ **Store all non-essential items out of sight.**

❏ **Check your ceremony cues with the wedding coordinator:**

❏ Where does the bride enter? _____
❏ Where does the wedding party enter? _____
❏ What is the cue for when the mothers and grandparents are being seated?
_____
❏ What will be the cue for when the mothers will approach the altar to light the unity candle? _____
❏ How will you know when to start playing for the processional? Will the celebrant walk down the aisle first? Or will he already be standing at the altar, so you will need another cue to know when the bridesmaids begin their walk?
_____
❏ Do you have the same number of bridesmaids, flower girls, and ring bearers as the wedding coordinator has in her notes? _____
❏ Confirm all song choices for the seating of the mothers, the processional, the bride's entrance, and the recessional

❏ **Check your ceremony cues with the celebrant:**

❏ If there is no wedding coordinator, review the above points with the celebrant
❏ When will the celebrant walk in?
_____
❏ Will the celebrant be asking the congregation to stand when the bride enters? _____
❏ Will the celebrant say anything else between the processional and the bride's entrance?
_____

❑ What are your music cues for traditions during the ceremony?

_____

_____

❑ Does the celebrant want you to play for any other wedding traditions that the bride and coordinator neglected to mention to you?

_____

_____

❑ How will the ceremony end? How will you know when to start playing the recessional music? Does the celebrant end the ceremony with the kiss, pronouncing the couple as man and wife, or by reciting a poem or prayer?

❑ Will the celebrant be making any announcements during the recessional? _____

❑ **Ceremony musicians: If the ceremony and reception are in the same room, when is the band or DJ to start playing for the reception? Are they scheduled to start playing before you are off the clock?** _____

❑ **Reception musicians: If the ceremony and reception are in the same room, when is the ceremony musician off the clock? Are you scheduled to start playing before the ceremony musician is done?** _____

❑ **Bandleaders and reception soloists: Check your reception itinerary with the wedding coordinator and the banquet captain:**

❑ Review your timeline of announcements and key songs to be played
❑ Do you have the correct start and finish times for your performance? _____
❑ Do you have the correct pronunciation of the names of the wedding party? Do you know their relation to the bride and groom? Include that information below:

_____

_____

❑ Review when you should not be playing any music (during the toast, prayer, etc.):

_____

❑ Confirm when food will be served to the wedding party: _____
❑ If there is a buffet service, is there a preference to the order of tables called up to the buffet line? _____
❑ If you and your group will be served meals,
When will the meals be available? _____, Where will you be seated for your meals?

_____

❑ **Keep the photographer posted about your agenda**

❑ **Order water, juice or soda from the bar**

❑ **If you are hungry, eat a quick snack that you brought from home**

❑ **Send your roadie(s) out of the room, unless they are helping to turn your sheet music pages or adjusting sound during your performance**

After Your Performance, Before You Leave:

❑ **Pay out your band members or ensemble members**

❑ **Compliment the bride, your client, and all others you come in contact with.**

❑ **Play an encore before finishing your performance**

❑ **Thank everyone by name with a smile, a handshake, or even a hug:**

❑ Thank the bride and groom for inviting you to perform
❑ Thank the person who wrote your check for their generosity.
❑ Thank the other wedding vendors for being so easy to work with.
❑ Thank the banquet captain for the wonderful meal if you were served food.
❑ Thank the other musicians who performed with you, followed your performance, or performed before you began playing.
❑ Thank the celebrant for a beautiful wedding service.
❑ Thank the wedding coordinator for their patience and solid organization.
❑ Thank the people who referred you to the wedding, if you haven't already done so.

❑ **When you congratulate the bride, give her a gift to remember you by. What will you give her? _____**

❑ **If the party is still going on, move your equipment out of the guests' view when you pack it up**

❑ **If you cannot move to another area to pack, work quickly and efficiently to pack things up**

❑ **Change into your street clothes after packing up equipment. If guests are still lingering, change into comfortable shoes and remove ties in order to move equipment.**

❑ **Bring around the car and load equipment into the same places in the car when you unloaded.**

❑ **Return to the performance area and do a quick walk-through to make sure you haven't left any equipment.**

Wow, Talk about followup!
*This one's from the Violinist who
played our wedding last year!*

CHAPTER 14

You're Not Done When the Gig Is Over: Keeping in Touch With Your Clients

"You are more attractive when you let your perfect customers know they are perfect."
—Stacey Hall & Jan Brogniez of Perfect Consulting Unlimited, experiential consulting and training company, from their book, "Attracting Perfect Customers"

"The letter possesses some practical virtues that you won't find in email...A handwritten note makes it personal."—David Shipley and Will Schwalbe, authors of Send: The Essential Guide to Email for Office and Home

Okay, so maybe your customers were not so very perfect. Maybe they were difficult, but you got through the gig, you were paid for your efforts, and you owe them a bit of thanks.

Of course, you thanked your clients verbally at the wedding. Now it's time to follow up with something in writing, and I don't mean by email. Show your gratitude in writing with an old-fashioned, hand-written note.

I am a fan of writing letters, although I fear it is a lost art. There is nothing to replace the feeling of receiving a letter, in handwriting. Open it up and hold it in your hands. Look at the personal flourishes of the pen. Cherish it and save it for years. It carries special meaning, particularly since handwritten letters are rarely sent anymore.

Try this experiment: Send a handwritten note to a friend that you haven't heard from in a while. Wait. The response will be a phone call, or maybe photos in the mail, or another note or postcard in kind. You won't get that level of response with an email thank-you.

A simple thank you on personal stationary will do. Thank the bride for inviting you to perform at her wedding. Tell her how beautiful the ceremony was, how gracious her guests were, and how much you enjoyed meeting everyone in attendance. Offer your congratulations and your good wishes.

Don't be afraid to ask her to think of you for future events and to pass your name along to friends interested in your music. Enclose a business card and drop it in the mailbox.

Magically, you may receive a thank-you note in return. You could use her kind words as a testimonial for your website and brochure. And even better, she will remember to recommend you. You might just get a call from her sister or best friend who becomes engaged and is looking for the right music for her wedding. By sending that little thank-you note to her, you are planting a seed for future referrals and gigs.

Here are some quick suggestions for writing thank-you notes, offered by Jeffrey Gitomer in his "Little Red Book of Sales Answers":

The shorter it is—the better it is.

The more handwritten it is—the better it is.

The more personalized it is—the better it is.

The more sincere it is—the better it is.

If for any reason your client is less than satisfied with your services, a thank you note will make it hard for her to complain. It's difficult for people to complain when they're being showered with gratitude.

Don't end your contact with the bride with a thank-you note. Add her to your email list (of course, let her opt out of your email list if she so chooses). Make up a newsletter to send to all your past clients. Send updates about your upcoming concerts, your newest album releases, and offer discounts that only are available to your past clients. Keep in touch with brides like they are old friends and new fans. They will sing your praises and refer you to others, bringing you ever more business.

Review Your Experience . . .
Now you've come full circle with the wedding gig. How did it go? What did you think? Are you ready to perform at more?

Many musicians make their careers out of performing at weddings. You may not have heard of these successful performers because they aren't famous in the way international touring recording artists are. But they make good money at it and are quite content.

Here are thoughts from some of the musicians who were interviewed for this book about why they took up performing at weddings:

"...It's my job, and I love it and love weddings. People are usually happy and a bit excited, the locations are usually beautiful, and music makes a meaningful contribution to the atmosphere of a significant event in people's lives. Through weddings, we have visited many lovely hotels, clubs, beaches and gardens that we would probably never have seen otherwise. While some brides-to-be can be difficult, I enjoy talking to most of them and have become really fond of a number of them. The positive responses which usually follow are very heartening and make me feel I'm doing something worthwhile—even important."—Gwyneth Evans, Concert and Celtic Harpist

"Making a living playing music at weddings is to move, touch, and inspire others."—Seán Cummings, eighth generation bagpiper

"You get the chance to make a real contribution to someone's very special day. You perform for a broader cross-section of people (from babies to great-grandfathers) than anywhere else I've ever played. You play for people who might not have heard live music in years. And when things go right (and they usually do) the room is filled with joyful tears and heartfelt laughter. What's not to like?"—Tim Goldsmith, Red Davidson Trio

"We are lifestylers and would rather not work structured lives."—Stephen Vardy, Sound Engineer for harpist Alison Vardy

"I found it to be a very immediate gratification for music. People come up to you right away and thank you and compliment you vs. the symphony where the people are distant and clap politely for 15 seconds and leave! You are an important part of the most important moment in most people's lives and have the chance to make it very memorable. They will remember that for a long, long time. Then I realized I had a chance to visit homes I normally wouldn't get to see, meet some VIPs, dine on fine food, make music with my friends and get paid for it. 'Bout as close to heaven as I can think..."—Van Vinikow, The Supreme Being of "The String Beings" string trio/quartet

"I love music!"—Destiny, Harpist from the Hood

And for me, it is never boring. Every wedding is different. I meet people from all walks of life, and I'm never playing to the same crowd. I get to provide music for a very special day in someone's life—quite an honor. I also get to work with a team of people who enjoy what they are doing, too. No sad sacks in the bunch! I love being part of the celebration.

I'll leave you with these positive thoughts as you embark or continue on your wedding music career. If you are reading this and are an experienced musician, I hope you've discovered some great new ideas to use at your next wedding gig. Whatever your level, I'd love to hear from you for the next edition of this book, especially if you have some additional ideas to make wedding gigs a bit easier for every musician.

Suggested Repertoire to Get You Started

"People who make music together cannot be enemies, at least not while the music lasts."
—Paul Hindemith, German composer and conductor]

The following are some wedding music standards that you might want to consider including in your repertoire:

WEDDING CEREMONY MUSIC—THE COMMON REQUESTS

The Top Ten Classical Music Requests (in order by composer):
1. "Air in G" from Orchestral Suite No. 3 in D (J. S. Bach)
2. "Ode to Joy" from Symphony No. 9 (Beethoven)
3. "Trumpet Voluntary" or "Prince of Denmark's March" (J. Clarke)
4. "Clair de Lune" (C. Debussy)
5. "Hornpipe" from Water Music Suite (G.F. Handel)
6. "Wedding March" from the incidental music for A Midsummer Night's Dream (F. Mendelssohn)
7. "Canon in D" (J. Pachelbel)
8. "Trumpet Tune" (H. Purcell)
9. "Allegro from Spring", first movement theme from The Four Seasons (A. Vivaldi)

10. "Bridal March" from the opera Lohengrin or "Here Comes the Bride" (R. Wagner)

WEDDING CEREMONY MUSIC ALTERNATIVES (BECAUSE NOT EVERY BRIDE WANTS TO ENTER TO "HERE COMES THE BRIDE")

Favorite choices for Christian weddings:
1. "Amazing Grace" (American Folk Melody)
2. "Ave Maria" (F. Shubert)
3. "Jesu, Joy of Man's Desiring" (J.S. Bach)
4. "The Lord's Prayer" (A.H. Malotte)
5. "Simple Gifts" (Elder Joseph)

Favorite choices for Jewish weddings:
1. "Dodi Li" (N. Chen)
2. "Erev Ba" (O. Avissar & A. Levanon)
3. "Siman Tov" (traditional Israeli song)
4. "Sunrise Sunset" from the musical "Fiddler on the Roof" (J. Bock)

Favorite choices for Celtic weddings
1. "Mairi's Wedding"
2. "Star of the County Down"
3. "When Irish Eyes are Smiling"
4. "Skye Boat Song"
5. "My Wild Irish Rose"

TIMELESS WEDDING RECEPTION FAVORITES

Ethnic favorites:
1. Mexican—"La Bamba"
2. Greek—"Never on Sunday" (M. Hadjidakis)
3. Italian—"Tarantella", the Italian Wedding Dance
4. Italian—"Musetta's Waltz" or "Quando Men Vo" (G. Puccini)
5. Scottish—"The Highland Fling"
6. Polish—"The Dollar Dance"

Silly dances to get everyone on the dance floor:
1. "The Chicken Dance"
2. "The Hokey Pokey"
3. "YMCA"
4. "Old Time Rock n Roll"

"...VERY SINCERELY YOURS,..."

Well, I guess her "Caps Lock" key is on...I can't think of any reason our wedding pianist would be shouting at us.

Netiquette for Wedding Musicians

"You demonstrate your intelligence by how well you convey your thoughts in writing."
—Richard Laermer, author of "Full Frontal PR: Building Buzz About Your Business, Your Product, or You"

"Netiquette" is proper Internet etiquette. Well-executed email correspondence can make your phone ring with inquiries. It generates business, which translates into income. Treat each email that you send off as a way to communicate your professionalism.

Before writing a single email, keep in mind that hitting the "send" button is the same as dropping a letter in a mailbox. You cannot retrieve it. It's gone.

If you need some basics on computer email use, check out the FAQs (Frequently Asked Questions) in the help section of your email program.

What follows are specifics for handling wedding business via email. This information does not necessarily apply to other types of business email correspondence or personal email correspondence.

HERE IS A LIST OF BASIC RULES GOVERNING PROPER BEHAVIOR FOR WEDDING BUSINESS COMMUNICATION ON THE INTERNET VIA EMAIL:

1. **Devise an all-purpose signature, and use it on all of your email correspondence.** Include your name, your business name or ensemble's name, your email address, your website address, your business phone number, and optionally your cell phone number and fax number. Don't forget to include at the bottom of your signature your benefit statement (discussed in Chapter 4, the example, "Cool Jazz for Swinging Receptions"), or a great recent testimonial ("Rockin' good time"—The Reno News and Review).

2. **Encourage the recipient to open your email.** Be specific in your subject line by saying something like "Wedding Music Suggestions for June 23, 2007", instead of just "Wedding Music Info". Include information in the subject line that makes the email easy for you and the recipient to file.

If you have difficulties coming up with a good subject line that is brief and specific, write it *after* you have written the body of the email. It will come easier to you.

3. **Include your name in the "sender" section of the emails that you mail. You can also include your name in the "reply to" section as well.** People delete emails when they can't readily identify who sent them.

4. **Do whatever it takes to insure that your email makes sense.** Use your computer's Spell Check and Grammar Check. Keep Strunk and White's "The Elements of Style" and any other grammar books handy. Carefully use punctuation. Read your email out loud before sending it along. If you are still unsure of how it looks, send it to yourself instead of the recipient, then look at it tomorrow. Keep it in your drafts folder until you are completely happy with the copy. Watch for typos that will make you look less than professional, and be careful of your use of capital letters (using too many capitals makes you look like you are SCREAMING).

5. **Assume that whatever you write in an email will be printed and passed around.** Nothing on the Internet, absolutely nothing, is private. Your clients can print your correspondence and editors can print your press releases. Anything on your website

"The Internet is just a world passing around notes in a classroom."—Jon Stewart, American comedian, host for the Comedy Central show, "The Daily Show"]

can be printed, and people can print cached pages (web pages stored in the computer's memory) long forgotten. Can your grandmother read it and your ten-year-old son read it without wincing? Be very, very careful about what you post and send.

6. **Avoid using fancy email stationery, graphics, or fonts.** Some email servers see these kinds of emails as questionable and they may end up in your recipient's junk email folders. These emails can also be difficult to read. They may look lovely on your computer when you send it, but when it is opened in someone else's email program, it can look like a mess.

Keep your outgoing email looking clean, just like a business letter on business stationery. Use the standard fonts that come with your email program, such as Helvetica and Courier, and set fonts to a readable size.

7. **Use "high priority" markers for your email sparingly.** Brides, and in fact all folks connected with weddings, want everything to go perfectly. Flagging an email as "high priority" when you send it may alarm some brides and clients who are a bit high-strung. Only use this marker for a very important issue, or perhaps pick up the phone instead.

An exception to this rule is if you are sending important information to a wedding coordinator or booking agent who gets tons of daily emails. For these professionals, you might want your important email to stand out in their inbox, if, of course, you have urgent information to convey. They are not as emotionally tied to the wedding as the bride, so they are not apt to be concerned about an email with a high priority flag on it.

8. **Heed the dangers of using "Reply All", cc and bcc.** What if you sent a wedding music list to the bride and everyone in her wedding party? What if she doesn't want her father to know what song she has selected for her ceremony entrance? The intended recipient may not want you to copy your correspondence to others. Furthermore, by using cc, some of those recipients may not want their email addresses available to everyone else who is receiving that email. Or maybe people you copy to on an email message may not interested in your information to begin with. When you hit "Reply All", you could be sharing a response from you that the recipient doesn't want you to share.

Using bcc is considered rude in one-on-one business correspondence. Its only place is in sending bulk emails to announce your upcoming appearances. It is more appropriate to "forward" pertinent email correspondence to individual parties, with an explanation from you about why you are sending the particular email message along. Make sure that the writer of the original email approves of the message being forwarded, or make the forwarded message anonymous by deleting all personal information from the original email (such as the original writer's email address).

My pet peeve is receiving forwarded emails that include the entire headers from the original email, along with the headers of all the other folks who have been forwarding that email along. It's easy to delete all kinds of information, including headers, from the original email before forwarding, and I cannot understand why more folks don't take the time to do this. Protect the sender's privacy when you forward along an email—do some editing and remove their email addresses.

9. **Use caution when sending to names in your address book.** If you have three people named Paul in your address book, or if one of those Pauls has a personal email address and two business email addresses, double check that you are sending the email message to the correct person and to the correct address. Really, your booking agent named Paul doesn't want to receive information that you meant to send to a banquet manager named Paul.

My email horror story: There is a minister I know who used to tell me, "Let's do lunch" every time I saw him at a wedding, but he would never name a date. I figured he was too busy or was having a good time teasing me. So, I emailed another friend of mine about this and asked what I should do. Well, wouldn't you know it, I sent that email to the minister instead of the friend whose opinion I was seeking. It took a long time to repair my relationship with that minister after I sent that email.

10. **Don't send sensitive information.** If there is any doubt in your mind that the information you send could upset or offend anyone if it falls into the wrong hands, don't put it into an email. You could send it to the wrong person accidentally, or the recipient could forward it to people who have no business reading it. Use another mode of communication instead. If the information is of a timely nature, use the phone. If the information is not, type a letter and send it via postal mail.

11. **Alert the recipient when you are including attachments, and avoid sending huge attachments.** Sometimes it is inevitable that you must send a music list to a bride who cannot download it off of your website. Just make sure she knows what kind of document you have attached (Word, PDF, etc.), so she will know what kind of software program to use to open it. As another example, perhaps you will need to send a large photo to a newspaper editor, so you can even alert them in the subject line, "Publicity Photo".

Some servers will not receive emails with large attachments, and large attachments can make some people's computers crash or freeze. Be conscious of the fact that not everyone is on a fast, broadband connection. When sending shorter documents, such as press releases, simply paste the body of the document into the email instead of attaching it. When sending photos, reduce the photo to a manageable size, below 1mb, and optimally, 250 kb.

12. **Utilize templates.** Make life easy for yourself. Save previously sent emails that contain information that you are likely to send along again, such as information about how to select wedding music. Then, you can simply copy and paste the information into a new email message and personalize it for the next recipient.

13. **Keep copies of all email correspondence on your computer hard drive. Download and print them as a backup in case questions arise at the wedding.** Having printed copies of email correspondence is not only important in the event of a computer crash, they may be very helpful at the wedding itself to review specific instructions. Clients can waffle back and forth about their music decisions, and bringing along previous correspondence will help everyone remember what was communicated.

14. **Mirror the same salutation used by the sender.** If the sender is formal and says, "Dear Ms. Musician," your response should be in kind, "Dear Ms. Bride," and should have an equally formal ending such as "Best regards". If you are sending an email to someone for the first time, you may use a more informal "Hi" or "Hello" for younger brides, but for mothers and more mature clients, it is my experience that it's better to start off with more formal salutations. If you are unsure, go with the more formal greeting.

15. **Mirror the same style as the sender.** If the sender writes in a formal business tone, giving you bare-bones specifics about

their daughter's wedding music selections, you should mirror that tone in your response, being formal, brief, and to-the-point. However, if the sender writes in a more laid-back style, mentioning how excited they are for the upcoming wedding, the beautiful view that they'll have at sunset, and how nice the minister has been over the phone, you can be a little more informal in your response.

16. **Avoid the use of chat acronyms (such as lol for "laughing out loud"), abbreviations, slang, jargon, or anything that may not be understood.** Assume that you are writing a formal letter to a client whose business is worth a lot of money, and you will find it easier to steer clear of the kinds of terms that a teenager might use when instant messaging to a friend. You *don't* want to sound like a teenager when corresponding to clients (even if you are one).

17. **Use emoticons and exclamation points sparingly.** It is ever so easy to be misunderstood in email communication. You can't hear inflections of voice, and humor can be misread and cause offense. It is fine to use exclamation points to express excitement, and certainly using a grin, expressed as <g> or a smiley face :-) to express humor is perfectly okay, as long as your message isn't riddled with these things. It can come off looking very unprofessional to have emoticons, especially the flashing kinds, all over your email letter to a prospective client.

18. **Include lots of pertinent information in your email messages.** Many email etiquette books say to be very brief, but I disagree. Brevity can generate a flurry of non-specific emails being exchanged. Your time is worth money, so why should you spend more time than necessary replying to emails? For instance, when a bride emails you just one sentence, "Are you available on June 23rd?", how will you answer her? If you answer with just one sentence, "When will your ceremony start?", she'll answer, "4 pm", and then you'll need to follow with, "Where is your ceremony being held?". You'll be going back and forth for days exchanging information by email in this manner.

Instead, respond with all of your questions that need to be answered in one email, so that you can verify if you are indeed available. Include in just one email message: "Where will your wedding be? What is the city and name of the wedding site or address of your wedding site? What time is your wedding scheduled to begin? Will you need just ceremony music or reception music, too? How many guests will be in attendance, so that I know how long I'll need to play for the prelude and postlude?". Your potential client will think it over, send you all your needed information in one email, and you'll be able to advise her of your availability.

19. **Be concise.** If you have a lot of information to convey, split the information into short, multiple paragraphs. Or number each point that you are making. Long paragraphs are difficult to digest when reading business emails (okay for personal emails, though).

20. **Avoid using a BlackBerry to reply to emails from clients.** It's easy to make spelling, grammar, and punctuation mistakes when typing a lengthy email on a BlackBerry. How can you be detailed about information when you're typing with your thumbs? How can you check for accuracy when trying to send a lengthy email on a BlackBerry? If you are on the road, certainly check your email with your BlackBerry, but go to the business office in a hotel or an Internet café and use a real computer to respond in detail.

21. **Invite the recipients of your emails to phone you.** Most of the time, wedding business can be concluded within a 20-minute phone call, instead of days of email correspondence to conclude the same business. Email does have a use for communicating very specific information, but it doesn't replace a phone call.

22. **Respond to emails within twenty-four hours.** People expect a quick turnaround on email inquiries, so if you are away from your desk and traveling on tour, set up an automated response that explains when you will be able to respond.

23. **Don't expect that your recipient has read your email within twenty-four hours.** Give them a break. Life happens, computers crash, servers go down. If you have a phone number for the recipient, follow up your email with a phone call. If you don't have a phone number, then you'll just have to wait to hear from them.

24. **Respect the fact that some people rarely use email to communicate.** Even if this is your primary way to be connected with your friends, don't assume everyone else is Internet savvy. These folks aren't prehistoric or technologically challenged; they just don't care to use email or don't have access to it. This

can be particularly true in rural areas where high speed or wireless connections are not available.

In general, if a potential client contacts you by phone initially, they probably prefer talking with you instead of using email. Believe it or not, some clients may only check their email inboxes once a week or don't even have email accounts. Of course, if a potential client emails mounds of questions to you, it's a sure bet they're online 24/7 and this is their preferred mode of communication.

Some reporters and editors prefer to receive press releases via fax. The fax machine is also popular among wedding coordinators and booking agents; I know several busy coordinators who send me job requests via fax machine. They reserve their telephone calls and email accounts for communication with brides, not wedding vendors.

25. **Get a life.** You don't need to eat, sleep, and breathe by email. You don't need to invest in a BlackBerry to succeed as a wedding musician. You can simply check email as little as once a day and be on top of things. What did people do before the Internet came into being? They spent time with their families, they exercised, and they enjoyed their vacations. And musicians practiced! Spending all day online seriously cuts into time spent enjoying music.

EMAIL CAN BE A GOOD TOOL WHEN USED FOR THE FOLLOWING TASKS:

1. **Distributing press releases:**

   a) **Get the correct spelling of the name of the proper contact, along with their email address.**

   b) **Address the email to a specific contact that will be likely to be interested in your press release.** If it is going to your local newspaper, think about which section your information is most likely to be printed. If you are sending a press release regarding an upcoming public performance, send the press release to the person who handles the entertainment calendar listings. If you are sending a press release about performing at your local hospice, you will want to send the press release to the editor of community events.

c) **Write a personal email to each recipient of your press release, addressed specifically to the recipient in the body of the email.** Do not send an email blast to every newspaper editor in your area; write a separate "cover letter" to each contact, using their name in the salutation and mentioning that you are including a press release below.

d) **Do not send your press release as an attachment.** It may not get through an email filter, and people who don't think you are a "trusted sender" may refuse to open your attached press release for fear of hidden viruses. Copy and paste your entire press release into the body of the email, just below your "cover letter".

e) **If you must send a press release as an attachment, make sure that you indicate in the body of the email what kind of attachment it is.** Also, do not send the attachment as a PDF file (Adobe Acrobat file). An editor can't directly change the copy in the document without copying and pasting it into another document first.

f) **Write a clever subject line (not "Press Release"), so that your email will get noticed and read.** If the headline of your press release is short, you can use it as your subject line.

g) **Only send the press release to your recipient ONCE.** Just because the editor hasn't responded to your email does not mean they haven't received it or aren't going to print your information. They're just busy. Phone them if you need to verify that your press release was received.

2. **Introducing Yourself to a Bride.** If you sign up for advertising on regional online directories that list services for the bride, there may be an added benefit. The website advertiser may send qualified leads to your inbox!

a) **Read the lead carefully.** You may find that the bride is looking for a jazz band when you are in a string quartet, you may find that she is having her wedding in a region or a wedding site where you don't want to perform, or she may simply be getting married on a date that you are booked. Obviously, delete the lead if you aren't interested.

b) **Send a letter of introduction to the bride.** Let her know which online directory informed you that she might be interested in your services. Tell her where she could learn more about you, by giving her your website URL and phone number in the text of the letter. Keep it short and end with your complete online signature. That's it!

c) **Save a sample of your email introduction letter to use as a template.** It will be ever so easy, in the future, to simply copy and paste the verbiage into the body of future email letters to brides (as long as you remember to personalize the email in the salutation).

d) **Do not share your leads with anyone else.** Advertisers get pretty testy if they find out you are passing leads along to people who have not paid for advertising on their sites.

How can advertisers find out? Brides who receive your introductory letter may check back on the original wedding directory website to view your advertisement to get more information. If you aren't listed there, she may contact the advertiser to find out how you received her email address. I know this for a fact, because I know of an instance when this actually happened. The bride was upset because she thought the advertiser was selling her email addresses to a third party.

3. **Sending an email reminder to brides after a bridal fair.**
When you are provided with a list of brides who attended a bridal fair, follow the same rules that you would use for introducing yourself to a bride. But here, you may send the email message to an entire group, since you may not have met most of the brides on the list. Place your own email address in the "To" field, and place all the brides addresses in the "Bcc" field, separated by commas. This way, each bride's address will remain private to anyone receiving the email blast.

Open with something like, "You may remember me from yesterday's Dream Wedding Show", and then detail the music services you provide. Be sure to invite her to phone you and visit your website.

4. **Contacting brides who entered your raffle at a bridal fair.**
Don't send an email blast using the "Bcc" field. In this case, send an email to each individual entrant. These brides were in your booth and were interested enough to linger and fill out an entry. They probably chatted with you about your services, too. Therefore, each of these brides deserves a personal response, thanking her for entering your contest and re-introducing yourself to her. Remind her of what you can provide for her special day and how to contact you for booking information.

5. **Sending general information to a group of brides or clients** (an email "blast" announcing that you will be exhibiting at the next Sacramento Bridal show to the Sacramento area brides on your mailing list)

6. **Supplying specific information to clients (answering clients' questions, confirming cancellation of a wedding in writing)**

7. **Responding to email inquiries.** The object of the email correspondence is to compel the bride to phone you. Close the sale by phone to prevent spending a lot of wasted time going back and forth with questions via email. Also, you will be able to tell if the bride is levelheaded by speaking with her directly.

Often, extraneous information about the wedding details seep out in conversation, information that might never have been disclosed via email. To the bride, it may be inconsequential information, but it could be information that is a deal-breaker for you. For instance, I might find out in the course of the conversation that, "Oh, by the way, you'll need to walk on a narrow trail down the cliff to the beach. It isn't really steep, though, and I figure you could get a harp down there." (This is a true example, and I've heard this more than once).

Always close the sale by phone, where you can give a sales presentation, and be selective when offering a specific quote by email. I believe it is fine to do so when the inquiry comes from a booking agent or a wedding coordinator. I don't have to sell these people on my services, and they are not going to let my quote go "stale" (in other words, they won't take so long to get back to me that I've changed my fees or have received other inquiries for the same date.). I also think it is fine when the bride lives overseas and it is obviously difficult to arrange a time to talk with her.

Professionals interviewed for this book were split as to whether they would send quotes via email. For instance, Destiny, the Harper from the Hood, only gives rate quotes over the phone or in person. She offers this story:

"I once sent a quote to a bride by email. She was a friend of mine, and I decided to give her a discount rate. She was so proud of the discount she received that she forwarded it to all her friends. They thought it was a great rate. So, when one of them wanted to get married, she thought she could hire me for the same rate. Sending any quotes by email can be dangerous, because you don't know where it will be forwarded. Besides, email is so impersonal."

Reverend David Beronio offers this anecdote:

"I am so tired of typing. It is easier to invite the bride to phone me at her convenience for a quote. Then, when she phones me, she is sincere about wanting me to be part of her wedding. Besides, I can hear the nuances in her voice to know who she is."

However, Jeff Leep, entertainment agent and musician, has a different take on this:

"I don't mind sending quotes by mail, because I can weed out the people who don't have the money for my services and are just going to waste my time on the phone."

When giving a quote by email, you can include one of these statements at the bottom of your signature: "All rates and specifications are confidential," or "This email and all of its contents is confidential," or "This is a one time only quote," or "This quote is good until _____," (and name a date). Then, if your quote gets forwarded in its entirety, you have already included a disclaimer regarding the fee you've quoted.

Whether the email inquiry comes from a bride, her mother or father, a wedding coordinator, or even a booking agent include these four points when responding:

a) **Start by thanking the writer for contacting you.** Or, you can end the email message with this, but I prefer to begin my message with a nice courtesy.

b) **Describe the entire package a bride will receive for that fee.** Let her know everything you will provide, all the wonderful benefits to having you perform for her special day. Then, at the end of your description, mention the fee.

c) **Indicate that you book weddings on a first come, first serve basis.** This kind of statement gets you off the hook in the event that someone else phones and books you before the bride with the email inquiry decides to phone you. "You snooze, you lose," as the saying goes.

d) **Include a statement that the fee you are quoting is subject to change.** If the bride takes months or even years to decide to phone you, she cannot expect you to hold to your original quote via email.

Also, if she has left some important details out of her email correspondence, you may need to adjust your quote once you discover this information in a phone conversation. A bride will think you are trying to pull the wool over her eyes if you mention a laundry list of extra charges that you didn't originally include in writing.

An example of when you may need to charge extra fees to a bride once you speak with her is when she tells you, "Oh, by the way, there is no loading zone at the church, and you can't double park in the city." Then, you realize that you need to charge for the extra set up time necessary to find a parking space and walk all your equipment from your car.

> e) **Finally, explain to the bride that when she decides to book your services, she must phone you to discuss the details.** Explain to her, "I do not handle booking arrangements via email, because it is much easier to get all our questions answered in one phone call."

HOW TO TELL WHETHER AN INQUIRY IS LEGITIMATE

Most email inquiries will include the question, "How much?" They will also include some information about time, date, and location. These are all good signs that the bride is genuinely interested in learning more about your talents.

However, on rare occasions, you will receive questionable inquiries. Actually, they are not inquiries at all—they are from scammers. As Steve Tetrault of GigSalad.com in Springfield, Missouri explains, "Their ultimate goal is to get you to receive a deposit check for an amount that is greater than what it should be, then ask you for the difference. Their check turns out to be fraudulent and they walk away with a few thousand bucks from you."

Pretty scary stuff, but true. Below is an example of a bogus email inquiry. It went through Steve Tetrault's system, and I was one of the many recipients of it. It's real and not a fictitious example:

Greetings to you,I am Mr.Robbin Mart from Louisville, KY.I will like to have your service for my son's Philip Wedding ceremony with her wife, named as Jessy.I found you at webpage saladgig. I am making an enquiry in regards to your services on my son's Wedding,We are having the party at his wife residence,in which i will like to get your price for 4 hours of service and we are having 120-140 guests in which the party will start at 11:00am by recption which is about 5 mins drive to the party venue and ends the party till 7:00pm and i will like the best of your performance on that date.Also let me know if there will be any little charges for your flight fee.What time will you show up for my event? What type of equipment do you use? Are you licensed, registered and insured? Do you want me to book a near by hotel we have here for you?And are you coming alone to perform at the party?Also i will like to know if you are available for the date 5th or 6th of July 2006. I await the best of your message soonest.The party venue is @ 4410 Shepherdsville Rd Louisville, KY 40218 Get back to me asap. NOTICE: Email me Reply me to robbinmart3@yahoo. com Engr.Robbin S. Mart.

The example includes many warning signs that this is a fake inquiry:

1. **The message is not addressed to anyone personally.** It just says, "Greetings" or "Hello", instead of "Greetings Anne" or "Hello Ms. Roos". It doesn't say that it is for my eyes only. This fact alone confirms that the email is probably a mass emailing.

You can also determine that the message is a mass mailing by looking at the "To:" field and the "Reply To:" or "From:" field in the header of the email. If these are all the same email addresses, the email was sent as a blind carbon copy (Bcc) to many email addresses.

Legitimate email inquiries will not be sent en masse to a number of wedding musicians, and the salutation, in the body of the email, will be addressed to you by name.

2. **The inquiry is riddled with exceptionally poor spelling, grammar, and punctuation.** True, some brides cannot spell worth beans and never use capital letters (or shamefully use all capital letters). But if you try to read the sentences out loud, and you find the urge to change the order of nouns and verbs within sentences, change plural nouns to singular nouns, fix misplaced capital letters, and simply edit the whole thing to get it to make sense, you don't have an email inquiry. You have spam.

3. **The email makes requests that do not apply to the services you offer.** I have received a number of fake inquiries that ask me to provide DJ services for a wedding. I'm a harpist, and it's obviously too big a mistake to take the email seriously.

The above example was sent to reception bands, DJs, and all kinds of entertainers who do not necessarily perform at wedding ceremonies at all. The scammer was just trying to cover all his bases and get someone, anyone, to take the bait and reply.

4. **The inquiry is missing important information, such as the event location or day of the wedding.** Notice in the above example, the date is either July 5th or 6th, and I've never personally seen a wedding "party" last from 11 am until 7 pm. Legitimate inquiries may say that the date has not yet been determined, or that the date will be sometime in June, but when several dates are given, it can be a red flag.

The address that is provided may not exist. Go to MapQuest.com, Yahoo Maps, or other map sites, plug in the address and see if it is a fake. If a phone number is provided, you can try phoning that number to see if someone answers. If you reach a disconnected number, a wrong number, or a generic answering machine, it can be yet another red flag.

5. **The message requests you reply by email only.** In legitimate email inquiries, it is implied that you can only respond to a client by email if they don't give you any other means for replying to them. If they offer their phone number in the email body or the signature of the email, then it is implied that you may go ahead and phone them. Real clients do not provide any additional personal information that they don't want you to know.

By contrast, a scammer may give you a lot of extraneous information, such as a mailing address and a phone number, only to say to contact them by email. They're trying to convince you that they're for real. Don't fall for it.

6. **Any email messages from overseas, claiming that they are willing to pay for your travel expenses and accommodations to perform in a foreign country.** Weddings are local events, and brides, event coordinators, and booking agents are most interested in booking local talent. It's pretty unlikely that a client will pay you thousands of dollars, put you up in a hotel, provide your meals, and take care of your expenses to travel overseas. Unless, of course, you are a very, very famous performer with a big name and the client has a bottomless wallet (in which case, you'd have an agent taking care of your booking calendar, weeding out illegitimate inquiries for you).

7. **Any email from a client or event planner who is itching to pay you upfront, without any previous correspondence or conversations with you.** People aren't that eager to part with their

money for any musician, and they like to do a bit of shopping around, asking questions, before they commit to spending money.

What should you do when you receive one of these bogus inquiries?

1. **Don't reply.** Once you reply, the scammer figures they've got you hooked. They'll keep responding to you, because they think they can get you to fall for their con job and send them money. The scammer may also put you on their email blast list, or send your address to their other scammer friends, and you'll receive ever more spam inquiries.

2. **Report it as spam.** If you received the spam inquiry through a wedding or music directory, alert them. In the above example, the spammer mentioned "saladgig". The true title of the directory is called "GigSalad.com", but that was certainly enough information for me. I knew that the folks at GigSalad.com needed to be alerted so that they could work to put a halt to it and report it to authorities.

And by the way, if you receive spam that mentions a legitimate online directory, don't blame them. These directories are victims as much as you are, because they don't want businesses that list with them to be subject to this spam.

There are other ways to report fake email inquiries. Depending upon what is contained in the body of the email, you can report it to the online FBI Internet Crime Complaint Center (ic3.gov), SpamCop.net, your own Internet Service Provider (ISP), and a host of other online agencies that exist to eradicate spam. If the spam meets their criteria, include the full headers (which contain the ISP numbers). Be careful, though, because sometimes the spammer uses your ISP address and email address as the "Reply to:" or the "From:" and you can end up putting your own email address on a blacklist!

WHAT TO DO WHEN A BRIDE BOMBARDS YOU WITH EMAIL

Brides that overwhelm me in email correspondence rub me the wrong way. I can say that about 3% of my brides bombard me with unnecessary emails. They send me so many that after I've downloaded and printed them, I could bind them into a thirty-page book by time the wedding day rolls around.

With these brides, I'm honest. I tell them, "I would prefer for you to phone me if you have a lot of questions. This way, I can answer them in one phone call instead of us going back and forth, one question at a time, by email. Also, I print all of your emails to keep a record of our correspondence. When I get too many emails, I can't keep track of it all and may misfile something important." I use my poor filing abilities as an excuse to get the bride to phone me, or at least to curtail her flurry of email messages. It works every time.

The funny thing is that when I arrive at the perpetually emailing bride's wedding, the other wedding professionals on the scene have also downloaded and printed her correspondence for their records. Invariably, we all take a moment to compare how many emails each of us received to see who was the "winner". I wonder whether brides would change their behaviors if they knew that their wedding vendors compare notes about them.

DO NOT use email in the following situations:

A. **Closing the sale with a bride or a client.** You need to get a read on who your client is, and you cannot do this by email. Use the phone or meet with her in person.

B. **Communicating potentially distressing or emotional information.** If you need to say, "I cannot play at your wedding and have found a substitute musician for you", email is definitely not the right tool. Use the telephone instead.

C. **When you are angry.** If you are seriously fuming about the behavior of a client or bride, stop and take a deep breath. Take out a pen and paper and scribble to your heart's content, then ball up the paper and throw it away. Go out and take a long walk in nature. But do not ever send an abusive or insulting email (a "flaming" email, in Internet lingo). It can be circulated to others and come back to haunt you for years. You can lose your reputation over it. You can lose work over it. You can lose money over it.

D. **Communicating time-sensitive information.** If you need to say to the bride, "It's raining today. What is your back-up plan for your outdoor wedding this afternoon?" use the telephone instead of email. She may not be checking her email on her wedding day.

E. **Saying "Thank you!"** A handwritten note is always the preferred way to receive a written response. The old-fashioned written word on paper always holds much more importance to the recipient than email.

Suggested Reading and Other Resources

THESE ARE USER-FRIENDLY REFERENCE GUIDES THAT YOU MAY FIND HANDY:

Baker, Bob. *Guerrilla Music Marketing Handbook: 201 Self-Promotion Ideas for Songwriters, Musicians, and Bands on a Budget, Revised Ed.* St. Louis, MO; Spotlight Publications, 2007.

———. *MySpace Music Marketing: How to Promote & Sell Your Music on the World's Biggest Networking Web Site.* St. Louis, MO: Spotlight Publications, 2006.

Bly, Robert W. *The Perfect Sales Piece: A Complete Do-It-Yourself Guide to Creating Brochures, Catalogs, Fliers, and Pamphlets.* New York, NY: John Wiley & Sons, Inc., 1994.

Editors of BottleTree Books LLC. *MySpace Maxed Out: Explode Your Popularity, Buzz Your Band and Secure Your Privacy on MySpace.* United Kingdom: BottleTree Books, LLC, 2006.

Dearing, James W. *Making Money Making Music (No Matter Where You Live).* Cincinnati, OH: Writer's Digest Books, 1990.

Francis, Jane. *Price Yourself Right: A Guide to Charging What You're Worth.* Lincoln, NE: iUniverse, Inc., 2006.

Gibson, James. *Playing for Pay: How to Be a Working Musician.* Cincinnati, OH: Writer's Digest Books, 1990.

Gitomer, Jeffrey. *Little Red Book of Sales Answers: 99.5 Real World Answers That Make Sense, Make Sales, and Make Money.* Upper Saddle River, NJ: Prentice Hall, 2005.

Hahn, Fred E. with Tom Davis, Bob Killian and Ken Magill. *Do-It-Yourself Advertising and Promotion: How to Produce Great Ads, Brochures, Catalogs, Direct Mail, Web Sites, and More!, 3rd Ed.* Hoboken, NJ: John Wiley & Sons, Inc., 2003.

Hall, Doug. *Jump Start Your Business Brain: Scientific Ideas and Advice That Will Immediately Double Your Business Success Rate.* Cincinnati, OH: Brain Brew Books, 2001.

———. *Jump Start Your Marketing Brain: Scientific Advice & Practical Ideas.* Cincinnati, OH: Brain Brew Books, 2005.

Hall, Stacey and Jan Brogniez. *Attracting Perfect Customers: The Power of Strategic Synchronicity.* San Francisco, CA: Berrett-Koehler Publishers, Inc., 2001.

Judy, Stephanie. *Making Music for the Joy of It.* Los Angeles, CA: Jeremy P. Tarcher, Inc., 1990.

Kaplan Thaler, Linda and Robin Koval. *The Power of Nice: How to Conquer the Business World With Kindness.* New York, NY: Currency Doubleday, 2006.

Laermer, Richard. *Full Frontal PR: Building Buzz About Your Business, Your Product, or You.* Princeton, NJ: Bloomberg Press, 2003.

Lawson, Ken. *Success in Dealing With Difficult People.* London, England: Axix Publishing Limited, 2006.

Levinson, Jay Conrad and Seth Godin. *The Guerrilla Marketing Handbook.* Chicago, IL: Dearborn Financial Publishing, Inc., 1992.

Levinson, Jay Conrad. *Guerrilla Marketing Weapons: 100 Affordable Marketing Methods for Maximizing Profits from your Small Business.* New York, NY: Penguin Books, 1990.

Maggio, Rosalie. *How to Say It: Choice Words, Phrases, Sentences & Paragraphs for Every Situation, Revised Ed.* Paramus, NJ: Prentice Hall Press, 2001.

Martin, Judith. *Miss Manners' Basic Training: Communication.* New York, NY: Crown Publishers, Inc., 1997.

McCormack, Mark H. *What They Don't Teach You At Harvard Business School, New Ed.* London, England: Profile Business, 1994.

Nevue, David. *How to Promote Your Music Successfully on the Internet.* Eugene, OR: Midnight Rain Productions, 2006.

Performance Research Associates, Inc. *Delivering Knock Your Socks Off Service, 4th Ed.* New York, NY: American Marketing Association (AMACOM), 2007.

Pincott, J., Ed. *Success: Advice for Achieving Your Goals From Remarkable Successful People.* New York, NY: Random House Reference, 2005.

Roney, Carley and the Editors of The Knot. *The Knot Guide to Wedding Vows and Traditions.* New York, NY: Broadway Books, 2000.

Rothstein, Barbara and Gloria Sklerov. *How to Set Your Wedding to Music.* Kansas City, MO: Andrews McMeel Publishing, 2002.

Sabath, Ann Marie. *Business Etiquette: 101 Ways to Conduct Business with Charm & Savvy, 2nd Ed.* Franklin Lakes, NJ: The Career Press, Inc., 2002.

Schiffman, Stephan. *The 25 Most Common Sales Mistakes and How to Avoid Them, 2nd Ed.* Avon, MA: Adams Media Corporation, 1995.

———. *The 25 Sales Habits of Highly Successful Salespeople, 2nd Ed.* Avon, MA: Adams Media Corporation, 1994.

Shih, Patricia. *Gigging: A Practical Guide for Musicians.* New York, NY: Allworth Press, 2003.

Shipley, David and Will Schwalbe. *Send: The Essential Guide to Email for Office and Home.* New York, NY: Alfred A. Knopf, 2007.

Stiernberg, John. *Succeeding in Music: A Business Handbook for Performers, Songwriters, Agents, Managers, & Promoters.* San Francisco, CA: Backbeat Books, 2001.

Stim, Richard. *Music Law: How to Run Your Band's Business, 5th Ed.* Berkeley, CA: Nolo Press, 2006.

University of Chicago Press Staff. *The Chicago Manual of Style: The Essential Guide for Writers, Editors, and Publishers, 15th Ed.* Chicago, IL. University of Chicago Press, 2003.

Yudkin, Marcia. *6 Steps to Free Publicity, Revised Ed.* Franklin Lakes, NJ: The Career Press, Inc., 2003.

Ziglar, Zig. *Selling 101: What Every Successful Sales Professional Needs to Know.* Nashville, TN: Thomas Nelson Publishers, 2003.

Zimmerman, Jan. *Web Marketing for Dummies.* Hoboken, NJ: Wiley Publishing, Inc., 2007.

Podcasts and Websites of Interest (Available through iTunes for free):

Artist Empowerment Radio—Gives musicians and other creative people marketing ideas and inspiration for success. Presented by Bob Baker and his websites, TheBuzzFactor.com, MusicPromotionBlog.com and PromoteYourCreativity.com.

Brain Brew Radio—Provides ideas and encouragement for helping you along your business ventures. Presented by Doug Hall.

PublicityHound.com—Publicity expert Joan Stewart shows you how to use free publicity. This is the site where you can sign up for her free online tutorial, "89 Ways to Write Powerful Press Releases".

Jump Start Your Brain—Twice a week, Doug Hall, star of ABC TV's American Inventor, scours the academic journals, business books, trend reports, and international marketplace for fresh ideas and opportunities for business growth.

Fake books by Hal Leonard filled with wedding and reception music:

All-Time Spanish Favorites in Fake Book Style
Classic Rock Fake Book
The Celtic Fake Book
The Classical Fake Book
The Hal Leonard Real Jazz Standards Fake Book
The Hymn Fake Book
The Latin Real Book
The Praise and Worship Fake Book: An Essential Tool for Worship Leaders,
    Praise Bands and Singers!
The Ultimate Broadway Fake Book
The Ultimate Country Fake Book
The Ultimate Fake Book
Wedding & Love Fake Book

Additional wedding sheet music books:

Coates, Dan. *Wedding Sheet Music Hits: Easy Piano.* Miami, FL: Warner Bros. Publications, 2004.

Hal Leonard Corporation. *The Bride's Guide to Wedding Music.* Milwaukee, WI: Hal Leonard Corporation, 2000.

Pasternak, Velvel. *The Jewish Fake Book.* Baltimore, MD: Tara Publications, 1997.

Index

About the Author

Anne Roos resides in South Lake Tahoe and has been playing the Celtic harp at weddings for more than twenty-five years. She regularly appears on radio and television programs. Roos has served on the Board of the Lake Tahoe Wedding and Honeymoon Association and is a member of the Association of Bridal Consultants. As a professional musician and arranger, she served on the Board of Governors of the San Francisco Chapter of the Recording Academy.

Among Anne's discography, she has arranged and recorded a special Celtic wedding CD called "*Haste to the Wedding*". It contains Celtic music performed on solo harp and within an ensemble of traditional instruments. It is packaged in a lovely 48-page hardcover book, written by Anne, containing wedding legends and lore. All of Anne's CDs, including "*Haste to the Wedding*", are available for purchase at www.celticharpmusic.com.

(photo: Angelene Hall)